MICROPROCESSOR
DATA MANUAL

From *ELECTRONIC DESIGN*

MICROPROCESSOR DATA MANUAL

From *ELECTRONIC DESIGN*

Edited by
DAVE BURSKY
Associate Editor, *Electronic Design*

HAYDEN BOOK COMPANY, INC.
Rochelle Park, New Jersey

ISBN   0-8104-5114-X
Library of Congress Catalog Card Number   77-92762

| 1 | 2 | 3 | 4 | 5 | 6 | 7 | 8 | 9 | PRINTING |
| 78 | 79 | 80 | 81 | 82 | 83 | 84 | 85 | 86 | YEAR |

Foreword

PETER ALFKE
Fairchild Semiconductor

In just twenty years, semiconductor technology has come around full circle. It started with the transistor, an extremely versatile nonspecialized device that performs a myriad of functions, limited only by the designer's imagination. From the transistor evolved specialized integrated circuits that soon developed into more complex MSI and LSI specialized building blocks.

Now the microprocessor has made the full swing back to the universal component, a device that can perform any digital function, given enough time and memory. This raises the question—why are there so many different microprocessors? Is this the result of avid competition or a ploy to confuse the potential user? While the number of incompatible microprocessors differing in architecture, instruction set, technology, and I/O capability seems larger than necessary, there is a good reason for diversity. A market exists for a spectrum of microprocessors, each geared to a specific kind of application, offering different performance tradeoffs between the following conflicting requirements.

■ Low hardware cost—low parts price, small number of pins, ease of interconnection, adequate drive capability, simple supply and clock requirements.

■ Low development cost—ease of programming, similarity to well-known minicomputer architectures and instruction sets, availability of applications software, simplicity of system design.

■ High performance—high execution speed, large memory address range, sophisticated interrupt structure, powerful instruction set.

Since these three requirements can never be optimized in one design, it is fortunate they need not all be optimized for any given application.

Today's microprocessors

When comparing microprocessors, from the simplest appliance controller to the most intricate 16-bit processor, it is surprising that there is little difference in size and complexity of the chips, package size and number of pins. The really significant differences lie in the size and complexity of the system for which the microprocessors are intended.

Semiconductor technology has not advanced, as yet, to the point where a complete 370 system can be built on a single chip. With today's technological constraints, the device designer must choose between functional completeness and complexity of the intended device application. Indeed, a complete computer can be built on one chip—CPU, RAM for data storage, ROM for program storage, and I/O circuits with practical drive capability to interface directly with LEDs and relays. Mundane functions can be included such as on-chip clock generation, power-on reset and direct-display drive, but this computer-on-a-chip is very limited in instruction set, memory size, word length, and speed.

The other extreme is the sophisticated microprocessor that does not even attempt to be a computer-on-a-chip, but is the central processing element of a far more complex multichip system. This microprocessor has an extensive instruction decoder, multiple accumulators, fast interrupt, efficient subroutine capabilities, a 16-bit program counter, and 16-bit address-bus drivers. Trivial features like simple clock generation, single power supply, and power-on reset are not always provided. This microprocessor forms the foundation for a powerful computer with up to 64-k bytes of ROM or RAM, multilevel prioritized interrupt structure, and almost unlimited I/O capability.

When evaluating microprocessors, it is important to consider the application complexity. Small controllers are dominated by hardware cost considerations and require a microprocessor that emphasizes hardware simplicity, operation efficiency, and functional completeness. Large data processing systems, on the other hand, tend to be dominated by software cost and development time. Here, a more regular minicomputer-like architecture is preferable.

Reprinted with permission from PROGRESS, July/August 1977.

Preface

With data about microprocessors scattered among 40 or so vendors, it's hard for you to get an overall picture of the different capabilities and limitations of each device. To help you compare features and capabilities of all microprocessors, microcomputers, and bit slices, this *MICROPROCESSOR DATA MANUAL* brings together the data necessary to get a good "feel" about any of the over 60 different processor types. By no means does this book cover every processor specification. To make a final device choice you should, of course, examine the actual processor data sheet and run some performance comparisons for the task you have planned.

This manual does provide much of the in-depth information you need to limit judiciously your field of target processors to several devices from a wide array of choices. The five sections in this manual provide different insights to the workings of the various processors. Section One examines the general microprocessor specifications to alert you as to what you should watch out for as you examine the detailed data for your target processor. Such specifications as execution time, the number of instructions, the number of I/O lines, clock frequency, and loading capability are closely examined. Also included in this section is a discussion of development software, development aids, and prototyping systems.

The next section of the book contains a short primer, designed to provide a refresher for the reader who is on shaky ground when the discussion turns to microprocessors. It starts with a "black box" definition of microprocessor and goes into a detailed explanation of the basic control signals typically encountered in most systems. A glossary of often-used microprocessor-related terms and their definitions is also included for handy reference.

After the primer, the next section contains the *MICROPROCESSOR DATA MANUAL* data pages, one page for each processor or family of processors from each original source vendor. Each data page highlights all the features and capabilities of the specific processor and includes tables detailing the main processor specifications and available support circuits, as well as an internal architecture drawing of the processor. Details of the software support and available design aids are also provided.

Section Four of the *MICROPROCESSOR DATA MANUAL* contains a report on specifying floppy-disc drives, the most popular bulk-storage device with microprocessor-based systems. This article steps through all the drive specifications that can be misleading or tricky to nail down. You face difficult choices when you must select a drive: i.e., do you want an 8-in. or 5.25-in. diameter model? single or dual density? single or double-sided recording? tunnel or straddle erase? and hard or soft-sectored units? You must examine, as well, such drive specifications as access time, power requirements, and performance over temperature.

Following the discussion of floppy-disc drives, Section Five provides articles on various aspects of microprocessor selection based on software and hardware. Included are six pieces that discuss low-cost microprocessor selection, microprocessor instruction evaluation sets, available program development aids, available hardware development aids, and microprocessor programming in assembly language. These articles help round out the *MICROPROCESSOR DATA MANUAL* and provide some final insights into the complexities of working with microprocessors.

DAVID BURSKY

Contents

MICROPROCESSOR
DATA MANUAL

Microprocessor Selection Guide

DAVE BURSKY *Electronic Design*

Every microprocessor can do a job—but with its own language, architecture, support circuits and development aids. Knowing one particular microprocessor's language (instruction set) doesn't mean you can easily switch to another.

Selecting the best microprocessor, microcomputer or bit slice has become a nightmare. Once you've selected one, you face another bad dream—testing it. Because a μP is designed to be general-purpose, it can handle a virtually unlimited number of code combinations. Some manufacturers have calculated that, even when operating the processor at top speed, it would take over 10 years to check all code combinations.

To help sort out the various models, word sizes and performance ranges, Hayden Book Company presents the *Microprocessor Data Manual*. In it you will find performance summaries of every available processor and summary tables to help you compare similar units. Also, to help you locate a processor by manufacturer or model number, we have included cross-reference tables and an alternate-source directory.

Three major classes of processor components are covered in this Manual:

1. **Microprocessor**—a general-purpose processor on one to three chips. It contains an arithmetic and logic unit (ALU), an address and data bus (sometimes multiplexed), a built-in instruction set, and the basic control logic.

2. **Microcomputer**—an all-in-one general-purpose processor that is similar to the microprocessor except that the chip contains the main control program in read-only memory (ROM) and possibly a clock oscillator, some input/output (I/O) capability, and some read-write random-access memory (RAM).

3. **Bit slice**—an enhanced subsection of the microprocessor's ALU. Besides the slice, which is available in two or four-bit sections, other circuits must be added to provide the basic control logic.

There are, of course, other classes of microprocessor components—dedicated controller chips that are either custom-designed or preprogrammed for specific applications. Calculator chips, floppy-disc controllers, microwave-oven controllers and many industrial process-control circuits are typical examples.

Selection can start with data-word size

To start selecting, many companies recommend that you first decide on the word size and the type of instructions needed. Then you can determine the execution speed and I/O capability needed. Once these four basics are nailed down, you're free to look at price, power drain, technology and available support.

Instruction-compatible microprocessors are available in more than one technology to provide per-

formance demanded by some applications. You can pick and choose from bipolar technology (ECL, I^2L, STTL or TTL) or MOS (CMOS, NMOS or PMOS).

If you plan to use an off-the-shelf processor, you can select data-word lengths of 1, 4, 8, 12 or 16 bits for microprocessor chips, 1, 4, 8 or 16 bits for microcomputer chips and 2 or 4 bits for bit slices. (An 8-bit ECL slice is expected next year from Fairchild.)

Performance summaries of the three processor types are provided in Tables 1, 2, and 3, respectively. While all performance specs have been normalized for easy comparison, you can still be misled by manufacturers if you don't read the fine print.

Computing speed is a case in point. Often, manufacturers use a basic cycle time or period—sometimes called a microcycle—to specify the instruction execution speed. But a microcycle is not necessarily the inverse of the clock frequency—it's often a multiple, possibly two or three times the clock frequency. Each instruction is then defined as requiring several microcycles for execution.

As a result, a three-microcycle instruction may actually require three, six or nine clock cycles. What's more, longer instructions such as multiply and divide can require tens or even hundreds of microcycles.

Clock speed can be misleading, too, if taken for a measure of processor speed. One microprocessor can perform basic operations—such as a register-to-register add—faster than another unit running at a higher clock because of variations in its internal architecture. In this instance a clock-rate spec is not very important.

Other speeds can give false indications of processor speed, including minimum instruction time, interrupt-response time, and addition time. Like cycle time and clock rate, these specs *don't* measure such important factors as the over-all time needed to perform critical routines in an application. Excluded, for instance, are the delays incurred when the processor must get data from memory. You can solve this dilemma by tailoring a program that compares the performance of several machines doing the same job.

Such a benchmark can help determine the power of the processor's instruction set, and circumvent another oft-abused spec—the number of instructions. Microprocessor comparisons based on this number abound, but don't make a choice based only on this number. Make sure you can use all the commands.

Examine the instruction set carefully

A number won't tell you which instructions are put aside for data movement and manipulation, for decision and control and for input and output. Some microprocessors have many more I/O commands than

Table 1. General-purpose microprocessors

Manufacturer	Processor	Process technology	Word size (data/instruction)	Direct addressing range (words)	Number of basic instructions	Maximum clock frequency (MHz)/phases	Instruction time shortest/longest[2] (μs)	TTL compatible	BCD arithmetic	On-chip interrupts/levels	Number of internal general-purpose registers	Number of stack registers	On-chip clock	DMA capability	Specialized memory & I/O circuits avail.	Prototyping system avail.	Package size (pins)	Voltages required (V)	Assembly language development system	High-level languages	Time-sharing cross software	Comments
Motorola	MC14500	CMOS	1/4	0	16	1/1	1/1	Yes	No	Yes/1	1	0	Yes	No	No[4]	No	16	3 to 18	No	No	No	Needs external program counter
Intel	4004	PMOS	4/8	4k	46	0.74/2	10.8/21.6	No	Yes	Yes/1	16	3x12	No	No	Yes	No	16	15	Yes	Yes	Yes	Superseded by 4040
Intel	4040	PMOS	4/8	8k	60	0.74/2	10.8/21.6	No	Yes	Yes/1	24	7x12	No	No	Yes	Yes	24	15	Yes	Yes	Yes	General-purpose 4-bit μP
NEC Microcomputers	μPD541	PMOS	4/8	4k	69	0.5/2	6.4/38.4	Yes	Yes	Yes/8	4	8x12	No	Yes	Yes	Yes	42	5,−5	Yes	No	No	Intended for electronic cash registers, etc.
Fairchild	2 chip F8	NMOS	8/8	64k	69	2/1	2/13	Yes	Yes	Yes/1	64	RAM	Yes	Yes	Yes	Yes	40	5,12	Yes	Yes	Yes	Usually used with program storage unit
General Instrument	8000	PMOS	8/8	1k	48	0.8/2	1.25/3.75	No	Yes	Yes/1	48	0	No	No	Yes	Yes	40	5,−12	No	Yes	Yes	Predecessor of F8
Intel	8008	PMOS	8/8	16k	48	0.8/2	12.5/37.5	No	Yes	Yes/1	6	7x14	No	No	Yes	Yes	18	5,−9	Yes	Yes	Yes	Predecessor of 8080, still in wide use
Intel	8080A	PMOS	8/8	64k	78	2.6/2	1.5/3.75	Yes[3]	Yes	Yes/1	8	RAM	No	Yes	Yes	Yes	40	5,12,−5	Yes	Yes	Yes	By and large, still the most popular
Intel	8085	NMOS	8/8	64k	80	3/1	1.3/5.85	Yes	Yes	Yes/4	8	RAM	Yes	Yes	Yes	Yes	40	5	Yes	Yes	Yes	8080 code compatible, has built-in clock
MOS Technology	MCS-650X	NMOS	8/8	64k	56	4/1	0.5/3.5	Yes	Yes	Yes/1	0	RAM	Yes	No	Yes	Yes	40	5	Yes	Yes	Yes	Provides 13 addressing modes
MOS Technology	MCS-651X	NMOS	8/8	64k	56	4/2	0.5/3.5	Yes	Yes	Yes/1	0	RAM	No	No	Yes	Yes	40	5	Yes	Yes	Yes	Similar to 650X but needs 2ϕ clock
Motorola	M6800	NMOS	8/8	64k	89	2/1	1/2.5	Yes	Yes	Yes/1	0	RAM	No	Yes	Yes	Yes	40	5	Yes	Yes	Yes	Available in new depletion-load version
Motorola	M6809	NMOS	8/8	64k	100+	2/1	2/5	Yes	Yes	Yes/1	0	RAM	Yes	Yes	Yes	Yes	40	5	Yes	Yes	Yes	Enhanced 6800 command set
Motorola	M6802	NMOS	8/8	64k	89	2/1	2/5	Yes	Yes	Yes/1	0	RAM	Yes	Yes	Yes	Yes	40	5	Yes	Yes	Yes	Has 128 x 8 on-chip RAM
National Semiconductor	SC/MP	PMOS NMOS	8/8	64k	46	4/1	5/10	NMOS only	Yes	Yes/1	0	RAM	Yes	Yes	No[4]	Yes	40	5,−7	Yes	Yes	Yes	Has handy daisy-chain capability
NEC Microcomputers	μPD 8080A	NMOS	8/8	64k	78	2/2	1.92/8.16	Yes[3]	Yes	Yes/1	8	RAM	No	Yes	Yes	Yes	40	5,12,−5	Yes	Yes	Yes	Pin compatible but does BCD subtraction
RCA	1802	CMOS	8/8	64k	91	6.4/1	2.5/3.75	Yes	Yes	Yes/1	16	RAM	Yes	Yes	Yes	Yes	40	3 to 12	Yes	Yes	Yes	Superseded two-chip version
RCA	1803	CMOS	8/8	64k	91	6.4/1	2.5/3.75	Yes	Yes	Yes/1	16	RAM	Yes	Yes	Yes	Yes	28	3 to 12	Yes	Yes	Yes	Trimmed down version of 1802
Scientific Microsystems	SMS-300	Bi-polar	8/8	8k+	8	10/1		Yes	No	No		0	No		Yes		50		No	Yes	Yes	Very specialized instruction set
Signetics	2650	NMOS	8/8	32k	75	1.2/1	4.8/9.6	Yes	Yes	Yes/1	7	8x15	No	Yes	Yes	Yes	40	5	Yes	Yes	Yes	Has two higher speed versions
Zilog	Z80	NMOS	8/8	64k	150+	4/1	1/5.75	Yes	Yes	Yes/1	14	RAM	No	Yes	Yes	Yes	40	5	Yes	Yes	Yes	8080 instructions are a subset
Intersil	6100	CMOS	12/12	4k	81	4/1	2.5/5.5	Yes	No	Yes/1	0	RAM	Yes	Yes	Yes	Yes	40	4 to 11	Yes	Yes	Yes	Emulates PDP-8 instruction set
Toshiba	T3190	PMOS NMOS	12/12	4k	108	2.5/1	10/30	Yes	No	Yes/8	8	RAM	No	Yes	Yes	Yes	36	5, −5	Yes	Yes	Yes	Has multiply and divide inst.
Data General	mN601	NMOS	16/16	32k	42	8.33/2	1.2/23.5	Yes	No	Yes/1	4	RAM	Yes	Yes	Yes	No	40	5,10,14,−4.25	Yes	Yes	Yes	Emulates NOVA instruction set
Fairchild	9440	I2L	16/16	64k	42	10/1		Yes	No	Yes/1	4	RAM	Yes	Yes	No[4]	No	40		No	No	No	Emulates NOVA instruction set
Ferranti	F100L	Bi-polar	16/16	32k	28	20/1	1.19/5.75	Yes	No	Yes/1	0	RAM	No	Yes	Yes	Yes	40	5	Yes	Yes	Yes	Can do double word operations
General Instrument	CP1600	NMOS	16/16	64k	87	4/2	1.6/48	Yes	No	Yes/1	8	RAM	No	Yes	Yes	Yes	40	5,12,−3	Yes	Yes	Yes	All internal registers can be accumulators
National Semiconductor	INS8900/PACE	NMOS/ PMOS	16/16	64k	45	2/2	2.5/5	No	Yes	Yes/6	4	10x16	No	Yes	Yes	Yes	40	5,8,−12	Yes	Yes	Yes	Architecture intended for data handling
Panafacom	MN1610	NMOS	16/16	64k	33	2/2	2/6	Yes[3]	No	Yes/3	5	RAM	No	No	Yes	No	40	5,12,−3	Yes	No	No	
Texas Instruments	TMS9980	NMOS	16/16[1]	16k	69	4/4	3.2/49.6	Yes[3]	No	Yes/4	16	RAM	Yes	Yes	Yes	No	40	5,12,−5	Yes	Yes	Yes	Small version of TMS 9900
Texas Instruments	TMS/SBP9900	NMOS I2L	16/16	32k	69	4/4	2/31	Yes[3]	No	Yes/16	16	RAM	Yes	Yes	Yes	No	64	5,12,−5	Yes	Yes	Yes	Emulates 990 mini instructions
Western Digital	WD-16	NMOS	16/16	64k	116	3.3/4	2.1/780	Yes	Yes	Yes/16	6	RAM	No	Yes	Yes	Yes	40	5,12,−5	Yes	Yes	No	Very similar to DEC LSI-11

1. Has 8-bit external buses and 16-bit internal buses   2. With maximum clock   3. Except clock lines   4. Standard TTL or MOS circuits will suffice

others, and are thus tailored for a specific group of applications. Instructions that you want but are not included in the instruction set can be provided with programmed routines, although you'll probably sacrifice some speed to get the extra commands.

Examine a particular unit's programming manual carefully. The number of instructions claimed for a processor can increase from one page to another. Often, this increase stems from the different ways used to define instructions. Many instructions are available in different modes or operate on different bits of a data word. Each variation in the same basic instruction produces a different operation code—a different instruction.

For example, the programming manual for a Z80 microprocessor says there are 158 "different" instructions. But taking into account all the possible addressing modes and variations, the 158 instructions become 696 operation codes. (Just to go back to the testing problem, there are 696! possible combinations of instructions. Multiply each instruction by 1.5 μs—assuming a 4-MHz clock—and then figure out how many years you'll need for a full test.)

Common addressing modes include direct, immediate and indirect, but many processors offer other modes, such as register, page 0, register indirect, extended, implied and relative.

Often, the most flexible instruction sets are available in 16-bit processors, since the units closely resemble minicomputers in both performance and design. For example, some 16-bit processors offer multiply and divide instructions that execute in tens of microseconds. Eight-bit processors can be programmed to do the same calculation, but take milliseconds to do the job. In general, processors with the same word length offer similar performance.

Analyze the μP's architecture

Chip vendors will tout the computer-like features of microprocessors every chance they get. These include the number and function of on-chip registers, the type and depth of the stack register, interrupt capability and the direct-memory-access feature. But when it comes to architecture, the chip vendors lose their voices to minicomputer manufacturers. They can't deliver as much performance.

The number of internal registers included in a processor is not really critical unless you are designing a minimal one or two-chip system. Essentially, the only register a processor needs is an accumulator. However, the accumulator must have access to memory, and an instruction set should permit immediate addressing and data manipulation between the memory and the accumulator. If indirect addressing is available, even special indexing registers can be imitated by using memory locations as registers.

The advantage of using on-chip registers instead of memory space is that the instructions are faster and the bits required are fewer. For example, not nearly as many bits are required to specify one of several predefined working registers as to specify a memory location. And since the registers are on-chip, access times are much shorter than for normal memory.

The type and flexibility—not just the quantity—of these on-chip registers is also important. Not every "general purpose" register can be incremented, tested for zero, decremented, or have other operations performed. Not every register can be used for program-loop control or counting or even indexed addressing, without some fancy programming tricks or excessive time delays.

Even the source and destination points for these registers must be examined. A processor should be able to load registers directly from memory—and memory from registers—without having the data first go into its accumulator.

Microprocessors are split about 50-50 between those that have on-chip subroutine stack registers and those that don't. The units without use memory as a subroutine stack, so they can handle an almost unlimited number of program subroutines. However, their chips must have a stack-pointer register, which must be set by one of the initialization instructions to point at the area of memory reserved for the stack. When the stack is on the processor chip, there is a limit to the number of subroutine levels that can be stored in the stack.

If an application involves asynchronous or unpredictable events, an interrupt capability on the processor is essential. Most units claim some form of interrupt capability, but only a few of the newer units can handle several levels of prioritized interrupt. Most of the processors announced in the last year can handle single-line, multilevel and vectored interrupts. And all their registers are automatically saved in the stack when an interrupt comes along; after the interrupt is serviced, the register contents are automatically restored.

When large amounts of data must be transferred back and forth between a μP's memory and peripherals, your processor should be able to withdraw itself from the loop and permit direct-memory accesses (DMAs). Most of the newer units can do that and even have one or two pins dedicated to a DMA-control function. A DMA transfer can often be five to ten times faster than transferring data through the processor itself for I/O applications.

Decide on the number of I/O lines

Most microprocessors provide the means to control input/output operations via specialized circuits. Microcomputers, on the other hand, usually have some of the I/O capability built in. If your application requires a fixed number of input lines and a fixed number of output lines, one of the all-in-one chips could be the answer, since they offer as many as 32 I/O lines in a single package. However, when your I/O requirements are subject to change, one of the

Table 2. All-in-one processors

Company	Device	Process technology	Word size in bits (data/inst.)	On-chip RAM size	On-chip ROM/ PROM size (words)	Off-chip memory expansion	Number of basic instructions	Maximum clock frequency (kHz)	On-chip clock	Instruction time (shortest/longest) μs	TTL compatible	BCD arithmetic	On-chip interrupts/levels	Subroutine nesting levels	General-purpose internal registers	Number of I/O lines	Additional special support circuits	Package size (DIP pins)	Voltages required (V)	Prototyping system avail.	Assembly language programming system	High-level language programming system	Time-sharing cross software	Comments
General Instrument	SBA	NMOS	1/8	120×1	1024×8	No	8	800	Yes	1.25/1.25	Yes	No	No	16	RAM	31	No	40	5,12	Yes	No	No	No	Will have expandable version
Essex International	SX-200	PMOS	4/8	64×4	1024×8	Yes	41	400	Yes	20/20	No	Yes	Yes/1	1	RAM	16	No	28	10 to 20	Yes	Yes	Yes	Yes	Has touch switch interface
ITT Semiconductor	7150	PMOS	?	?	N.A.[1]	?	?	25	Yes	?	?	?	?	?	?	14	Yes	14/18/24	−15	No	No	No	No	Designed for washing machines
National Semi	MM57109	PMOS	4/8	5×32	N.A.	Yes	70	400	No	1220/1 S	Yes	Yes	Yes/1	4	1	11	Yes	28	9	No	No	No	No	Has scientific calculation ability
	MM57140/57152	PMOS	4/8	55×4	630×8	No	35	280	Yes	16/16	Opt.	Yes	0	2	4	24	No	28	7.9 to 9.5	Yes	Yes	No	Yes	Drives LEDs or fluorescents
	MM5799	PMOS	4/8	96×4	1536×8	No	35	400	Yes	10/20	Opt.	Yes	0	2	5	23	Yes	28	7.9 to 9.5	Yes	Yes	No	Yes	Serial I/O and LED drive
	MM5731/82	PMOS	4/8	160×4	2048×8	Yes	35	400	No	10/20	Opt.	Yes	0	2	5	24	Yes	28	7.9 to 9.5	Yes	Yes	No	Yes	Two chip set
NEC Microcomputers	μPD548	PMOS	4/10	96×4	1920×10	Yes	72	200	No	10/20	Yes	Yes	Yes/2	4	RAM	35	No	42	−10	Yes	Yes	No	No	Can interface to keyboard
	μPD546	PMOS	4/8	96×4	2000×8	No	80	440	No	10/40	Yes	Yes	Yes/1	3	6	35	No	42	−10	Yes	Yes	No	Yes	Has 6-bit programmable timer
	μPD547	PMOS	4/8	64×4	1000×8	No	58	440	No	10/40	Yes	Yes	Yes/1	1	RAM	35	No	42	−10	Yes	Yes	No	Yes	Instructions are 546 subset
	μPD545	PMOS	4/8	32×4	640×8	No	58	440	No	10/40	Yes	Yes	Yes/1	1	RAM	21	No	28	−10	Yes	Yes	No	Yes	Can handle high voltages
Panasonic	MN1400	NMOS	4/8	64×4	1024×8	No	75	300	Yes	10/20	Yes	Yes	Yes/1	2	RAM	30	No	40	5	No	Yes	Yes	Yes	Complete all-in-one controller
	MN1402	NMOS	4/8	32×4	768×8	No	57	300	Yes	10/20	Yes	Yes	Yes/1	2	RAM	19	No	28	5	No	Yes	Yes	Yes	Smaller I/O version of 1400
	MN1498	NMOS	4/8	64×4	N.A.	Yes	68	300	Yes	10/20	Yes	Yes	Yes/1	2	RAM	18	No	40	5	No	Yes	Yes	Yes	Handles 1024 bytes of external memory
	MN1499	NMOS	4/8	64×4	N.A.	Yes	75	300	Yes	10/20	Yes	Yes	Yes/1	2	RAM	31	No	64	5	No	Yes	Yes	Yes	Handles 2048 bytes of external memory
Rockwell	PPS-4	PMOS	4/8	0	0	Yes	50	200/400 Two clocks	No	5/15	No	Yes	Yes/1	2	1	12+	Yes	42	−17/+5,−12	Yes	Yes	No	Yes	Combination ROM/RAM/I/O available
	PPS 4/2	PMOS	4/8	0	0	Yes	50	200/400	Yes	5/15	No	Yes	No	2	1	12+	Yes	42	−17/+5,−12	Yes	Yes	No	Yes	Same as PPS-4 but has internal clk
	PPS-4/1 MM77	PMOS	4/8	96×4	1344×8	RAM only	50	100/4	Yes	10/40	Yes	Yes	Yes/1	2	2+RAM	31	Yes	42	−15/+5,−10	Yes	Yes	No	Yes	I/O includes serial channel
	MM78	PMOS	4/8	128×4	2048×8	RAM only	50	100/4	Yes	10/40	Yes	Yes	Yes/1	2	2+RAM	31	Yes	42	−15/+5,−10	Yes	Yes	No	Yes	Software compatible with 77
	MM76	PMOS	4/8	48×4	640×8	RAM only	50	100/4	Yes	10/40	Yes	Yes	Yes/1	1	1+RAM	31	Yes	42	−15/+5,−10	Yes	Yes	No	Yes	Primarily used for keyboard display
	MM76/C	PMOS	4/8	48×4	640×8	RAM only	50	100/4	Yes	10/30	Yes	Yes	Yes/1	1	1+RAM	39	Yes	52	−15/+5,−10	Yes	Yes	No	Yes	Has high-speed counter
	MM76/D	PMOS	4/8	48×4	640×8	RAM only	50	100/4	Yes	10/30	Yes	Yes	Yes/1	1	1+RAM	37	Yes	52	−15/+5,−10	Yes	Yes	No	Yes	Has a/d converter on chip
	MM76/E	PMOS	4/8	48×4	1024×8	RAM only	50	100/4	Yes	10/30	Yes	Yes	Yes/1	1	1+RAM	31	Yes	42	−15/+5,−10	Yes	Yes	No	Yes	Larger ROM than MM76
	MM76/L	PMOS	4/8	48×4	640×8	RAM only	50	100/4	Yes	10/30	Yes	Yes	Yes/1	1	1+RAM	31	Yes	40	6 to 11	Yes	Yes	No	Yes	Low voltage version of 76
	MM75	PMOS	4/8	48×4	670×8	RAM only	50	100/4	Yes	10/40	Yes	Yes	Yes/1	1	1+RAM	22	Yes	28	−15/+5,−10	Yes	Yes	No	Yes	Reduced I/O version of 76
Texas Instruments	TMS-1000	PMOS/NMOS	4/8	64×4	1024×8	No	43	400	Yes	15/15	Yes	Yes	Yes/1	1	2	23/25	Yes	28/40	15	Yes	Yes	Yes	Yes	Also a 35 V family and a low voltage family TMS 1070/1270 and TMS 1100/1300
	TMS-1100	PMOS/NMOS	4/8	128×8	2048×8	No	40	400	Yes	15/15	Yes	Yes	Yes/1	1	2	23/28	Yes	28/40	15	Yes	Yes	Yes	Yes	Pin compatible with TMS-1000
	TMS-1018	PMOS	4/8	64×4	N.A.	No	43	400	Yes	15/15	Yes	Yes	No	N.A.	N.A.	4	No	28	15					Dedicated number cruncher

	Device	Tech		RAM	ROM																			Comments
	TMS-1022	PMOS	4/8	64×4	1024×4	No	43	400	Yes	15/15	Yes	Yes	Yes/1	1	2	N.A.	No	28	15					Dedicated CB PLL controller
	TMS-1117	PMOS	4/8	128×8	N.A.	No	43	400	Yes	15/15	Yes	Yes	No	N.A.	N.A.	19	Yes	28	15					Dedicated controller for microwave ovens
	TMS-1121	PMOS	4/8	128×4	2048×8	No	42	400	Yes	15/15	Yes	Yes	Yes/1	RAM	RAM	N.A.	Yes	40	15					Dedicated multiappliance timer/controller
	TMS-1330	PMOS	4/8	128×4	2048×8	No	42	400	Yes	15/15	Yes	Yes	Yes/1	RAM	RAM	31	Yes	40	15	Yes	Yes	No	Yes	Has on chip 5-bit a/d converter
Toshiba	T3444	NMOS	4/8	16×8	256×24	Yes	[3]	800	Yes	[3]	Yes	[3]	Yes/1	8	RAM	16	No	40	5	Yes	Yes	Yes	Yes	Intended for dedicated controllers
	T3472	NMOS	4/8	16×4	256×24	Yes	67	1000	Yes	33/360	Yes	Yes	Yes/2	8	RAM	16	Yes	42	5	Yes	Yes	Yes	Yes	Designed for keyboard/display interfacing
Western Digital	1872	PMOS	4/10	4×32	512×10	No	37	150	Yes	6.25/12.5	Yes	Yes	Yes/1	1	RAM	27	No	40	12	Yes	Yes	Yes	Yes	RAM holds BCD numbers
General Instrument	PIC-1650	NMOS	8/12	32×8	512×12	Yes	31	1000	Yes	4/8	Yes	Yes	Yes/1	2	RAM	32	No	40	5	Yes	Yes	Yes	Yes	Smaller I/O and larger ROMs avail
Intel	8041/8741	NMOS	8/8	64×8	1024×8	Yes	90	6000	Yes	2.5/5	Yes	Yes	Yes/1	RAM	RAM	18	Yes	40	5	Yes	Yes	Yes	Yes	Both a ROM and EPROM version are available
	8048/8748	NMOS	8/8	64×8	1024×8	Yes	96	6000	Yes	2.5/5	Yes	Yes	Yes/1	8	RAM	27	Yes	40	5	Yes	Yes	Yes	Yes	8748 has uv PROM
Mostek 1 chip F-8	3870	NMOS	8/8	64×8	2048×8	Yes	70+	4000	Yes	1/6.5	Yes	Yes	Yes/4	RAM	RAM	32	Yes	40	5	Yes	Yes	Yes	Yes	Software compatible with F8
Motorola	6400	NMOS	8/8	32×8	1024×8	Yes	?	8000	Yes	?	Yes	?	?	?	RAM	?	Yes	?	5	Yes	1978	1978	1978	Intended for controller use
	6801	NMOS	8/8	?	?	Yes	?	2000	?	?	Yes	?	?	?	?	?	Yes	40	5	No	1978	1978	1978	Available 1978
Rockwell	PPS-8	PMOS	8/8	0	0	Yes	100	256/4	No	4/12	No	Yes	Yes/3	16	2	0+	Yes	42	−17/+5,−12	Yes	Yes	No	Yes	Combination RAM/ROM/I/O support
	PPS-8/2	PMOS	8/8	0	0	Yes	100	200/4	No	5/15	No	Yes	Yes/3	16	2	0+	Yes	42	−17/+5,−12	Yes	Yes	No	Yes	I/O chip includes clock
Zilog	Z8	NMOS	8/8	96×8	2048×8	Yes	?	4000	Yes	0.75/?	Yes	Yes	Yes/?	?	RAM	32	Yes	40	5	1978	1978	1978	1978	Has two counter/timers
Texas Instruments	TMS 9940	NMOS	[2]	128×8	2048×8	No	68	5000	Yes	2/452	Yes	Yes	Yes/4	64	RAM	16	No	40	5	Yes	Yes	Yes	Yes	Two versions available, one has a 2 k EPROM, the other a 2 k ROM

1 Not applicable   ? Not available   2 Externally 8 bits, internally 16 bits   3 User defined

more general-purpose units would probably be better.

Ideally, when you pick a processor with I/O lines on the same chip, you'd like to be able to configure each line as you need it. With some processors, you can configure each line to act as either an input or an output. But many processors don't have this capability—and skimming the data sheet may not uncover this deficiency.

Often, the I/O lines are already dedicated—some fixed as outputs and the rest as inputs. And, even if they are programmable, they might be programmable only on a word basis. Individual lines cannot be set as input or output. Some all-in-one circuits can be expanded beyond their limited on-chip I/O capability, but by the time you add all the necessary expansion circuits, you'll be wishing that you had used a general-purpose chip instead.

While you're checking the capabilities of the I/O lines, check the capabilities of the I/O instructions. Processors with dedicated I/O lines usually have special instructions for manipulating bits, setting mask codes and even performing operations directly on the bits in the port. General-purpose processors usually don't have any I/O port lines, but there are many specially designed support circuits available to provide both serial and parallel I/O ports.

Serial I/O capability is available only on a few processor chips but if you need only one serial port along with some parallel I/O lines you should consider a processor with serial I/O to keep the chip count minimal. Controlling the serial port is done via the program so no extra hardware is needed, except for a buffer or level shifter.

For almost all processors, data sheets claim TTL compatibility—but don't expect most MOS processors to drive more than one normalized or low-power TTL load. Older processors can't even drive that much of a load without pull-up resistors or MOS-to-TTL level shifters and buffers.

Few microprocessor spec sheets deal with noise immunity—an important spec if your processor will be used in industrial environments. Comparing input levels for peripheral circuits with the address-output levels of a certain processor may reveal little or no protection against unwanted transients. If you don't have the needed noise immunity, you will quickly discover the need when you move the prototype from the lab bench to the factory floor.

However, some CMOS processors can provide noise immunity without much strain since the signal swings typically range from the supply to ground. Of course, you can get around the noise problem by using inexpensive level shifters and pull-up resistors, but they take up valuable board space and power.

You can also roll your own processor

Now that bit-slice chips are available, you can design your own multichip processor. A bit-slice-based processor will be two to five times faster than NMOS processors since just about every slice is bipolar and takes under 100 ns to execute an instruction. Right?

Wrong. The 100 ns refers to a microinstruction—not a complete instruction as in microprocessors.

In a microprocessor, microprograms tell the logic circuits in the chip how to route data and set up the ALU to perform an operation. In a bit slice, you must program these instructions into the microprogram memory. (The microprogram memory consists of a ROM array that is not part of the addressable RAM or major program space.)

Normally, a programmed bit-slice processor may require anywhere from 100 to 1024 words of microprogram memory to control all the operations. Each word, in turn, can consist of many bits since it can be used to control more than just the processor slice. It can also control peripherals, memories and other processor subfunctions. Depending on the application, a microprogram-control word can be from about 10 to 60 bits long.

The advantages of microprogramming your own processor versus buying a programmed chip include the ability to write your own macroinstructions and thus customize for your application.

With microprogramming, you don't need as much control hardware either—software does more of the peripheral control than with a macroprogrammed processor. This proves invaluable in applications requiring in excess of tens of thousands of units. Microprogramming also presents a good alternative when a system must be emulated or when critical short routines must be executed rapidly.

However, microprogramming does have a drawback. Since the programmer works very closely with the timing relationships of the machine itself and on a machine-language level (the 1's and 0's), developing a program is difficult. Each application requires a different microprogram, with a different instruction set, so designs cannot be transferred readily. Nor can software design aids, most of which are geared for a fixed in-

Table 3. Bit-slice families

Company	Series	Process technology	ALU part number	ALU word size (bits)	Number of ALU instructions	Can ALU do BCD arithmetic	Maximum ALU clock rate (MHz)	General-purpose registers in ALU	ALU package size (DIP pins)	Microprogram sequencer number	Number of address bits	Maximum sequencer clock rate (MHz)	Number of sequencer commands	Sequencer stack size	Sequence package size (DIP pins)	Are parts TTL compatible	Voltages required (V)	Prototyping system available	Development software available	Specialized support circuits available	Comments
Advanced Micro Devices	2900	STTL	2901A	4	16	No	10	16	40	2909/11	4	10	12	4×4	28/20	Yes	5	Yes	Yes	Yes	Has widest number of second sources
		STTL	2903	4	25	No	10	16	48												ALU has nine more instructions than 2901, including multiply and divide.
Fairchild	Macrologic	STTL/CMOS	9405/34705	4	64	No	10	8	24	9406	4	10	4	16×4	24	Yes	5	Yes	Yes	Yes	CMOS version (34705) operates at 2 MHz
	100k 8-bit	ECL	ADIU	8	27	Yes	20	1	*	*	*	*	*	*	*	*	−4,5,−2	1978	1978	1978	Only 8-bit slice
Intel	3000	STTL	3002	2	40	No	10	11	28	3001	9	10+	11	0	40	Yes	5	Yes	Yes	Yes	Only 2-bit ALU available
Monolithic Memories	5700/6700	STTL	57/6701	4	32	No	5	16	40	6710	9	10+	8	0	40	Yes	5	Yes	?	No	Has double-addressing capability
Motorola	10800	ECL	10800	4	100+	Yes	20	0	48	10801	4	20	16	4×4	48	No	−2,−5.2	Yes	Yes	Yes	Fastest bit slice available
National Semiconductor	IMP-4	PMOS	00A/520	4	8	No	5.714	20	24	4A/521	4	5.714	100+	in ALU	24	Yes	+5,−12,	Yes	Yes	No	Need external register file
	IMP-8	PMOS	00A/520	4	8	No	5.714	20	24	8A/521	8	5.714	100+	in ALU	24	Yes	+5,−12	Yes	Yes	No	Uses IMP-4 ALUs with big ROM
	IMP-16	PMOS	00A/520	4	8	No	5.714	20	24	16A/521	16	5.714	100+	in ALU	24	Yes	+5,−12	Yes	Yes	No	Two development systems available
Texas Instruments	SBP-0400A	I²L	SBP 0400	4	512	No	5	10	40	74S482	4	20	64	4×4	20	Yes	Current	Yes	No	No	Has pipeline register
	SBP-0401A	I²L	SBP 0401	4	512	No	5	10	40	74S482	4	20	64	4×4	20	Yes	Current	Yes	No	No	Does not have pipeline register
	74S481	STTL	74S481	4	24,780	No	10	0	48	74S482	4	20	64	4×4	20	Yes	5	Yes	No	Yes	Very flexible instruction set

*In definition stage

struction set, be used with a bit-slice processor's alterable macroinstruction set.

What's happening

Even in the short interval since mid-summer 1977, new microprocessors and microcomputers have been introduced.

For example, Texas Instruments claims a first with its TMS9940—the first 16-bit microcomputer chip. It is instruction compatible with the other TMS9900 products except for four instructions. The development version puts a 2048-byte erasable PROM and the processor on the same chip, while the production version puts a mask-programmed ROM on the chip.

Drifting down to the low-end microcontrollers: Both Toshiba and Panasonic (Matsushita) have introduced 4-bit processors for dedicated-control applications. Toshiba offers the T3444 and 3472 processors for high-speed data handling and man/machine interfacing, respectively. Preprogrammed versions of the T3444 are available as floppy-disc controllers and cassette controllers.

Panasonic's MN1400 family consists of four models, each with a different amount of on-board memory and different features. The MN1499 is the prototyping unit and has provisions for external memory and 75 instructions.

The other newcomer is the 4-bit S2000 developed by American Microsystems. It is a display-oriented microcomputer with a 1 k × 8 on-chip ROM and drivers for either a LED or vacuum fluorescent display. Meanwhile, more details have finally come out about the 2903, an enhanced version of the 2901A bit slice from Advanced Micro Devices. The 2903 has nine additional instructions—unsigned multiply, two's complement multiply, increment by one or two, sign/magnitude two's complement, two's complement multiply correction, single length normalize, double length normalize and first divide op., two's complement divide, and two's complement divide, correction, and remainder. No other processor slice has multiplication or division routines.

Products that will appear in early 1978 include an 8-bit ECL processor slice currently being developed by Fairchild, the Z8 microcomputer from Zilog, and a 2-k × 8 version of the 8048 from Intel.

More details of the Zilog Z8 all-in-one microcomputer have been released since the product was brought to light in the middle of the summer in 1977. The 8-bit processor chip includes a 96-byte RAM, where each byte can act as an accumulator. Data can be transferred back and forth to any RAM word by the I/O ports or ALU. Although the Z8's instruction set has fewer basic instructions than the Z80, more variations are possible. So the number of op codes increases.

Of the 32 I/O lines on the Z8, 16 are set up to be individual-line programmable as input or output, eight lines are set to be byte-programmable as input, output or bidirectional, and eight can be divided into 4-bit sections, each of which can be either input, output or bidirectional lines. Software controls all the port I/O lines and the control commands can be either mask-programmed on the processor chip or stored in external memory.

External memory for the Z8 can be expanded so that the processor addresses both 65 kbytes of ROM and another 65 kbytes of RAM or ROM. The processor also has an on-chip prioritized interrupt structure that is software-controllable. Up to six interrupts can be handled without any support circuits.

The processor executes its instructions fairly fast —the shortest instruction can run in 0.75 μs and the longest in 1.9 μs.

Also on the Z8 chip are two software-controllable 8-bit counter/timers that can interrupt the processor. One timer has an 8-bit prescaler that is also software programmable so that large timing loops can be used.

Zilog is also readying the Z8000, an NMOS 16-bit microprocessor with the equivalent processing power of a minicomputer such as the 11/70 made by Digital Equipment Corp. (Maynard, MA). The Z8000 will have a RAM-addressing capability of millions of bytes (with the use of a special memory-expander chip) and have advanced instructions such as hardware multiply and divide.

The processor has been optimized to execute compiler-generated code, according to company officials. It can perform instructions in less than 1 μs (for the shortest instruction). Still, the processor instructions will be compatible with the assembly-level mnemonics already in use on the Z80. A translator program will also by available to transfer assembly-level Z80 programs into Z8000 op code.

Both the Z8 and Z8000 will not be available until 1978, with the Z8 scheduled for early 1978 and the Z8000 for late 1978.

This year has been a good one for alternate-source agreements. Even Intel has selected a few companies to whom it will provide masks for its 8048 and 8085 microprocessors. Monolithic Memories has finally found an alternate source—ITT—for its 5701/6701 bit slice just as it starts manufacturing the 2901A bit slice as an alternate source to AMD.

In the 4-bit area, Texas Instruments has quietly postponed its introduction of NMOS equivalents to its TMS-1000 family. But even more quietly, TI has announced a CMOS equivalent. The only 4-bit CMOS processor on the market, it should find a home in many portable and battery-operated items.

Take a close look at some units

Most of this year's development activity has been in 8-bit microprocessors and microcomputers. The Mostek 3870 single-chip microcomputer is in a head-to-head confrontation with the Intel 8048. Both units have many of the same features, with the Mostek chip

Processor alternate source directory

Generic type number	Data word size (bits)	Technology	Original source	Alternate sources	Data manual page number
1600, 1610	16	NMOS	General Instrument	EM&M Semiconductor	62
1650, 1655	8	NMOS	General Instrument	EM&M Semiconductor	33
1802, 1803	8	CMOS	RCA	Hughes & Solid State Scientific	45
1872	4	PMOS	Western Digital	None	38
2650	8	NMOS	Signetics	Advanced Memory Systems National Semiconductor	52
2900	4	STTL	Advanced Micro Devices	Fairchild, Monolithic Memories, Motorola, National Semiconductor, Raytheon, Sescosem, Signetics	70
3000	2	STTL	Intel	Signetics	68
3850	8	NMOS	Fairchild	Mostek, Motorola	46
3859	8	NMOS	Fairchild	Discontinued	—
3870	8	NMOS	Mostek	Fairchild, Motorola	35
4040/4004	4	PMOS	Intel	National Semiconductor	42
5701/6701	4	STTL	Monolithic Memories	ITT Semiconductor	71
6100	12	CMOS	Intersil	Harris Semiconductor	57
6400	8	NMOS	Motorola	None	—
65XX	8	NMOS	MOS Technology	Rockwell, Synertek	49
6800, 68A00, 68B00	8	NMOS	Motorola	American Microsystems, Fairchild, Fujitsu, Hitachi, Sescosem Thompson CSF	50
6801	8	NMOS	Motorola	None*	—
6802	8	NMOS	Motorola	None	51
6809	8	NMOS	Motorola	None*	39
7150	4	PMOS	ITT Semiconductor	None	
8000	8	PMOS	General Instrument	AEG, SGS-ATEs	36
8008	8	PMOS	Intel	None	54
8035, 8048, 8748	8	NMOS	Intel	Advanced Micro Devices, NEC and Signetics	34
8041, 8741	8	NMOS	Intel	None	40
8080A	8	NMOS	Intel	Advanced Micro Devices, NEC, National Semiconductor, Signetics, Texas Instruments	47
8085	8	NMOS	Intel	Advanced Micro Devices, NEC	48
8900	16	PMOS	National Semiconductor	None	63
9002	8	NMOS	Electronic Arrays	Discontinued	—
9080	8	NMOS	Advanced Micro Devices	Actually an alternate source for 8080	47
9405, 34705	4	STTL/CMOS	Fairchild (Macrologic)	Signetics	69
9440	16	I²L	Fairchild	None	60

*This product is still in development

offering double the ROM capacity and the Intel device a larger instruction set.

Intel introduced the 8048 and 8085 processor families last year, with a flurry of industry firsts. A pin-compatible unit with the 8048, the 8748 has all the features of the 8048, but instead of containing 1024 bytes of mask-programmable ROM, the 8748 contains 1024 bytes of ultraviolet, erasable, programmable read-only memory. Not only is the PROM included on the chip, but the chip itself can operate from a single 5-V supply—another first.

Support for the 8048 and 8085 comes from a family of 8-bit auxiliary chips, including the 8155, a 256 × 8 static RAM with programmable 14-bit timer and 22 lines of programmable I/O—all on one chip. There's also the 8355/8755, a 2048 × 8 ROM with 16 lines of programmable I/O, or a 2048 × 8 UV EPROM with 16 lines of programmable I/O. Both the 8155 and 8355/8755 also help simplify the interface between Intel's other new processor, the 8085, and the outside world.

The 8085 is a souped-up 8080A with two more instructions, some new control lines, an on-chip clock oscillator, and a faster instruction-execution speed. However, to get the additional control capability while keeping the processor in its 40-pin package, something

Processor alternate source directory

Generic type number	Data word size (bits)	Technology	Original source	Alternate sources	Data manual page number
9900	16	I²L/NMOS	Texas Instruments	American Microsystems (NMOS version)	65
9940	16	NMOS	Texas Instruments	None*	37
9980	16	NMOS	Texas Instruments	None	66
10800	4	ECL	Motorola	None	72
14500	1	CMOS	Motorola	None	41
8X300	8	STTL	Signetics	None	44
74S481	4	STTL	Texas Instruments	None	74
100 K	8	ECL	Fairchild	None*	29
COPS	4	PMOS	National Semiconductor	None	—
F8	8	NMOS	Fairchild	See 3850	59
F100L	16	Bipolar	Ferranti	None	75
IMP-4, 8, 16	4, 8, 16	PMOS	National Semiconductor	Rockwell	
Macrologic	4	STTL/CMOS	Fairchild	See 9405, 34705	—
MCP-1600/WD-16	16	NMOS	Western Digital	None	67
Micromachine	8	NMOS	Fairchild	See 3859	—
mN601	16	NMOS	Data General	None	61
MN1400	4	NMOS	Panasonic	None	25
MN1610	16	NMOS	Panafacom	None	64
PACE	16	PMOS	National Semiconductor	Rockwell	
PPS-4	4	PMOS	Rockwell	National Semiconductor	43
PPS-4/1	4	PMOS	Rockwell	None	32
PPS-4/2	4	PMOS	Rockwell	None	43
PPS-8	8	PMOS	Rockwell	National Semiconductor	56
PPS-8/2	8	PMOS	Rockwell	None	56
S2000	4	NMOS	American Microsystems	None	24
SBA	1	NMOS	General Instrument	None	22
SBP0400A/ 0401A	4	I²L	Texas Instruments	None	73
SC/MP, SC/MPII	8	NMOS/PMOS	National Semiconductor	Rockwell, Signetics, Western Digital	55
SMS-300	8	STTL	Scientific Microsystems	Signetics	—
SX200	4	PMOS	Essex International	None	28
T3190	12	PMOS, NMOS	Toshiba	None	59
T3444	4	NMOS	Toshiba	None	26
T3472	4	NMOS	Toshiba	None	27
TMS1000, 1100, 1200, 1300	4	CMOS, NMOS or PMOS	Texas Instruments	Motorola for CMOS version	23
uCOM 42	4	PMOS	NEC	None	30
uCOM 43, 44, 45	4	PMOS	NEC	None	31
Z8	8	NMOS	Zilog	None*	—
Z80	8	NMOS·	Zilog	Mostek, Sharp	53

had to be forfeited.

So the 8080A's totally separate data and address buses had to go. The 8085 has the eight most-significant address bits brought out to their own pins, but the eight least-significant address bits are multiplexed on the eight data-bus lines. So that a complete system can be formed with only two chips, the 8355/8755 and the 8155 have internal address latches that can hold the first eight bits of the address.

The 8085 contains the equivalent of the bus controller and clock generator on its chip. All the 8080A's software is compatible with the 8085. The only changes you may have to make are in timing loops since the time will change with the higher clock frequency. The processor chips, of course, are not pin-compatible, so upgrading the system really means redesigning the circuit board. However, all chips in the 8085 can operate from a single 5-V supply.

Mostek's 3870 doesn't have any new specialized support circuits, but it is compatible with all the older F8 processor circuits and software. So popular is the 3870, in fact, that Fairchild, the original developer of the F8, has scratched plans to market its own one-chip microcomputer, the 3859. Instead it will alternate-source the 3870, currently the only 8-bit microcomputer with 2048 bytes of on-chip storage.

Table 4. Directory of µPs by vendor

Manufacturer	Microprocessor model number
AEG Telefunken	Series 8000*
Advanced Micro Devices	2900, 8048*, 8080*, 8085*
Advanced Memory Systems (Intersil)	2650*
American Microsystems	6800*, 9900*, S2000
Data General	mN601 (microNova)
EM&M Semi	CP1600*, 1610*, 1650*, 1655*
Essex International	SX200
Fairchild	Macrologic (9405), 100K, 2900*, 3850(F8), 3870*, 6800*, 9440
Ferranti	F100-L
Fujitsu	6800*
General Instrument	CP1600, 1610, 1650, 1655, SBA
Harris Semiconductor	6100*
Hitachi	6800*
Hughes	1802*
Intel	3000, 4004/4040, 8008, 8048, 8080A, 8085
Intersil	IM6100
ITT	1600*, 5701/6701*, 7150
Monolithic Memories	2900*, 5701/6701
MOS Technology	65XX
Mostek	3850*, 3870, Z80*
Motorola	2900*, 3850*, 3870*, 6400, 6800, 6801, 6802, 6809, 10800, 14500
National Semiconductor	2650*, 2900*, 4004/4040*, 8080A* COPS, IMP-4, 8, 16, INS8900, PACE,
NEC	8048*, 8080A*, uCOM 42, 43, 44, 45
Panafacom	MN1610
Panasonic	MN1400
Philips	8080A*
RCA	CDP1802
Raytheon	2900*
Rockwell	65XX*, PPS 4, 4/1, 4/2, 8, 8/2, SC/MP II*
SGS-ATES	Series 8000*
Scientific Microsystems	SMS-300
Sharp	Z80*
Siemens	8080A*
Signetics	8X300, 2650A, 2900*, 8048*, 8080A*, 8085*, 9405*, 34705*, SMS-300*
Solid State Scientific	1802*
Synertek	65XX*
Texas Instruments	74S481, 8080A*, SBP-0400A/0401A, TMS-1000, TMS-9900, 9940, 9980
Thomson CSF/Sescosem	2900*, 6800*
Toshiba	T3190, T3444, T3472
Western Digital	1872, MCP1600/WD-16, SC/MP II*
Zilog	Z8, Z80, Z8000

*Alternate source product

Meanwhile, no 16-bit processor has captured a dominant market share. The biggest 16-bit trend is price reductions. General Instrument, for instance, recently introduced an $8 version (100 qty) of its CP1600 16-bit microprocessor. The low-cost 1610 is totally pin and software-compatible. Performance, however, was traded off for low cost—the 1610 operates at a 2-MHz maximum clock instead of 4 MHz, and comes in a plastic—not ceramic—40-pin DIP.

National Semiconductor has upgraded its PMOS 16-bit microprocessor, the PACE, with an NMOS equivalent, the INS8900, which performs better for the same price.

Ferranti's bipolar 16-bit processor, the F100L, is not well known in the U.S. But with its rapid clock speed, it can provide high performance, and since it's a bipolar device, it can operate over the full military temperature range.

The only other 16-bit bipolar processor is the SBP9900 from TI. The SBP9900 and its NMOS equivalent, the TMS9900, as well as a "shrink" (16-bit internal data bus, 8-bit external) version, the TMS9980, are all software-compatible with each other and with TI's 990 series of minicomputers. Software-development costs for the 9900 can be kept down since the 990 minicomputers have an extensive program library.

The same is true for the mN601 (microNova) from Data General. The 16-bit mN601 is software-compatible with the company's Nova series of mini-computers, so it has a vast repertoire of applications software. Also available are all the peripheral devices and interface circuits already designed for the Nova minicomputers.

Fairchild has announced a bipolar (I³L) 16-bit machine, the 9440, that emulates the Nova 1200 minicomputer-instruction set. However, due to patent-infringement lawsuits brought on by Data General (the developer of the Nova), the 9440 will not be available for a while.

Getting all the hardware together for a prototype system is probably the easier half of system design. The harder half is getting the software to control the system. Writing the code to control the micro-processor, microcomputer or bit slice can take about double the time you typically allot for it—and possibly cost as much as $100,000. However, the software cost can be amortized by the number of systems produced since it is a one-shot expense.

Speed program development with design aids

Almost every manufacturer of a processor product —and several other manufacturers—offer some form of development system to help you develop both hardware and software for the processor. However, features vary considerably from one manufacturer's system to the next. Depending on the features each system offers, be prepared to spend anywhere from

$6000 to $15,000 for a system that permits you to program only one manufacturer's processor.

Only one or two systems can program more than one manufacturer's processor—that capability will cost you about $25,000. But what do you get for the money? Typically you're buying a microcomputer with about 32 kwords of RAM, several kwords of ROM, a dual floppy-disc system, a CRT terminal and a printer, paper-tape reader/punch and possibly a PROM programmer. The floppy-disc memory and the ROMs contain most of the control programs needed to develop your own programs.

If you don't want to invest in major equipment such as a development system, you can use a computer (usually a large one) to develop your programs. But depending on how long it takes to develop your program, going this route could be more expensive in the long run.

Typical programs you would use during a program-development cycle include an assembler, editor and a compiler. There are also large programs written in Basic, variations of PL/1 and Fortran that are used first to develop programs in these higher-level languages, then to translate the instructions down to the actual operation code needed to control the processor. These languages, though, generate more code than is necessary. But that's the price you pay if you don't want to work in the assembly language of the processor itself.

An assembler is a program that translates assembly-language statements into machine code that your processor can execute. However, there are many types of assemblers, each with its idiosyncrasies.

Essentially, an assembler reads statements written in mnemonic or symbolic form and produces the op codes necessary to run the processor. Errors due to misuse of the assembly language can be detected by the better assemblers and pointed out before the code is programmed into the processor.

Most assemblers offered require two passes through the mnemonics to be assembled before they complete their job. Usually, on the first pass the assembler assigns addresses to all jump symbols and labels used in the program. On the second pass, all instructions are converted into binary, with all the correct jump locations inserted into the proper places.

More efficient assemblers require only one pass through the mnemonic listings to do the job completely, which cuts the time needed to obtain binary codes. Many of the assemblers also offer the convenience of transferring the binary codes directly to a paper tape or PROM, thus providing a permanent record of the program and putting it in a form easy for the processor to digest.

The more powerful assemblers often include another feature, called macro capability. This feature permits short, oft-used mnemonic routines to be represented by a new mnemonic that can then be substituted into the program under development. When the final program is assembled, the macroassembler automatically substitutes the proper code sequence.

Editor programs permit you to write programs in assembly language and to change them at will with simple commands. They are available either on time-sharing systems or on most of the purchasable development systems. With editors, you can add documentation; store, combine and retrieve programs; and deliver programs to paper tape or printers.

The coding process is usually completed with a loader. Usually stored in ROM, a loader transfers the binary programs from paper tape into RAM, from ROM into RAM or from some form of magnetic storage into the computer. A relocating loader automatically readjusts program addresses and loads the resulting instructions into the computer. Another feature some loaders offer is a linking capability, which lets you use routines with undefined labels. Missing label definitions are filled in as the program is loaded.

Compiler programs let you develop your program in a higher-level language. Since many programmers are familiar with languages such as Fortran or PL or Basic, this capability cuts development time. The biggest factors in deciding whether or not to use a high-level language are turnaround time and memory size. (Code generated by high-level languages can require about 20 to 50% more memory space than assembly-language-generated programs.)

In addition to the basic development aids, simulators, emulators and debuggers are usually mandatory to track down errors that might still remain in the code. For the same reason hardware emulators and in-circuit emulation are handy capabilities to have in a development system.

Don't overlook the learning aids

Anyone interested in designing μP-based equipment is immediately confronted with a bewildering variety of evaluation kits, learning aids, design aids, teaching aids and programming aids. Because the μP market has grown so rapidly, there are no exact definitions for the aids.

"Aids" currently range from under $200 to well over $20,000 depending on the features. But one subgroup, from $100 to $900, permits just about anyone to get "hands on" experience with a particular processor.

Almost all the inexpensive microprocessor design aids are aimed at 8-bit devices—there are no 4-bit microprocessor or microcomputer design aids. There are, however, several inexpensive evaluation kits for the two-bit Series 3000 bit slice and the 2900 4-bit slice.

For the 8-bit processors, Intel offers several kits as well as preassembled boards for its 8080A and 8085. Motorola offers several kits for its 6800. National Semiconductor offers a kit and some boards for the SC/MP. RCA offers a designer's kit for its 1802. Intersil offers a learning system for its 6100. MOS Technology offers a system for its 6502. Both Fairchild and Mostek offer boards for the F8. Zilog offers a family of boards for the Z80. Signetics offers a board for the 2650 and another for its 8X300. American Microsystems offers several kits for the 6800. And the list of "offerings" keeps growing as more processors are developed.

Software for microprocessors can also be as confusing to select as design aids. Basically, software is available in resident and nonresident forms—and there are several hundred variations in each form. Resident software consists of programs written in the instructions of a specific microprocessor and ready to run on a system that uses that micro. Nonresident software consists of programs that run on one processor (typically, a minicomputer or larger processor) to help you develop the software of another processor (typically at μP).

Most microprocessor-development systems, which range from the $100 kit to the $20,000 work station, come with some form of resident software—if the system is designed to develop code for one type of microprocessor. Some development stations, though, don't have truly resident software. For example, the 8002 universal microprocessor development system from Tektronix (Beaverton, OR) uses the 2650 as the main controller, but it can also be used to develop code for the 8080A, 6800, Z80 and TMS9900 processors.

For less expensive systems, the software included is usually minimal and often stored in ROMs (sometimes referred to as firmware). The more expensive systems usually contain either a paper-tape reader or a floppy-disc drive to permit large programs to be entered and help you develop software.

Firmware on most of the smaller development systems usually consists of a monitor program that permits you to use either a TTY or CRT terminal with the board and write your programs in machine code. Such commands as examine a memory location, change its contents and examine the next location, start execution at a specific location, and establish breakpoints to allow selected program sections to be executed are available on most monitors.

However, if you want the convenience of working in assembly language, you'll have to use a fairly large development system, since most assembly-language programs require several thousand bytes of RAM. Extensive program-development systems are available from most processor vendors, but other alternatives are available from many companies. Futuredata Computer Corp. (formerly Microkit) in Los Angeles offers a flexible system that provides assembly-language capability for the 8080, Z80 and the 6800. Other companies offering systems include muPro (Cupertino, CA) and Wintek (Lafayette, IN). The μPro System 80, intended for 8080A users, not only lets you develop programs for the 8080A, but also contains an in-circuit emulator, a field-test system, and an 8080 microcomputer. The system uses a language developed by muPro called BSAL-80, a nonmnemonic language.

The Wintek systems use the 6800 and, since they are designed on a standard 44-pin circuit card (dual 22-pin), can be installed in a standard card rack.

Although not quite design aids, some of the newer microcomputer systems such as the PET made by Commodore (Palo Alto, CA) and the TRS-80 made by Radio Shack (Fort Worth, TX) come ready-to-use and let you write programs in Basic and load or store the programs on a magnetic-cassette transport. The 6502-based PET has an IEEE-488 interface bus, so it can figure in many instrumentation applications. What's more, the price for the processor with integral CRT, 12 k of ROM, 4 k of RAM, cassette deck and 70-key keyboard is only $595.

The Z80-based Radio Shack system also includes 4 k of RAM and 4 k of ROM, but has a separate video monitor, cassette deck and keyboard/CPU as well.

Don't want hardware? Try time-sharing

The accessibility of large computers and time-sharing services has sparked the processor manufacturers to develop higher-level programs that can run on the large machines and be shared by hundreds of users at the same time. Programs are now available in machine language, forms of PL/1, Fortran and Cobol to permit you not only to develop programs in higher languages but also to get processor-compatible code when you're done.

Such programs are usually not as efficient as assembly-language programs. However, some time-sharing companies have helped reduce the inefficiencies by developing their own software for program development. For instance, the Boston Systems Office uses large minicomputers in its time-sharing network, and develops its own software in the minicomputers' assembly language. What this means is more efficient use of the computer's time and thus smaller time-sharing bills.

Some of the other larger companies that offer μP-development programs include National CSS (Norwalk, CT), General Electric Information Services (Bethesda, MD), First Data (Waltham, MA), United Computer Systems (Kansas City, MO) and Tymshare (Cupertino, CA). Each company's original programs will offer different features, so you must get each company's manual and compare features to make sure you get what you need.

A high-level system often lets you develop the program for your system before the hardware can be prototyped—sometimes even before a dollar is spent for hardware—since complete simulators and emulators are available for many processors. Cross-assemblers are commonly available in Fortran, versions of PL/1 and assembly language. Some assemblers even provide more than one machine-code format for absolute and relocatable code listings.

Compiler and integrator programs are available in PL/M, PL/W, PL/Z, MPL, Fortran, Cobol, Forth. And if that isn't enough alphabet soup, there are at least as many that have gone unnamed.

However, all isn't roses with time-sharing services —computer time is expensive. If you're concerned with CPU time, keep a careful watch over the use of a terminal with a time-shared computer. And CPU time isn't the only big expense. Storage space reserved, output time and communication links, and manpower will also cost you dearly.

Software costs can vary widely, depending on the design approach taken by the programmer. Some programmers can also keep the hardware cost down by transferring some of the hardware into software routines handled by the microcomputer. Often, the more functions you can assign to software, the more flexible the final system. Of course, you shouldn't burden the processor with so many little things that it can't do the job you originally wanted it for.

Software cost can get bothersome if you saddle capable programmers with a new and totally un-familiar instruction set. The learning curve starts at the peak cost and must be given time to work its way back to average as the programmers become familiar with each processor's language. And with the approx-imately 40 languages that have appeared the last six years, it will take a while before they catch up.

When you start a microprocessor development pro-gram, don't just consider the circuit hardware and the programming language—look at the development sys-tem itself. One of the most overlooked items is some form of high-speed, hard-copy output device. Sure, the ASR-33 teletypewriter is the industry workhorse— but it's too slow for many program-development uses.

Say you've spent the day working on a program and you want to get a printout of your 2000-line program with all comment notes to check out. If you're using a 10 to 50 character-per-second printer, forget it. Assuming each line has about 50 characters and the printer chugs away at 10 cps, you'll have to wait about three hours for the listing. With a 50-cps printer the delay is less—only half an hour.

Does your system use a cassette, cartridge or disc-file system? Floppy-disc operating systems usually offer the fastest performance, but they're also the most expensive. But in a dual-disc system one disc holds main operating programs, while the other stores user programs. This method helps reduce access time, while providing a more flexible development system.

If there is an ideal development system, it hasn't been put on the market yet. Ideally, the basic hard-ware should include a universal CPU, a full comple-ment of RAM and ROM-based bootstrap-loader pro-grams, general-purpose interfaces for terminals, printers, disc drivers, PROM programmers, paper-tape readers/punches, etc., a CRT terminal with a few programmable keys and a high-speed printer capable of 50 to 100-cps hard-copy outputs. Of course, the floppy discs that come with the system should hold the development programs you'll need to write the software for your system. ■■

Original Source Microprocessor Manufacturers

The products cited in this report don't represent the manufacturers' full lines. For data sheets and more vendors, consult ELECTRONIC DESIGN'S GOLD BOOK.

AEG Telefunken, 6 Frankfurt 70, AEG Hochhaus, Federal Republic of Ger-many.

Advanced Memory Systems, 1215 Hammerwood Rd., Sunnyvale, CA 94086. (408) 734-4330.

Advanced Micro Devices, 901 Thompson Pl., Sunnyvale, CA 94086. (408) 732-2400.

American Microsystems, 3800 Homestead Rd., Santa Clara, CA 95051. (408) 246-0330.

Data General, Route 9, Southboro, MA 01772. (617) 485-9100.

Electronic Memories & Magnetics, Semiconductor Div., 12621 Chadron Ave., Hawthorne, CA 90250. (213) 644-9881.

Essex International, 564 Alpha Dr., Pittsburgh, PA 15238. (412) 963-9322.

Fairchild, 1725 Technology Dr., San Jose, CA 95110. (408) 998-0123. (MOS)

Fairchild Semiconductor, 464 Ellis St., Mountain View, CA 94042. (415) 962-3816. (Bipolar).

Ferranti Ltd., Western Rd., Bracknell, Berkshire RG12 1RA, England.

Fujitsu Ltd., 6-1, Marunouchi 2 Chome, Chiyoda-ku, Tokyo, Japan.

General Instrument, 600 W. John St., Hicksville, NY 11802. (516) 733-3130.

Harris Semiconductor, P.O. Box 883, Melbourne, FL 32901. (305) 727-5400.

Hitachi, Ltd., Nippon Building, No. 6-2, 2-Chome, Ohtemachie, Chiyoda-ku, Tokyo 100, Japan.

Hughes, Solid State Div., 2601 Campus Dr., Irvine, CA 92715. (714) 752-6396.

ITT Semiconductor, 74 Commerce Way, Woburn, MA 01801. (617) 935-7910.

Intel, 3065 Bowers Ave., Santa Clara, CA 95051. (408) 246-7501.

Intersil, 10900 N. Tantau Ave., Cupertino, CA 95014. (408) 996-5000.

MOS Technology, Valley Forge Corporate Center, 950 Rittenhouse Rd., Nor-ristown, PA 19401. (215) 666-7950.

Monolithic Memories, 1165 E. Arques Ave., Sunnyvale, CA 94086. (408) 739-3535.

Mostek, 1215 W. Crosby Rd., Carrollton, TX 75006. (214) 242-0444.

Motorola Semiconductor, 3501 Ed Bluestein Blvd., Austin, TX 78721. (512) 928-2600. (MOS)

Motorola Semiconductor, 5005 E. McDowell Rd., Phoenix, AZ 85008. (602) 244-6900. (Bipolar).

NEC Microcomputers, 5 Militia Dr., Lexington, MA 02173. (617) 862-6410.

National Semiconductor, 2900 Semiconductor Dr., Santa Clara, CA 95050. (408) 737-5000.

Panafacom Ltd., 2-10-16 Jiyuzaoka, Mezuro-ku Tokyo, Japan 152.

Panasonic, 50 Meadowland Parkway, Secaucus, NJ 07094. (201) 348-7276.

Philips Industries, Electronic Components and Materials Div., P.O. Box 523, Eindhoven, the Netherlands.

RCA, Box 3200, Route 202, Somerville, NJ 08876. (201) 685-6423.

Raytheon, 350 Ellis St., Mountain View, CA 94040. (415) 968-9211.

Rockwell International, P.O. Box 3669, RCOI-Dept. 720, Anaheim, CA 92803. (714) 632-2321.

SGS-ATES, Via C Olivetti 1/20041, Agrate Brianza, Italy.

Scientific Microsystems, 520 Clyde St., Mountain View, CA 94043. (415) 964-5700.

Sharp, 22-22 Nagaike-Cho, Abeno-ku, Osaka, 545, Japan.

Siemens AG, Central Information Dept., Oskar-von-Miller Ring 18, D-8000 Munchen 2, Federal Republic of Germany.

Signetics, 811 E. Arques Ave., Sunnyvale, CA 94086. (408) 739-7700.

Solid State Scientific, Montgomeryville Industrial Park, Montgomeryville, PA 18936. (215) 855-8400.

Synertek, 3050 Coronado Dr., Santa Clara, CA 95051. (408) 241-4300.

Texas Instruments, 13500 North Central Expressway, M/S 308, Dallas, TX 75222. (214) 238-2011.

Thomson-CSF, Sescosem, 101 Boulevard Murat, 75781 Paris Cedex 16, France.

Toshiba Transistor Works, 1 Komukai Toshiba-cho, Kawasaki-shi Kanagana-ken, Japan.

Western Digital, 3128 Red Hill Ave., Newport Beach, CA 92663. (714) 557-3550.

Zilog Microcomputers, 10460 Bubb Rd., Cupertino, CA 95014. (408) 446-4666.

Learn Microprocessor Fundamentals

EDWARD GELLENDER
Roslyn, N.Y.

As microprocessors (μPs) become more and more acceptable as basic building blocks for all kinds of "intelligent" systems there is a tendency to assume that all engineers have a working knowledge of them. As a result, many μP articles that appear today—even many of the so-called "basics"—unexpectedly leave some readers in a dust cloud of vectored interrupts.

For those of you who missed the primer article about μP fundamentals in Microprocessors: New Directions for Designers *the following article will introduce the basics. While no prior knowledge of μPs is required, a little knowledge of computer programming and basic digital logic will help. A brief glossary of terms is included to summarize many of the buzz words.*

A microprocessor can be thought of as a box with three sets of signal lines coming out of it (Fig. 1):

1. Address lines (often 16 of them), are all outputs and at any time may be at a logic 1 or 0, which indicates a binary number from 0 to 65,535 ("64 k").

2. "Data" lines (usually eight for an 8-bit μP) can act as inputs or outputs (bidirectional).

To find out what they are doing, look at

3. The control bus, whose most important segment is the read/write line. This output indicates whether the data lines are outputting (writing) or acting as inputs (reading).

At a given time, a μP will output an address between zero and 64 k, a read or write status, then will either output an 8-bit data word onto the data lines or accept data from the lines. The control bus also contains control lines for interrupts, resets, and other features, depending on the particular processor.

The memory is organized like this...

There are 64-k possible memory addresses, typically organized in groups of 8 bits (Fig. 2). A group of bits in parallel is called a "word," but the 8-bit word occurs so frequently that it has its own name—a byte.

Each byte of memory is accessed by the address lines. Until its individual address is called, it appears open-circuited. The byte being addressed is either pulled from the memory location onto the data lines or changed to match the byte of data on the data lines, depending on the status of the read/write line, shown in the block diagram of Fig. 3.

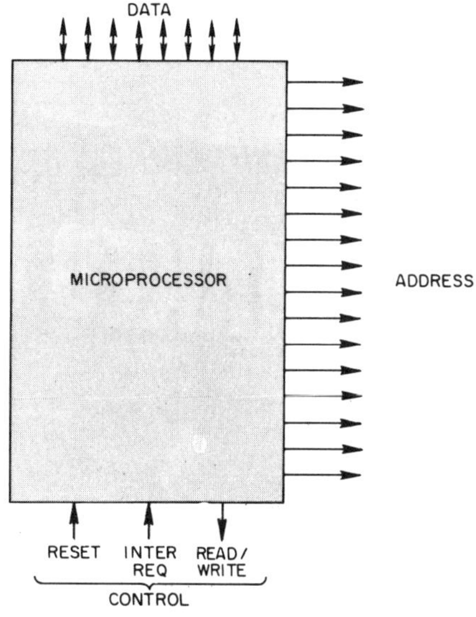

1. **A microprocessor, in its simplest form,** can be thought of as a black box with three sets of wires coming out of it.

Rarely will all 64 kbytes of addressable memory be used. The capability is there, but only as much memory as is required by the application is ever used—sometimes less than 1024 bytes. Often in such systems, decoding is simplified by not using all 16 address bits.

To deal with large binary numbers, certain simplifications are extremely helpful. To this end, hexadecimal notation is often used (see box, p. 75).

A microprocessor's memory is generally organized into blocks of addresses that serve specific areas:

1. Program.
2. Scratchpad and data storage.
3. The "stack."
4. Input/output (I/O) ports.

The program is a series of instructions to direct processing. Each instruction can contain one or more bytes. The first byte of a multibyte instruction provides the basic information, including the number of additional bytes in the instruction. Steps within an instruction proceed serially byte by byte. And unless otherwise indicated, a μP will "look" at the instructions sequentially, starting with a specific memory address and incrementing the address.

In most cases, a μP reads only from the program section of memory since programs are often stored in read-only memories (ROMs). In developmental systems, however, more flexible program storage is usually required. To this end, read/write random-access memories (RAMs) should be used. However, this permits the original program to be stored on a magnetic cassette, so that it can be entered each time the power is turned on. This inconvenience is compensated by ability to change the program at will and rerecord it on the cassette. The corrected tape can be generated by one of several means—sometimes from a program already in the development systems, called a resident assembler, or from a "cross-assembler" program on a large computer. Or from a number of time-sharing services that have various cross-assemblers in their software arsenals. And simpler pad and pencil techniques can also be used quite successfully for short programs.

An intermediate programming step is to use EPROMs (erasable programmable read-only memories), which can be erased with ultraviolet light. Once programmed, however, they can retain their information indefinitely. With μPs that serve to control routine operations, use of factory-programmed ROMs will minimize cost, but sacrifice flexibility.

Examine a typical program sequence

Having come this far, consider a program sequence that illustrates a simple procedure. Suppose a byte of data were to be moved from one memory location to another. Assume that the address of the previous instruction is 0100 and that the contents of byte 24F1 are to be moved into 2407, neither address being in the program section of memory. Table 1 shows how it's done.

Step 1. The next consecutive address after 0100, 0101, is read. Its contents are 7A, which is interpreted as "Read data from the address given by the next two bytes."

Step 2. The least significant byte (F1) is read.

Step 3. The most significant byte (24) is read.

Step 4. The consecutive-address sequence on the

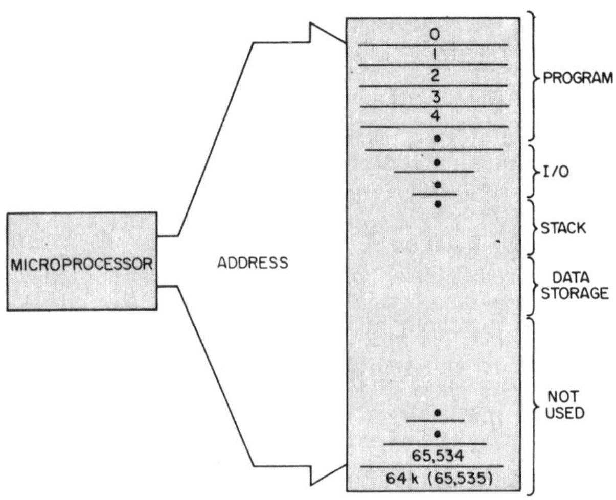

2. Everything the microprocessor is hooked into fits into the category of memory organized into specialized blocks.

Hex notation explained

Hexadecimal notation groups together four binary digits to form one digit representing a count from zero to 15. Obviously, some one-digit characters are needed to represent the decimal two-digit numbers from 10 to 15. The six letters, A through F, are used for this.

Hexadecimal notation is very convenient for microprocessors since it gives good counting densities and works very well with the multiples-of-four binary words usually encountered in a μP.

To understand the hexadecimal notation, take a number like 107. In binary notation, this becomes 1101011. Breaking this number into two groups of four digits, you get 0110 and 1011. The first of these is equal to 6, while the second one is 11. In hexadecimal notation, 107 becomes 6B.

Note that the highest memory address in a micro is hexadecimal FFFF.

To convert from decimal to hexadecimal, or vice versa, you must first convert the number into binary and then into hexadecimal as previously illustrated.

Decimal conversion guide

Decimal	Hex	Binary
0	0	0000
1	1	0001
2	2	0010
3	3	0011
4	4	0100
5	5	0101
6	6	0110
7	7	0111
8	8	1000
9	9	1001
10	A	1010
11	B	1011
12	C	1100
13	D	1101
14	E	1110
15	F	1111

Glossary of some microprocessor related terms

Category I: Basics

Bit: a minimum logic element. A binary number of either 0 or 1.

Word: any group of bits indicating a single number or expression.

Byte: a word consisting of eight bits.

Address: a specific memory location that is called out by the program counter.

Hex: short for hexadecimal: numbers calculated to the base 16.

Register: a device that stores one word of data, and often consists of several flip-flops.

RAM (random-access memory): a data-storage device that can retain and produce on demand any data placed in it.

ROM (read-only memory): a device that has data permanently entered into it to be outputted on demand.

PROM: a programmable ROM in which a program is entered by the user before installation into equipment, as opposed to a factory-programmed ROM.

EPROM: A PROM that can be erased and reused indefinitely. Most EPROMs are erased under ultraviolet light and can be recognized by the clear cover over the silicon ''chip.''

Decoder: usually a device that detects a certain specific address on the address bus.

Bus: a group of wires that carry related binary signals, usually a word, as in a 16-wire address bus. A bus can be bidirectional, as in the case of a data bus.

Category II: Parts of a microprocessor

Accumulator: a register in the microprocessor that operates on data. It is so-called because these registers were first used to accumulate totals.

ALU (arithmetic and logic unit): the circuitry that performs the manipulations on data held in the accumulator.

I/O (input/output): hardware that interfaces a microprocessor system with the outside world.

Port: a place through which inputs and outputs—either data or instructions—are channeled. A µP can have more than one port or can address many. Port size, though, is often specified in bits, ranging from 4 to 16 bits.

Processor Status Word (PSW): a word of readily available status information provided to indicate the result of specific operations.

Program Counter: two 8-bit registers used to generate the 16-bit address. The registers are called PCH and PCL and are used for the higher-order and lower-order bytes, respectively.

R/W (read/write): a control output of the microprocessor that indicates if data are being transferred from the microprocessor to memory, or vice versa.

Scratchpad: an area of the main memory set aside for short and often done calculations.

Stack: storage for data during subroutines or interrupts.

Stack Pointer: two 8-byte registers containing the address of the top (most recent end) of the stack.

Category III: Programming

Assembly Language: a compromise between the user's thoughts and the numerical notation of the microprocessor. Assembly language is the closest technique to the actual numerical codes that still retains some speaking-language characteristics.

Branch: depending on the status of a particular bit in the status register, the program will jump by the indicated amount if the condition is met, or merely increment if not.

Cross-Assembler: a program on a larger computer that allows a microprocessor programmer to use assembly language. The assembler reduces the program to the machine language.

DMA (direct memory access): a process in which a microprocessor is removed temporarily from a system to allow data to be transferred rapidly in or out of memory without microprocessor control.

Interrupt: an external signal that causes a microprocessor to jump to a specific subroutine. Interrupts are maskable or nonmaskable. A maskable interrupt may be delayed until a mask bit is lowered.

Iterative Loop: a programming technique whereby a process is repeated a specified number of times.

Jump: a programming instruction that breaks the consecutive-instruction programming sequence and resumes elsewhere in the program.

Machine Language: Numerical coding, representing instructions, usually in the form of groups of bytes, used by the microprocessor.

Peripheral: a unit operated with a microprocessor system such as a keyboard or a printer.

Program: a set of sequential instructions that a computer follows.

Subroutine: a program within a program that performs a specific, often-used function.

Vector: a specific address loaded into a microprocessor's program counter to force the µP to start processing at a specific address.

address bus is momentarily interrupted, and the contents of byte 24F1 are read. The contents are 7A — but now the 7A represents data, not an instruction as in Step 1.

Step 5. The consecutive-address count resumes at 0104. The next instruction, 4A, is interpreted as "Write the data stored in the processor into the address given by the next two bytes."

Step 6. The least significant byte (07) is read.

Step 7. The most significant byte (24) is read.

Step 8. The consecutive addresses are interrupted again, while 7A is placed into address 2407.

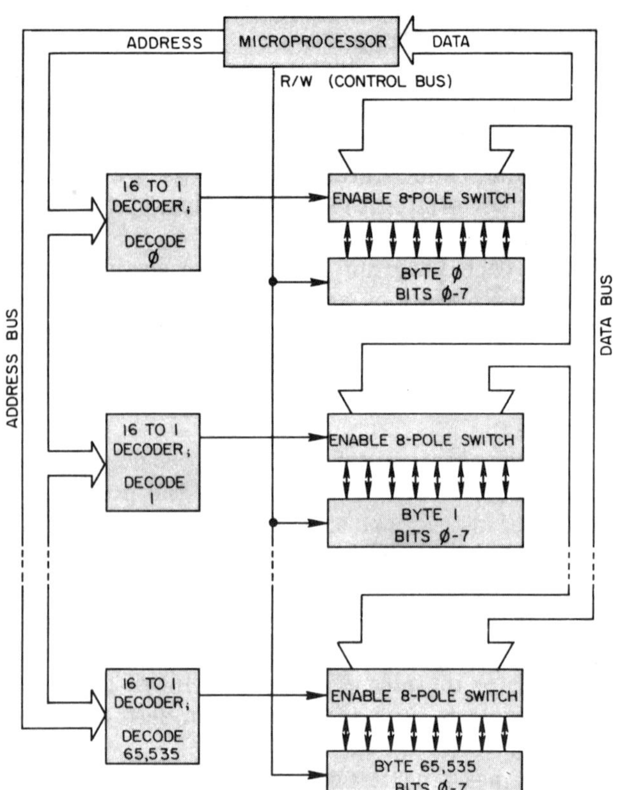

3. **Microprocessor-to-memory connection** via the buses can be thought of as shown above. Note that each 8-pole switch can be closed one pole at a time.

A simple machine program

Step no.	Address bus	Data lines	R/W
1	0101	7A	R
2	0102	F1	R
3	0103	24	R
4	24F1	7A	R
5	0104	4A	R
6	0105	07	R
7	0106	24	R
8	2407	7A	W
9	0107	...	

Step 9. The consecutive addresses resume.

Note that the μP follows a rigid sequence to keep track of which bytes are instructions, which are data, which are addresses, and so on. Thus, the same byte (7A in the example) can be placed on the data lines at two different times and have two separate meanings.

Note also, that the least significant byte of an address is handled first, although it isn't crucial. Some processors do it this way while other processors do it the reverse. Just make sure to check which way it should be done when you start to program.

The *scratchpad and data storage* serve to store data temporarily. "Scratchpad memory" usually designates an area of memory used for many quick data transfers. It is the most frequently used memory segment. Some microprocessors have simplified instructions that can only be used in a certain small part of the memory (say, the first 256 bytes), where the most significant byte of the addresses is zero. The scratchpad is usually placed in such a location.

The data-storage area is similar to the scratchpad, except that just the usual processor instructions can be used. Thus data may be addressed slower than in the scratchpad area. Data storage is used for the bulk of the memory, and RAM is most often used for data storage.

The *stack* is a read/write block of memory used to "remember" the next consecutive address and associated data when the address lines are taken over by a sequence of nonconsecutive addresses, as in a subroutine. More will be said about the stack when subroutines are discussed.

I/O ports are simply a means for getting into and out of a μP, which is virtually a closed system with no way of communicating with the outside world. A typical port is an 8-bit register that can have data loaded into it or read out by means of external signals. It also has an address decoder to detect when the μP is addressing it. At such a time, either the contents of the data bus are put into the register (output port) or the contents of the register are placed on the data bus (input port).

If, for the program sequence of Table 1, address 2407 does not go to a RAM but is decoded and used to load the contents of the data lines (7A) into a register, the data are accessible at the outputs of the register (an output port) until the register is supplied with new data. Thus the data stored in memory at address 24F1 and accessible only by programming are now available to the outside world via an output port (Fig. 4a). If such a register's address is called with the outputs connected to the data lines, the register would be an input port (Fig. 4b).

What goes on inside?

So far the microprocessor has been treated as a "black box" that always knows which words to place on the address and data lines. Look inside to see how the μP figures out what to to.

The simplest μP consists of a program counter, a controller and an accumulator (Fig. 5a). The program counter often consists of two cascaded 8-bit counters —the low and high-byte registers (or the least and most significant bytes). When power is applied, the program counter is forced to a particular starting address that holds the first line of the program. The first line is then read into and interpreted by the controller. The program counter is then increased by one count unless that line has information that drastically modifies the counter.

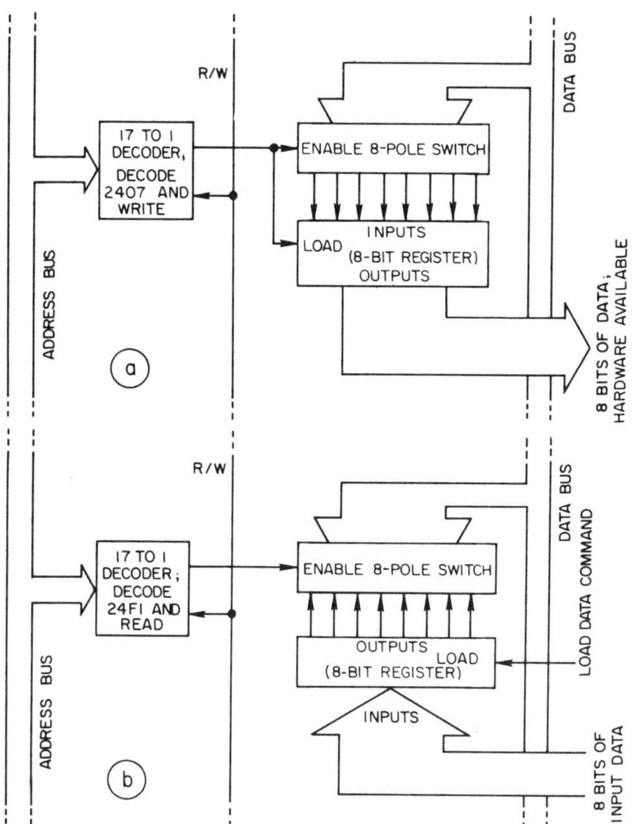

4. Output (a) and input (b) ports provide the means for communicating with the outside world. In "a," address 2407 and a WRITE command load the data bus into a register. In "b," data are loaded into the register. Address 24F1 places them onto the data bus.

Any data read in or out via data lines are read to or from the accumulator, which is also an 8-bit register. All logic and math manipulations occur in the accumulator. For example, a word can be read from memory and added to one already in the accumulator. The result is stored in the place of data used to generate it.

Fig. 5b depicts a more complex microprocessor. Certain tests on the accumulator such as checking for zero, a positive result, a negative result, or something else, are often needed, and indicators are provided by bits in the status register. A carry bit for additions indicates sums in excess of the accumulator capacity. Another bit indicates when the accumulator holds all zeros. Certain program instructions require the instruction decoder to monitor those status bits and a few others.

A number of auxiliary registers can be provided for modifying the program counter, additional accumulators, or readily available scratchpad memories.

Control the μP with a program

Having covered the basics, you are ready to learn about basic programming instructions to move and process data, and modify a program.

Data-move instructions transfer data from memory into the accumulator and vice versa, or from the accumulator to an auxiliary register or other combinations. Data-processing instructions include adding, logic ANDing and rotating data around the accumulator. Those instructions are carried out in the arithmetic and logic unit (ALU), which consists of the accumulator and status register, as well as the circuitry performing the mathematical operations to the accumulator.

After each program step, the program counter usually increments by one count. When data are read into the processor from the memory, the program counter may momentarily be set to some different value. But then it is restored to the last instruction plus one.

If you want to, you can change the program counter to continue at some other point in the program. A number of instructions will help. Unconditional jumps are used to change the program counter to some entirely new value.

Conditional jumps, or branches, can force a program jump under specific conditions. For instance, when the accumulator contains zero the zero bit of the status register detects that and a jump on zero command can divert program flow.

Sometimes a particular process is repeated many times during the program. Rather than repeat the program section each time, the program can call a subroutine (a subservient program) whenever it is needed. This particular process is written in a separate part of program memory, usually after the main program. Getting to the subroutine is similar to the unconditional jump. Bear in mind, however, that the present location of the program sequence must be memorized for the program to return to where it left off after completing the subroutine.

The stack is used for this purpose. It is an area of memory reserved primarily, but not exclusively, for program addresses. A stack pointer, which refers to addresses placed in the stack, is initialized to a desired value at the beginning of the program to the starting point of the block of memory locations reserved for the stack. When a subroutine is called, the contents of the program counter are incremented and placed in two bytes of the stack memory (16 address bits in two bytes). The stack pointer is lowered by two counts. At the end of the subroutine, the two bytes are read from the stack into the program counter to call the next consecutive instruction as if no change had taken place. Of course, the stack pointer is brought back up to keep the bookkeeping up-to-date.

But suppose the contents of the accumulator, status register or other registers are needed later and cannot be kept in their present locations while the subroutine is being executed. The first instructions in the subroutine may also load these contents onto the stack. The last instruction in the subroutine will have to restore these registers to their original status. The stack pointer, of course, will be changed accordingly.

Another alternative is for subroutines to call other subroutines to be performed, then return first to the original, or main subroutine, and finally to the main program. Calling subroutines within subroutines, or nesting, can continue indefinitely, as long as there is enough room in the stack. Each time an address is loaded onto the stack, the stack pointer is decremented by two bytes. The next address is then placed in the next two bytes, and the stack pointer is decremented again. Each time a return from subroutine is executed, the top address is taken from the stack and the stack pointer is incremented twice. When the main program is running again, the stack pointer will return to its initial value.

Sometimes, the program can be modified by data stored in a particular memory location. For instance, data stored in one place can indicate the address where some other data are to be sent. The programming steps described so far do not allow for this.

Indirect addressing helps

Some sort of indirect addressing is included in a μP, to allow the data to provide some form of steering to the program. One technique is to place a byte of data into one byte of the program counter, and then have the μP read or write data between that composite address and the accumulator. At the end of that step, the old program counter contents (plus one) are reintroduced.

I/O ports are often used for data transfer into and out of the system. However, the μP must determine whether or not an input has occurred and data have been loaded into an input port.

One way to determine if data are present is to allow the processor program to test one bit of an input port periodically. If data are brought in, that bit can be set to 1 by external circuitry and reset to 0 via an output port after the data are entered. This approach is very slow, however, so a faster method is generally used.

The essence of the faster method is to provide a special input to a μP. It is called an interrupt input. During normal operation, the processor ignores all input ports. Should data be entered, an external signal is brought to the interrupt input, without going through the program.

Once the instruction in progress is completed, the processor acts as if a "call subroutine" is being read. The program counter and status-register contents are placed on the stack and the program counter is forced (or vectored) to the address where a program servicing the interrupt begins. The interrupt is serviced and a return from interrupt, similar to a return from subroutine, restores the program counter and status registers to the initial values.

In general, when one of several inputs causes an interrupt, the interrupt program scans the inputs to determine which one has new information. The most time-critical input is scanned first, then successively less critical inputs.

When a high-priority input is completed, scanning

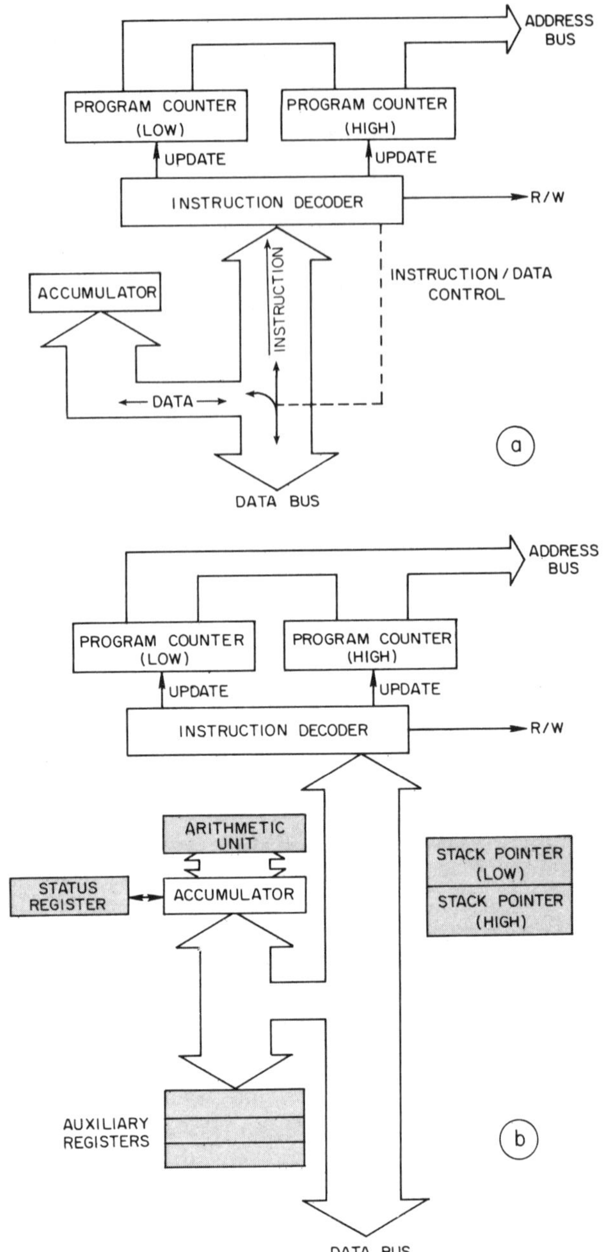

5. **A simple microprocessor** consists of just a few basic blocks (a). A more realistic μP (b) includes a few "frills" that make it operational.

resumes. Eventually, all the inputs are serviced according to their relative priority. High-priority interrupts can break in on lower-priority interrupts. As with subroutines, interrupts can be nested.

Interrupts can be either maskable or nonmaskable. A mask bit can delay servicing of an interrupt until the bit is lowered. Nonmaskable interrupts do not respond to a mask bit and are serviced immediately.

Sometimes, data or programs must be quickly loaded from memory into an external unit, or vice versa. These are jobs for direct memory access (DMA). DMA capability means that a μP can be effectively decoupled from the address, data, and read/write buses. An external device will control those lines to rapidly transfer blocks of data directly into memory, and bypass the μP.■■

Microprocessor Data Pages

The Data Manual microprocessor data pages are organized first by processor data-word size, then by generic family, by technology and finally by original source manufacturer (within each generic family processors are listed alphabetically by original manufacturer). Generic families included in the manual are:

Processor generic family	Pages	Processor generic family	Pages
1-bit microcomputer, NMOS	page 22	8-bit microprocessor, CMOS	page 45
4-bit microcomputer, CMOS	page 23	8-bit microprocessor, NMOS	pages 46 to 53
4-bit microcomputer, NMOS	pages 24 to 27		
4-bit microcomputer, PMOS	pages 28 to 32	8-bit microprocessor, PMOS	pages 54 to 56
8-bit microcomputer, NMOS	pages 33 to 35	12-bit microprocessor, CMOS	page 57
		12-bit microprocessor, PMOS	page 58
8-bit microcomputer, PMOS	page 36	16-bit microprocessor, Bipolar	pages 59 to 60
16-bit microcomputer, NMOS	page 37		
4-bit microcontroller, PMOS	pages 38 to 39	16-bit microprocessor, NMOS	pages 61 to 67
8-bit microcontroller, NMOS	page 40		
1-bit microprocessor, CMOS	page 41	2-bit processor slice, Bipolar	page 68
4-bit microprocessor, PMOS	pages 42 to 43	4-bit processor slice, Bipolar	pages 69 to 74
8-bit microcontroller, Bipolar	page 44	4-bit processor slice, PMOS	page 75

Here's what's on a manual page

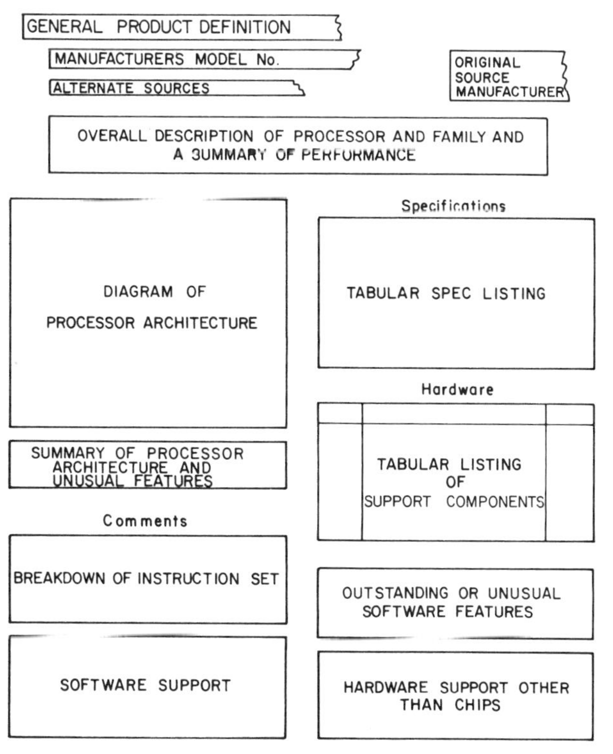

1-bit microcomputer, NMOS

SBA (Sequential Boolean Analyzer)

General Instrument Corp.
600 West John St.
Hicksville, NY 11802
(516) 733-3107

Alternate sources: None.

A simple, low-cost single-bit processor, the SBA can directly evaluate a set of Boolean equations. Thirty programmable inputs and outputs as well as memory make the SBA a true 1-bit microcomputer. An n-channel, ion-implanted device, the SBA is designed for ease of use, in simple control applications.

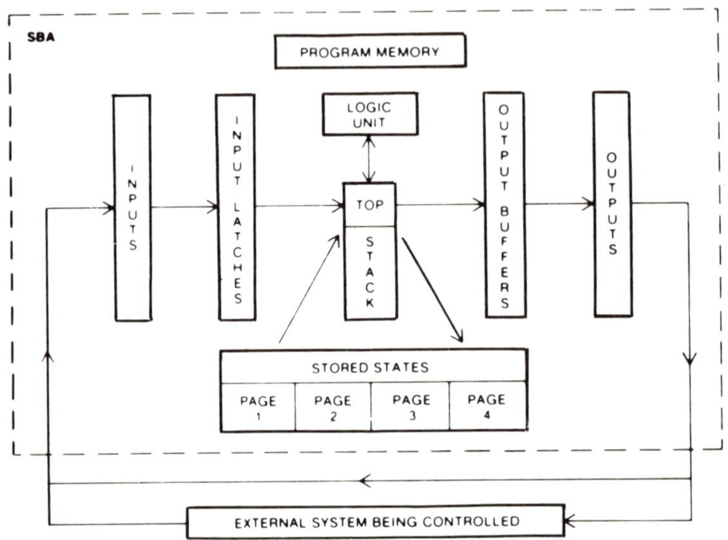

The Sequential Boolean Analyzer consists of a program memory that holds a set of Boolean functions that define system operation as well as 30 input buffers that are latched at the start of the evaluation of Boolean equations, and four pages of 30 stored-state flip-flops which can be grouped to emulate counters and shift registers. Also included are a logic unit that can perform the logic functions and a stack that holds a set of Boolean values used to evaluate the input equation.

for logic operations are from the stack or memory, or from inputs. The stack is 16 x 1 bit and the state store is 120 x 1 bit. There are 24 basic instructions, all of which execute in the same amount of time. The processor is designed to process Boolean equations based on the status of the 30 I/O lines.

An SBA Compiler produces optimized codes from Boolean equation inputs, and an SBA simulator provides software simulation of the SBA.

The programming for the SBA is via Boolean expressions. An 8-bit word provides the instruction code, five bits of the code provide an address for the inputs, outputs or stored states and, if two of the 32 available addresses are reserved for address-less instructions, the remaining three bits of the code enable a total of 24 instructions to be made available. Most of the instructions are AND, NAND, OR, Ex-OR, and stack or I/O operations.

Hardware support will be the SBA-1, a version with external RAM or PROM for prototyping, otherwise there are no prototyping systems available.

Specifications

Data word size:	1 bit
Address bus size:	None*
Direct addressing range:	None*
Instruction word size:	8 bits*
Number of basic instructions:	24
Shortest instruction/time (All):	1.25 μs
Clock frequency (min/max):	10 kHz/ 800 kHz
Clock phases/voltage swing:	Internal
Dedicated I/O control lines:	30
Package:	40-pin DIP
Power requirements:	12 V/? mA
	5 V/? mA

* No external address lines are available but the SBA can address up to 1023 words of on-chip program memory.

Comments

The results of Compare and Invert instructions are stored in either the stack, memory or output. Inputs

Hardware

Model	Description	Price
SBA	CPU	$4 (2500 qty)
SBA-1	Same as SBA but uses external PROM/RAM	N/A

4-bit microcomputer, CMOS, NMOS or PMOS

TMS1000 family

Alternate sources: Motorola for CMOS version.

Texas Instruments Inc.
P.O. Box 5012, M/S308
Dallas, TX 75222
(214) 238-2011

The TMS1000 family of single chip microcomputers is available in about 35 models —the unprogrammed evaluation processors (the TMS1099/SE1 and 1098/SE2), the general purpose family (the TMS1000, 1070, 1100, 1200, 1270, 1300 and other models) and some already preprogrammed units that can go right into an application (the TMS1018, 1022, 1117 and 1121). All processors have on-chip ROMs that range from 1024 × 8 to 2048 × 8 and on-board RAMs of either 64 × 4 or 128 × 4. Also, versions with up to 16 output lines can be had.

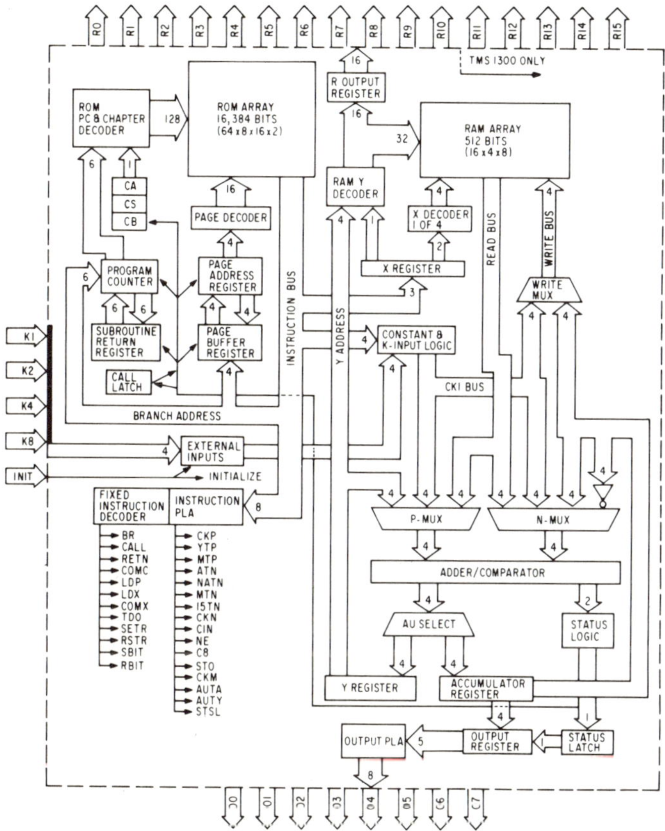

The architecture of all the TMS1000 products is very similar, with the main differences appearing in the size of the RAM and ROM and the number of I/O lines. All processors have an internal clock generator, but can accept a single-phase clock signal if timing must be generated externally. Just the single chip is needed to form a minimal working system.

Comments

The instruction set contains a total of 54 commands that are divided into five basic groups: 12 register reference instructions, 27 arithmetic and logic operations, three bit-manipulation commands, five I/O instructions and seven memory addressing.

Software support for the TMS1000 family consists of an assembler, simulator, a high-level language compiler (TIML) and a variety of utility programs. There is no program library available.

Special features of the software include the wide variety of register and accumulator operations possible as well as the individual bit set, reset and test operations on the contents of a memory location.

Hardware support for the TMS1000 family starts with the 64-pin system evaluator chips that permit external RAM and ROM interfaces and prototype boards for the evaluation chips. Also available is the AMPL development system which permits assembly and simulation and will soon permit in-circuit emulation.

Specifications

Data word size:	4 bits
Address bus size:	Internal
Direct addressing range:	2048 words, max
Instruction word size:	8 bits
Number of basic instructions:	54
Shortest instruction/time (All instructions):	6 µs min.
Clock frequency (min/max):	50 kHz/1 MHz
Clock phase/voltage swing:	$1/V_{supply}$
Dedicated I/O control lines:	16 max.
Package:	28 or 40-pin DIPS or 64-pin evaluator
Power requirements:	3 to 35 V at 1 to 10 mA, depending on model

Hardware

Model	Description	Price (5000 qty)
TMS1000	28-pin microcomputer	Under $4.
TMS1070	28-pin microcomputer	Under $4.
TMS1100	28-pin microcomputer	Under $4.
TMS1200	40-pin microcomputer	Under $4.
TMS1270	40-pin microcomputer	Under $4.
TMS1300	40-pin microcomputer	Under $4.
TMS1098/ SE1	64-pin evaluator	N/A
TMS1099/ SE2	64-pin evaluator	N/A
TMS1330	Combo CPU, a/d converter and keyboard controller	$7.
TMS1024	4 x 4 I/O expander	Under $3.
TMS1025	4 x 7 I/O expander	Under $3.
TMS1976	CPU to capacitive keyboard interface	Under $3.

4-bit microcomputer, NMOS
S2000

American Microsystems Inc.
3800 Homestead Rd.
Santa Clara, CA 95051
(408) 246-0330

Alternate sources: None.

A single-chip, 4-bit microcomputer built with silicon-gate, depletion-load NMOS technology, the S2000 includes, on-chip, a 1 k x 8-bit ROM, 64 x 4-bit RAM, 50/60-Hz timer and clock oscillator. Most of its 61 instructions are executed in 4 μs. Among 29 I/O lines are LED drivers (and a 7-segment display decoder), as well as a touch-control interface. The device operates from a 9-V supply and has power-on reset circuitry.

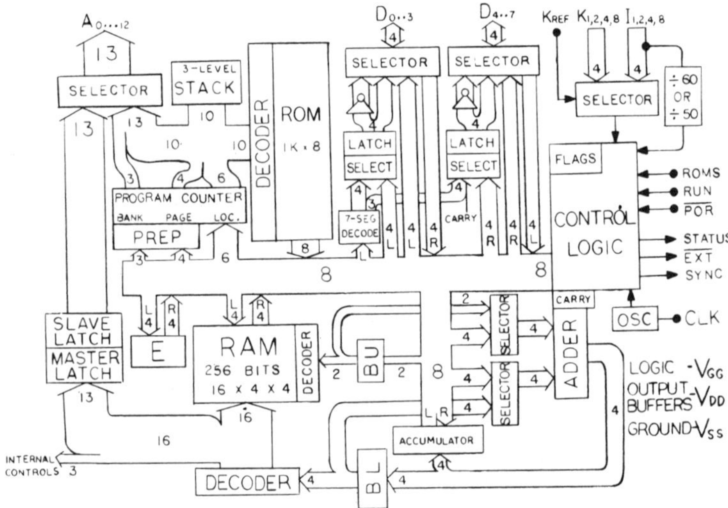

The architecture of the S2000 microcomputer includes I/O ports for almost every application—there are seven-segment display outputs, touch-control inputs, LED or vacuum-flourescent drivers (S2000A), a voltage comparator, a 64 × 4 RAM, a three-level stack and an on-chip clock oscillator. All lines are TTL compatible and the eight D lines also have three-state capability.

Comments

The instruction set for the S2000 processor consists of 61 commands that are divided into the following groups: 14 ROM and RAM instructions, 13 conditional skip commands, 12 arithmetic and logic operations, 11 I/O directives and 11 register instructions.

Software support includes a text editor, assembler, real-time debugger, floppy-disc operating system, software simulator, macroprogram library, self-diagnostic programs and many applications oriented programs. All these programs are designed to run on the MDC, a microcomputer development center.

Special features of the software include the fact that all but two instructions execute in one machine cycle and that some instructions can do several jobs simultaneously. For instance, the XCD command exchanges the accumulator contents with a RAM location, decrements register BL, modifies register BU and does a conditional jump.

Hardware support consists of the MDC microcomputer development center, which includes a CRT terminal, a dual-floppy-disc system, the DEV-2000 real-time debug breadboard, printer and logic analyzer (40 channels × 1024 events). There is also a single-board S2000 evaluator that uses a UV EPROM memory to permit program testing.

Specifications

Data word size:	4 bits
Address bus size:	13 bits
Direct addressing range:	8192 words
Instruction word size:	8 bits
Number of basic instructions:	61
Shortest instruction/time (Most):	4 μs
Longest instruction/time (Jump to subroutine):	8 μs
Clock frequency (min/max):	Dc/1 MHz
Clock phases/voltage swing:	1/internal
Dedicated I/O control lines:	29
Package:	40-pin DIP
Power requirements:	9 V/26 mA

Hardware

Model	Description	Price
S2000	4-bit microcomputer	$3.50 (100-k qty)
	No special interface circuits are needed.	

4-bit microcomputers, NMOS

MN1400 series

Alternate sources: None.

Panasonic Co.
50 Meadowland Parkway
Secaucus, NJ 07094
(201) 348-7276

The MN1400 series of microcomputers consists of four models, each with different amounts of on-chip program memory. The "standard" model is the MN1400, with a 1k x 8 on-chip mask-programmed ROM and 75 instructions. A "shrink" version of the unit, dubbed the MN1402 offers 57 instructions and only a 768 x 8 program memory. Also available are two versions that have no on-chip memory. The MN1498 can address 1 k x 8 of external memory and offers 68 instructions. The largest processor is the MN1499, with an addressing capability of 2 k x 8 and 75 instructions. All processors have a two-level subroutine stack and on-board RAMs of 64 x 4 bits, except for the 1402, which has a 32 x 4 bit RAM.

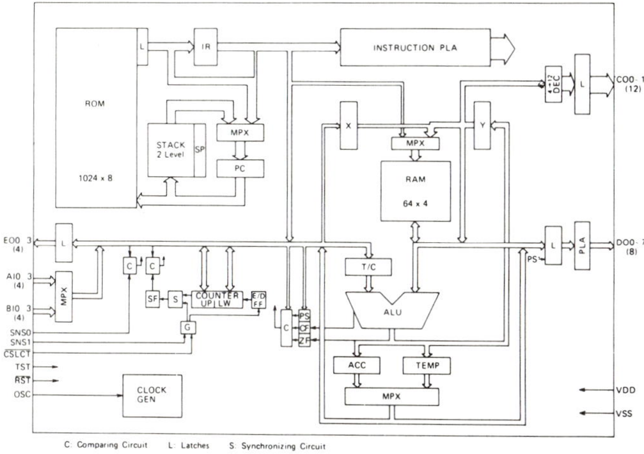

Complete all-in-one microcomputers on a chip, all parts in the MN1400 family have on-board clock generators, and up to 64 x 4 bits of RAM. All units have a two-level subroutine stack and different amounts of I/O capability. The MN1400 provides 12 individually settable latched output lines on one of its ports, eight simultaneously settable lines on another output port, four more lines on another output port and two sets of four lines each on two input ports. The 1402 has two 4-bit input ports, two 4-bit output ports and one 5-bit output port. The 1498 has fewer ports since the program memory must be externally addressed—it has one 4-bit input port, one 4-bit output port and one 9-bit output port.

Lastly, the 1499 has all the ports of the 1400 and in addition has the interface necessary to handle external memory.

Comments

Both the MN1400 and 1499 have a set of 75 instructions that are divided into four basic groups: 18 data transfer commands, 18 arithmetic and logic directions, nine I/O instructions, and 30 control commands. Both the 1402 and 1498 instruction sets are subsets of the 75 commands of the 1400.

Support software for the MN1400 family consists of a cross-assembler program for use on large computer systems. The cross-assembler contains error diagnostic and macro instructions, and is written in Fortran. Additional support is also available on minicomputers such as the PFL-16A made by Panafacom Ltd. Hardware simulation as well as editing and debug routines are available. There is no formal program library, but various application programs are available on request.

Special instructions in the MN1400 family include bit reset and bit set commands for data stored in memory as well as a wide choice of I/O commands. The built-in counter/timer is totally software controller—special instructions are used to preset the circuit or to enable or disable the counter.

Hardware support is performed by the MN1499, a system evaluator circuit. The 1499 requires external memory but to help debug programs it has a single-step control line that can be used to go through programs one line at a time.

Specifications

Data word size:	4 bits
Address bus size:	11 bits (max)
Direct addressing range:	2 k (max)
Instruction word size:	8 bits
Number of basic instructions:	57 to 75
Shortest instruction/time (several commands):	10 μs
Longest instruction/time (Branch/Jump):	20 μs
Clock frequency (min/max):	dc/300 kHz
Clock phases/voltage swing:	1/5 V
Dedicated I/O control lines:	20
Package:	28, 40 or 64-pin DIP
Power requirements:	5 V/100 mA

Hardware

Model	Description	Price
MN1400	CPU, 40-pin, 75 instructions	approx. $8 (1000 qty)
MN1402	CPU, 28-pin, 57 instructions	same.
MN1498	CPU, 40-pin, 68 instructions	consult factory
MN1499	CPU, 64-pin, 75 instructions	$75. unit qty

4-bit microcomputer, NMOS

T3444

Toshiba Transistor Works
1 Komukai Toshiba-cho Kawasaki-shi
Kanagawa-ken Japan
044-511-3111

Alternate sources: None.

The T3444 is a general-purpose microprogrammable controller and is available either unprogrammed or in two preprogrammed versions: The T3444A is designed as a floppy-disc controller, and the T3444B as a digital cassette controller. All inputs and outputs are TTL compatible and both chips have a 4-bit data bus and the 8-bit command bus. Both buses have three-state capability.

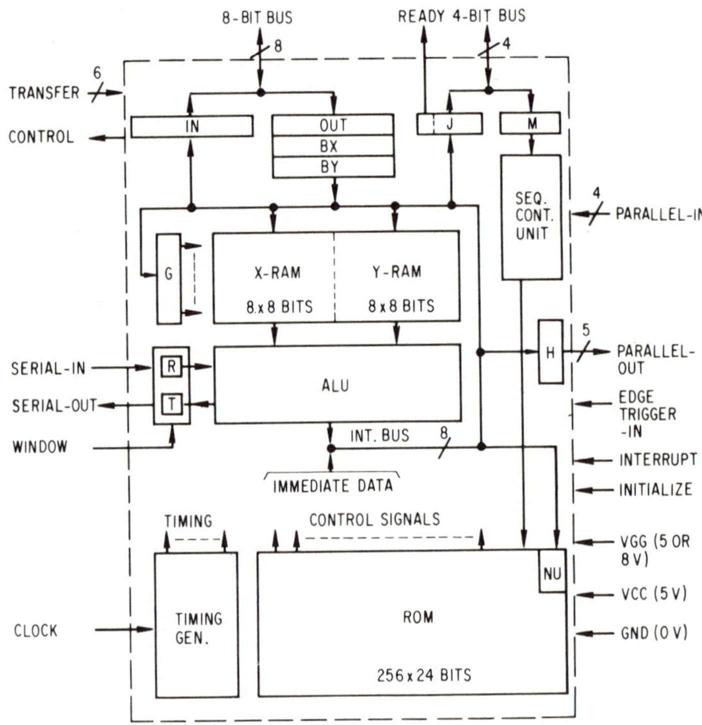

The architecture of the T3444 revolves around two 8 × 8 bit data RAMs that feed in to the ALU. There are 16 lines for dedicated inputs and eight lines dedicated as outputs. The processor also has a separate serial I/O section as well as an on-board clock circuit.

Comments

The software set of the T3444 is user determined since the processor is microprogrammable. Program storage space consists of an on-board 256 x 24 bit control memory.

Software support consists of a microassembler in Fortran and in G-MAP (Honeywell Computer's assembly language). There is no program library.

Special features of the software include a cyclic-redundancy-check capability as well as special functions.

Hardware support includes a breadboard circuit consisting of about 110 TTL devices on a board. Program development proceeds by using PROMs in the TTL equivalent.

Specifications

Data word size:	4 bits
Address bus size:	8 bits
Direct addressing range:	Internal
Instruction word size:	4 bits
Number of basic instructions:	N/A
Shortest instruction/time	N/A
Longest instruction/time	N/A
Clock frequency (min/max):	Dc/0.8 MHz
Clock phases/voltage swing:	1/TTL
Dedicated I/O control lines:	24
Package:	40-pin DIP
Power requirements:	5 V/200 mA

Hardware

Model	Description	Price (100 qty)
T3444	Controller, any version	$23.

4-bit microprocessor, NMOS

T3472

Toshiba Transistor Works
1 Komukai Toshiba-cho Kawasaki-shi
Kanagawa-ken, Japan
044-511-3111

Alternate sources: None.

This microprogrammable 4-bit processor is intended to provide up to a 16-digit numeric display and handle a 64-key input. It is a silicon-gate NMOS device, operates from a single 5-V supply, and its data bus is three-state. A large instruction set (67) includes advanced instructions, like variable-length (1 to 16 digits) decimal/binary arithmetic operations. All inputs and outputs are TTL compatible. A two-level interrupt and 12-bit address bus are other features.

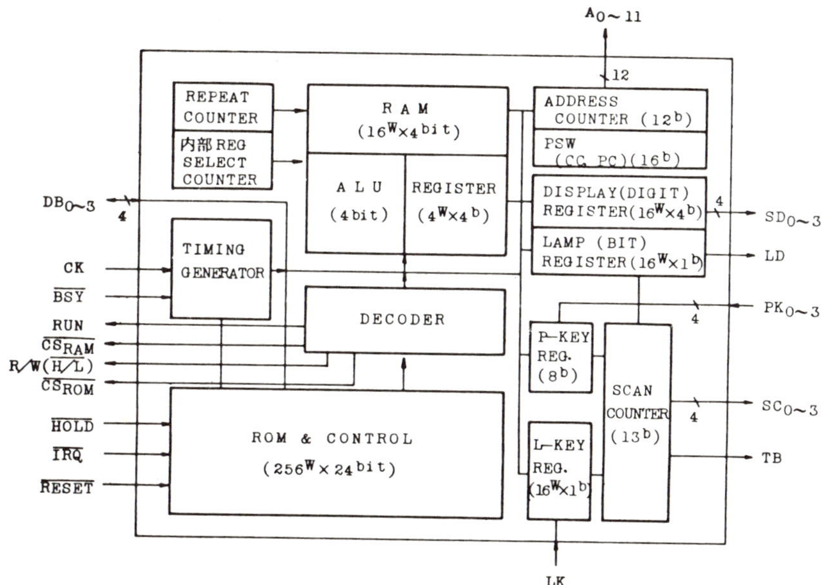

The architecture of the T3472 is oriented for binary and BCD data manipulation and display. All I/O lines are TTL compatible and the data bus has three-state capability. Display control logic and the clock as well as the keyboard scan control circuitry are included on the processor chip.

Comments

The instruction set of the T3472 contains a total of 67 commands divided up as follows: 17 data transfer commands, 17 arithmetic instructions, 11 logic operations, four I/O commands, nine branch instructions and nine control operations.

Software support for the T3472 consists of a cross-assembler written in Fortran. There is no program library available.

Special features of the software include the capability of instructions to handle variable length data (from 1 to 16 digits), and the capability to handle both binary and BCD arithmetic operations.

Hardware support for the T3472 consists of the EX-4/01, a board containing 4096 words of RAM, 4096 words of PROM, a control panel with numeric display and a keyboard.

Specifications

Data word size:	4 bits
Address bus size:	12 bits
Direct addressing range:	4096 words
Instruction word size:	8 bits
Number of basic instructions:	67
Shortest instruction/time (Load immediate):	33 μs
Longest instruction/time (Compare 16 bits):	360 μs
Clock frequency (min/max):	Dc/1 MHz
Clock phases/voltage swing:	1/TTL
Dedicated I/O control lines:	16
Package:	42-pin DIP
Power requirements:	5 V/195 mA

Hardware

Model	Description	Price (100 qty)
T3472	Microprocessor	$13.00
T3473	Printer controller (for Seiko CR-101T)	$6.50
T3538	Printer controller (for Seiko CR-330)	$6.50
T3474	16 kbit mask-programmable ROM	$9.50

4-bit microcomputer, PMOS

SX 200

Essex Group Wire Assembly Division
Semiconductor Operations
564 Alpha Drive
Pittsburgh, PA 15238
(412) 963-9322

Alternate sources: None.

A 4-bit PMOS microcomputer in a single 28-pin package, the SX 200, combines CPU with 1024 × 8 bits of ROM and 64 × 4 bits of RAM. In addition to data storage, there are 16 individually settable, resettable and testable flag bits for program control. The outputs are mask programmable via a PLA; some outputs are individually settable and resettable under program control and others output parallel data. Direct input is provided for capacitive touchplates.

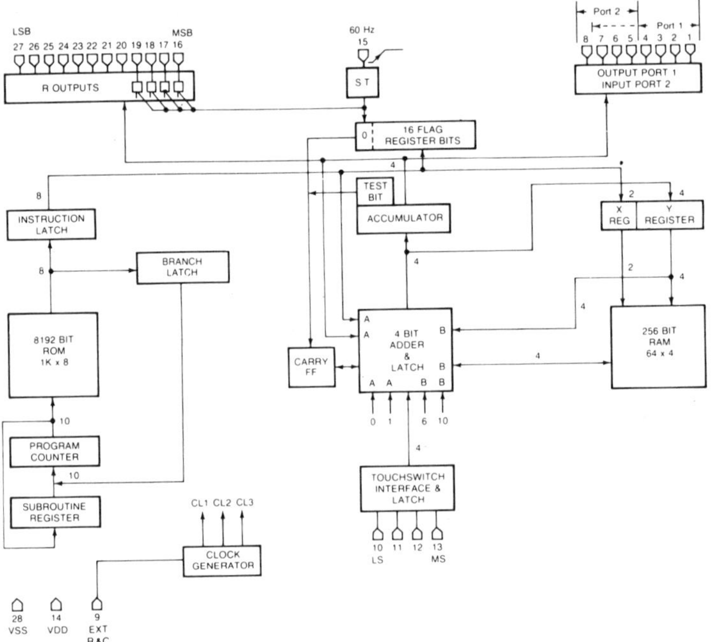

The architecture of the SX 200 processor is typical of the small all-in-one microcomputers—the on-chip ROM feeds instructions to the ALU and to the flag register while the RAM provides the workspace. The processor contains its own clock and touch-switch interface to make a complete system using capacitive touchplates to enter data. The output section contains three ports—a 12-bit output port, a 7-bit output port and a 4-bit input port.

Comments

The instruction set contains 41 basic instructions that all execute in one cycle. The instructions can be split into the following groups: three branch instructions, eight constant operations, two bit-manipulation operations, 20 register, accumulator and RAM operations, and eight control and I/O instructions.

Software support is provided by the company for the SX 200 in the form of assembly and high-level assembler and simulator programs. There is no program library available.

Special features of the software start with the fact that all instructions require the same amount of time to execute. The 16 individually settable, resettable and testable flag bits greatly improve program control. Data can be input in BCD, thus simplifying many interfaces.

Hardware support consists of a programmable emulator that is used to verify the system and program design.

Specifications

Data word size:	4 bits
Address bus size:	4 bits
Direct addressing range:	1024 bytes (internal)
Instruction word size:	8 bits
Number of basic instructions:	41
Shortest instruction/time (Any):	20 μs
Clock frequency (min/max):	Dc/400 kHz
Clock phases/voltage swing:	1/internal
Dedicated I/O control lines:	24
Package:	28-pin DIP
Power requirements:	10 to 18.5 V/25 mA

Hardware

Model	Description	Price
SX 200	4-bit CPU There are no support circuits available.	N/A

4-bit microcomputer, PMOS

COPS series

Alternate sources: None.

National Semiconductor, Inc.
2900 Semiconductor Dr.
Santa Clara, CA 95051
(408) 737-5000

The COPS family of PMOS processor chips consists of four different processor circuits or circuit combinations—the MM5781 and 5782 combination processor and ROM circuits, the MM5799 all-in-one processor, the MM57140/57152 single-chip processor (the 140 drives LEDs, the 152 handles fluorescents) and the MM57109 single-chip number cruncher. The 5782 is the processor half of the two chip set and contains a 160×4 bit RAM. The 5781 is the ROM half and can hold up to 2048×8 bits (an expansion chip, the 57129, can hold up to 4096×8 bits). On the 5799 up to 1500×8 bits of ROM are available and on the 57140 only 630×8 bits. RAM space on the 5799 and 57140 decreases to 96×4 and 55×4, respectively.

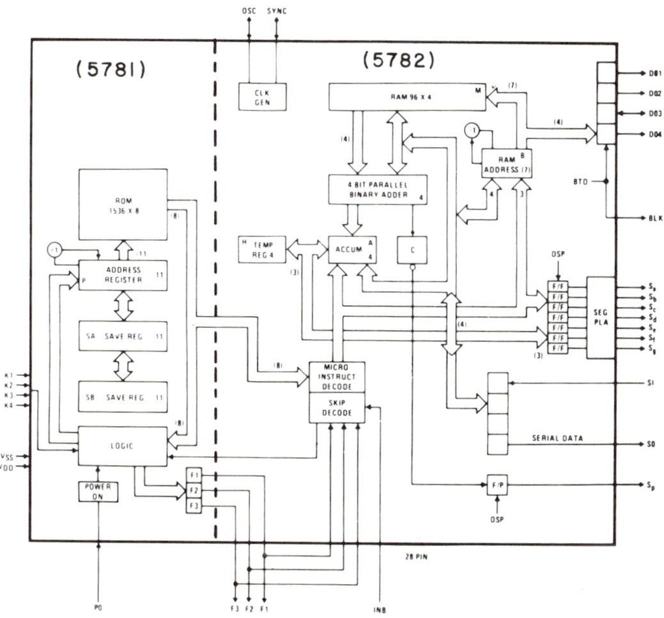

The architectures of the devices in the COPS family of processors are similar. Variations in memory size and I/O capability are the major differences. Most of the processors provide BCD or seven-segment outputs plus all can handle a direct keyboard interface. Only the MM5782 requires an external clock oscillator all other circuits have internal clocks.

Special features of the software include simple BCD data handling and serial as well as parallel data handling instructions. All instructions require either one or two clock cycles.

Hardware support includes the IMP-16P micro-based hardware and software development system, including a ROM simulation capability. Chips without ROMs are also available so that external RAM and PROM can be used for program development.

Specifications

Data word size:	4 bits
Address bus size:	Internal
Direct addressing range:	Up to 4096 bytes
Instruction word size:	8 bits
Number of basic instructions:	33 to 41
Shortest instruction/time (Single word):	10 μs
Longest instruction/time (Double word):	50 μs
Clock frequency (min/max):	70/400 kHz
Clock phases/voltage swing:	4 internal
Dedicated I/O control lines:	11 to 24
Package:	28-pin DIP
Power requirements:	9 V/8 to 15 mA

Comments

The instruction set between all four processor models is compatible—the instructions of the smaller processors are a subset of the larger chips. The largest processor MM5799 offers 41 instructions that can be broken down as follows: 18 control and ALU commands, 10 I/O directions and 13 memory operations. The other processors have 36 and 33 (for the 57140 and 5782, respectively). The 57109 has 70 pre-programmed commands to handle calculations.

Software support for the COPS series consists of a cross assembler and simulator program available on an IMP-16 computer system. No program library is available.

Hardware

Model	Description	Price (100 qty)
MM5781	2 k x 8 ROM & I/O	N/A
MM5782	4-bit microcomputer	$14.35
MM5799	4-bit microcomputer	N/A
MM57109	4-bit number cruncher	12.00
MM57140	4-bit microcomputer, LED	N/A
MM57152	Same as 140 but fluoresc.	N/A
MM5785	Interface to RAMs	N/A
MM5788	Interface to printer	N/A
MM57129	4 k x 8 ROM & I/O	N/A

4-bit microcomputer, PMOS

uCOM-42 (uPD548C)

NEC Microcomputers, Inc.
5 Militia Dr.
Lexington, MA 02173
(617) 862-6410

Alternate sources: None.

The uCOM-42 is a 4-bit single-chip microcomputer designed for electronic cash register and vending applications. Containing an on-chip ROM of 1920 × 10 bits and a 96 × 4 bit RAM, the processor still has 35 lines available for I/O operations. The I/O lines can handle an 8 × 4 key keyboard as well as an eight-digit LED display and electronic printer without any additional support circuits.

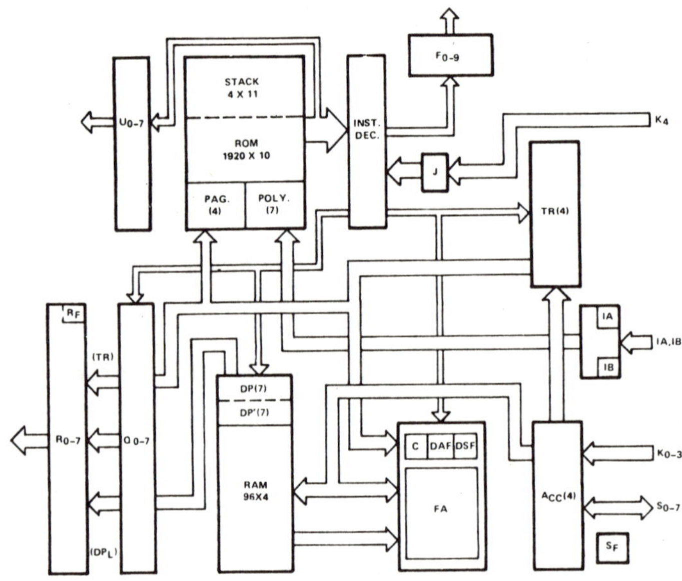

The architecture of the uCOM-42 is designed directly for the electronic cash register market and keyboard controllable appliances. The I/O structure handles an 8 × 4 keyboard, an 8-digit LED display and peripherals. The on-board RAM can also be expanded off the chip. All I/O lines are TTL compatible and all outputs can handle up to −35 V.

prepare the program. It also has a hold line to stop operation so that instruction execution can be examined. The other aid is an evaluation kit that provides single-step, breakpoint and register display capabilities.

Comments

The instruction set of the uCOM-42 processor contains 72 instructions divided as follows: 11 accumulator manipulation commands, five load/store directives, five data pointer manipulation directions, four register manipulation instructions, three bit manipulation operations, seven skip and jump instructions, three subroutine commands, four interrupt directives, nine I/O operations, 20 port manipulation instructions and one no-operation command.

Software support for the uCOM-42 consists of a cross assembler that runs on the company's 8080A-based PDA-80 program development system. Also available is the PDA editor program. There is no program library available.

Important software features include the fact that all instructions require just a single cycle. And, many commands are multifunction and have auto increment and auto-decrement capability.

Hardware support comes in two forms—an evaluation chip or an evaluation kit. The chip is available so that external ROM or PROM can be used to

Specifications

Data word size:	4 bits
Address bus size:	11 bits (internal)
Direct addressing range:	1920 words (internal)
Instruction word size:	10 bits
Number of basic instructions:	72
Shortest instruction/time (Add):	10 μs
Longest instruction/time (Return from subroutine):	20 μs
Clock frequency (min/max):	100/200 kHz
Clock phases/voltage swing:	1/TTL
Dedicated I/O control lines:	15
Package:	42-pin DIP
Power requirements:	−10 V/−30 mA

Hardware

Model	Description	Price
uCOM-42	Microcomputer (5000 qty) There are no specialized support circuits.	$5.50

4-bit microcomputer, PMOS

NEC Microcomputers
5 Militia Dr.
Lexington, MA 02173
(617) 862-6410

uCOM-43, uCOM-44, uCOM-45 (uPD546C, 547C, 550C)

Alternate sources: None.

The uCOM-43, 44 and 45 family of all-in-one 4-bit microcomputers is designed for dedicated controller applications. The major differences between the different models is the amount of memory space available on each chip—the 43 is the largest with 2000 $\times$ 8 bits of ROM and 96 $\times$ 4 bits of RAM. Next step down is the 44 with 1000 $\times$ 8 of ROM and 64 $\times$ 4 of RAM. The smallest chip is the 45, with a 640 $\times$ 8 ROM and a 32 $\times$ 4 RAM. Other differences are in the number of I/O lines and a timer included on the uCOM-43 chip.

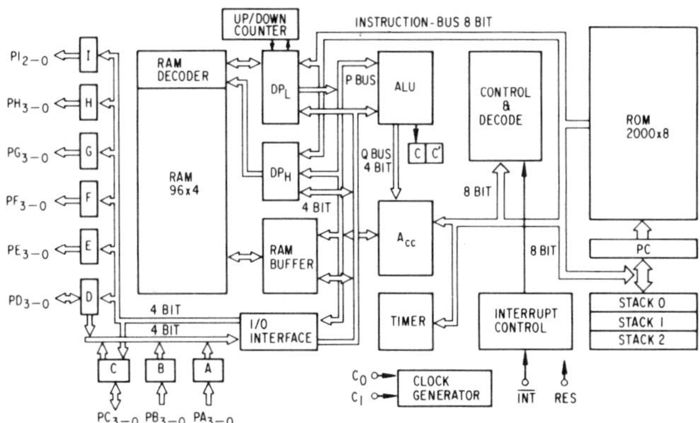

The architecture of the uCOM 43, 44 and 45 all-in-one processors is the same except for varying amounts of ROM and RAM. All chips have an on-board clock circuit and have TTL compatible I/O lines. The largest circuit, the 43, has an on-board programmable timer, a three-level stack, a flag register and six working registers. The I/O ports are divided as follows: two 4-bit input ports, two 4-bit I/O ports, four 4-bit outputs and one 3-bit output.

Comments

The instruction set consists of 80 commands for the uCOM-43 and each of the instruction sets for the 44 and 45 are just subsets of the 80. The 44 and 45 have 58 instructions in their repertoire. The major instruction set is broken down as follows: six arithmetic, 11 jump, branch and skip, 11 I/O, two timer, 26 register and memory manipulation, three comparison and 10 register exchange operations.

Software support is provided by a cross assembler that runs on the company's 8080A-based PDA-80 hardware and software development system. Also available is the PDA-80 editor program and a Fortran IV cross assembler for a 16-bit host computer. There is no program library available.

Special features of the software start with the fact that 73 of the 80 instructions require just a single byte. Six instructions provide multiple functions. There are also a total of 25 test-and-skip directions.

Hardware support for the uCOM-43, 44 and 45 starts with the uPD556D evaluation chip, which is the same as the uCOM-43 except that the address lines

for the ROM are now available for external program memory. Also available is an evaluation kit that provides single-step, breakpoint and register display operations to aid program development.

Specifications

Data word size:	4 bits
Address bus size:	Internal
Direct addressing range:	Up to 2000 bytes
Instruction word size:	8 bits
Number of basic instructions:	80 (max.)
Shortest instruction/time (Clear accumulator):	9.1 μs
Longest instruction/time (Return to subroutine):	36.4 μs
Clock frequency (min/max):	150/440 kHz
Clock phases/voltage swing:	1/Internal
Dedicated I/O control lines:	21 to 35
Package:	42-pin DIP
Power requirements:	−10 V/−30 mA

Hardware

Model	Description	Price
uCOM-43	4-bit microcomputer	$5.50
uCOM-44	4-bit microcomputer	3.40
uCOM-45	4-bit microcomputer	2.70
	All prices are for 50,000 qty purchases.	
	There are no support circuits available.	

4-bit microcomputer, PMOS

PPS-4/1 family

Rockwell International
P.O. Box 3669
Anaheim, CA 92803
(714) 632-3729

Alternate sources: AEG Telefunken.

A family of 4-bit, single-chip, microcomputers, the PPS-4/1 Models MM75, 76, 77 and 78 include CPU, RAM, ROM, I/O and clock circuitry on a single chip. On-board ROM ranges from 640 to 2048 bytes and on-chip RAM spans 48 to 128 4-bit words. Three special versions of the MM76 are also available—the E version with an expanded ROM, the D version with an a/d converter and the C model with a high-speed counter.

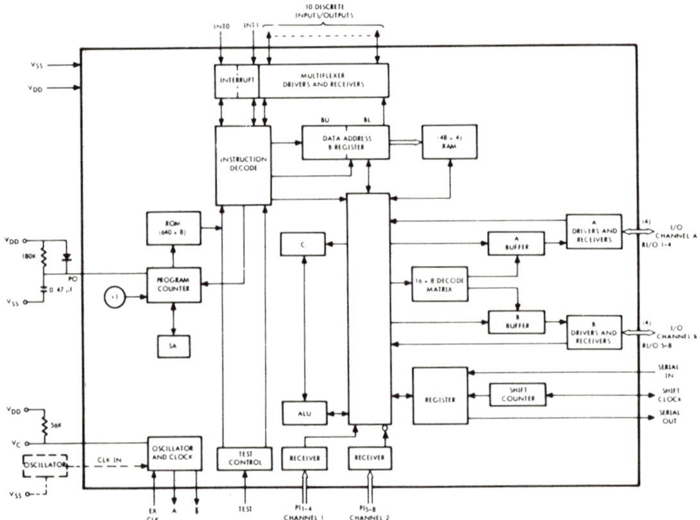

The architecture of the PPS-4/1 devices resembles that of a complete minicomputer—all the necessary circuits are included on a single chip. All chips except the MM77 and 78 have a 48 × 4 bit on-board RAM. The 77 and 78 contain 96 × 4 and 128 × 4 RAMs, respectively. All chips have one 8-bit bidirectional port as well as two conditional interrupt lines, except for the MM75 which has only one interrupt.

Comments

The instruction set of the PPS-4/1 processors is divided into nine basic categories—RAM addressing commands, bit-manipulation directions, register-to-register operations, arithmetic instructions, ROM addressing commands, logic comparison instructions, I/O directions, conditional transfer operations and register/memory instructions.

Software support for the PPS-4/1 family consists of a Fortran IV cross assembler available either for direct purchase or on time-sharing networks (GE and Tymshare). Also available is the PPS MP Universal Assemulator that contains supervisors, assemblers, and a text editor as well as debug routines.

Software features include specialized instructions for the software controllable converter and counter in the MM76D and C versions, as well as a large number of general-purpose I/O commands.

Hardware support for the PPS-4/1 family consists of various processor modules that plug into the PPS MP Universal Assemulator—the complete resident development system for the family. There are also a wide number of support modules for the Assemulator—memory, I/O, personality and prototyping cards are available.

Specifications

Data word size:	4 bits
Address bus size:	Internal
Direct addressing range:	Internal
Instruction word size:	8 bits
Number of basic instructions:	67 to 69
Shortest instruction/time (Most):	12.5 μs
Clock frequency (min/max):	40/120 kHz
Clock phases/voltage swing:	Internal
Dedicated I/O control lines:	22 to 39
Package:	28 pin DIP or 42 and 52-pin QUILs
Power requirements:	15 V/5 mA

Hardware

Model	Description	Price (1000 qty)
MM75	CPU with 640 bytes of ROM	$6.10
MM76	CPU with 640 bytes of ROM	8.00
MM76C	CPU with counter	
MM76D	CPU with a/d converter	
MM76E	CPU (expanded MM76)	
MM77	CPU with 1344 bytes of ROM	9.50
MM78	CPU with 2048 bytes of ROM	10.75

8-bit microcomputer, NMOS

PIC 1650/PIC 1655

General Instrument Corp.
600 W. John St.
Hicksville, NY 11802
(516) 733-3000

Alternate sources: None.

Manufactured with ion-implant, n-channel processing, the PIC 1650 and PIC 1655 are byte-oriented, stand-alone processors that include 512-word user-defined ROMs for program storage and 32 eight-bit internal registers (RAM), all on-chip. The 1650 has 32 user-defined I/O lines and the 1655 has 20 lines.

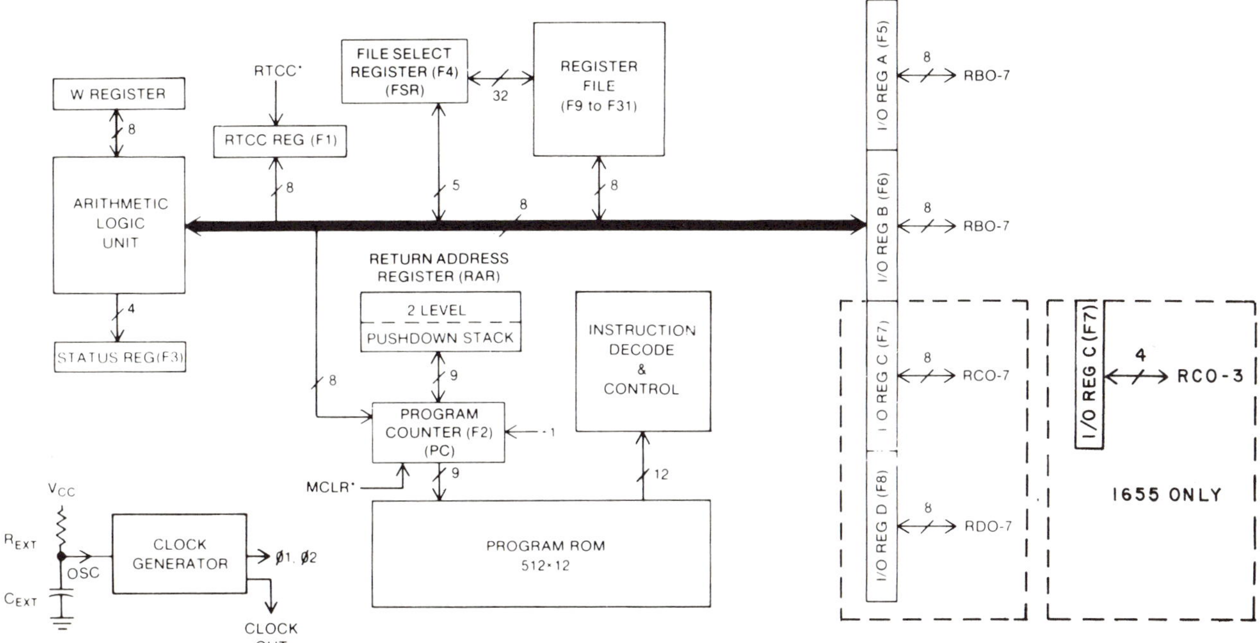

The PIC 1655 differs from the 1650 only in the number of I/O lines. All lines are TTL compatible. There are four 8-bit parallel ports on the 1650 as well as 32 8-bit general-purpose registers and a built-in clock generator to supply all the timing signals. The 1655 has only two 8-bit and one 4-bit ports.

Comments

The instruction set of the PIC 1650/1655 contains 30 commands, including 18 for arithmetic and logic operations on the 32 internal registers. Another group of four operates on individual bits, while a third group of eight is for literals, subroutine stacking, and program control.

The software available includes an assembler (PICAL), a debugger (PICBUG), and a software simulator (PICSIM) that are written to run on the Gimini 16-bit microcomputer system. A Fortran version of PICSIM is also available.

Software features of the PIC1650/1655 instruction set include individual bit set, reset and test operations as well as BCD arithmetic capability in the accumulator. The general purpose input/output lines can be programmed to scan keyboards, drive multiplexed displays, etc.

Hardware support is provided with the PIC Emulator, a single-board development tool with software debugger, Teletype interface, and in-circuit emulation. Also available is the PIC 1664 a version of the 1650 that uses external PROM or RAM for prototyping.

Specifications

Data word size:	8 bits
Address bus size:	Internal
Direct addressing range:	—
Instruction word size:	12 bits
Number of basic instructions:	30
Shortest instruction/time (Most):	4 μs
Longest instruction/time (Program counter skips):	8 μs
Clock frequency (min/max):	0.1/1 MHz
Clock phases/voltage swing:	Internal
Dedicated I/O control lines:	32 or 20
Package:	28-pin DIP(1655)
	40-pin DIP(1650)
Power requirements:	5 V/50 mA

Hardware

Model	Description	Price
PIC 1650	CPU (2500 min order)	$8.00
PIC 1655	CPU (2500 min order)	$6.00
PIC 1664	CPU with ext. memory (for prog. dev.)	N/A

8-bit microcomputer, NMOS
MCS-48 (8035, 8048 and 8748)

Intel Corp.
3065 Bowers Ave.
Santa Clara, CA 95051
(408) 246-7501

Alternate sources: Advanced Micro Devices, NEC and Signetics (Philips) are official second sources via mask exchange.

There are three versions of the basic processor available—the 8035, which is just a processor without any on-chip program memory; the 8048, which has the processor along with 1024 bytes of mask-programmable ROM on the same chip; and the 8748, which contains the processor and 1024 bytes of UV erasable PROM on the same chip. All three versions are made via an NMOS silicon-gate process and contain a 64 × 8 data RAM, 27 I/O lines, a counter/timer and an on-board clock generator in addition to the processor. And, all three versions of the processor are pin-compatible.

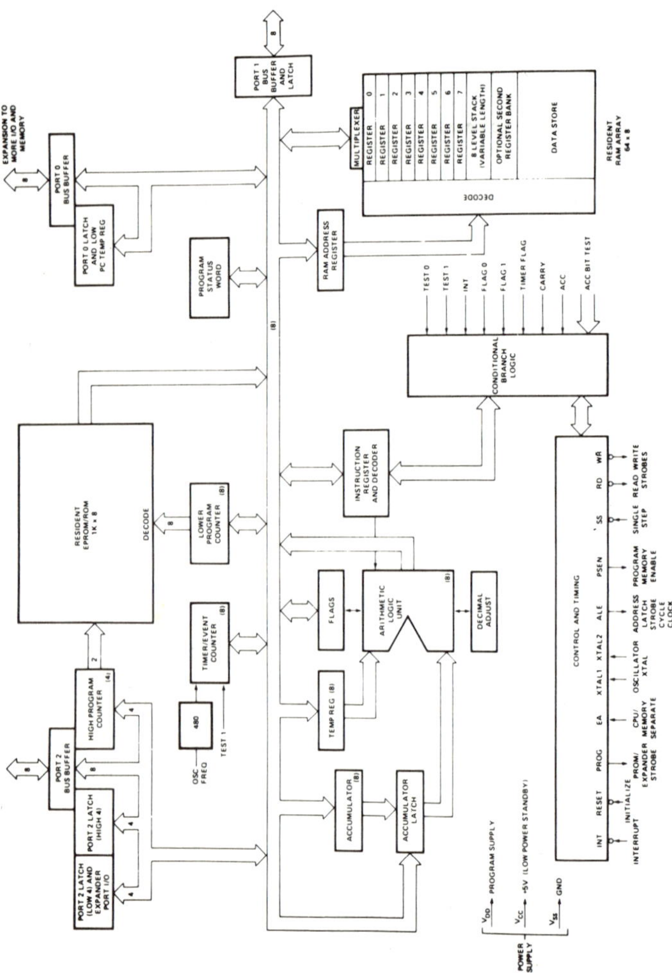

Debug software as part of the ICE-48 in-circuit emulator system. Also, MCS-48 programs are available through the company's Insite program library, which contains over 350 programs.

Unique features of the software include AND and OR operations directly to the I/O ports for bit set and reset operations. Accumulator bit test operations and indirect fetch for table look-ups are also possible.

Hardware support includes the Prompt-48, a benchtop stand-alone development system and the Intellec Microprocessor Development System (MDS), a full microcomputer based system with 16 k of RAM and 2 k of ROM and software and hardware interfaces for peripherals.

Specifications

Data word size:	8 bits
Address bus size:	12 bits
Direct addressing range:	4096 words
Instruction word size:	8 bits
Number of basic instructions:	96
Shortest instruction/time (50% of commands):	2.5 μs
Longest instruction/time (remaining 50%):	5 μs
Clock frequency (min/max):	1/6 MHz
Clock phases/voltage swing:	Internal/TTL
Dedicated I/O control lines:	27
Package:	40-pin DIP
Power requirements:	5 V/65 mA

Hardware

Model	Description	Price (100 qty)
8035	CPU without ROM	$13.55
8048	CPU with mask-programmed ROM	consult factory
8748	CPU with UV PROM	$175.00
8155	RAM, I/O & timer	14.00
8205	1 of 8 binary decoder	2.80
8212	8-bit I/O port	2.90
8214	priority interrupt	4.65
8216	Bidirectional bus drive	2.75
8226	Inverting bus driver	2.75
8243	I/O expander	5.00
8253	Programmable timer	17.55
8259	Interrupt controller	17.20
8279	Keyboard/display interface	14.10
8355	ROM & I/O expander	c.f.
8755	UV PROM & I/O	125.00

The basic architecture of the MCS-48 family is highly bus oriented, with almost every sub block tied into the bus. All three eight-bit ports provide latched outputs. If more program memory is needed than is on the chip, ports 0 and 2 can be used to output an address to external memory.

Comments

The instruction set of the MCS-48 family consists of 96 instructions split into 24 register operations, 26 accumulator operations, 23 conditional and unconditional transfers, 13 I/O control instructions and 10 other system control instructions.

Software support for processors includes a macroassembler on paper tape or floppy disc, a resident text editor in the MDS development system and

8-bit microcomputer, NMOS

MK3870

Alternate sources: Fairchild and Motorola.

Mostek Corp.
1215 W. Crosby Rd.
Carrollton, TX 75006
(214) 242-0444

A complete microcomputer on a single chip, the MK3870, can execute the instruction set of the F8. The 8-bit device executes more than 70 instructions, allowing expansion into multichip configurations with software compatibility. Featured on-board are 2048 bytes of ROM and 64 bytes of scratchpad RAM. The processor operates from a single 5-V supply and contains 32 lines of bidirectional I/O and a programmable timer.

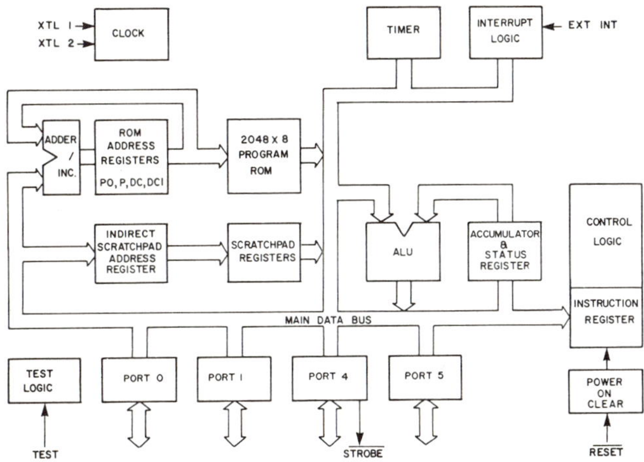

The architecture of the 3870 is identical to that of the original F8, with the extra features of ROM and RAM added to the original chip. Also included on the chip is an 8-bit timer and an 8-bit prescaler. The 3870 can form a complete processor system without any other additional circuits aside from the power supply. All lines are TTL compatible.

software development board. The largest system is the AIM-70, a complete real-time emulation system that provides snapshot software in ROM.

Comments

The instruction set of the 3870 is compatible with that of the F8 processor. There are 76 basic instructions, divided as follows: 15 accumulator reference, eight memory reference, 12 branch and jump, 13 address modification, 15 scratchpad memory reference and 13 miscellaneous control instructions.

Software support for the 3870 processor includes resident debug, edit and assembly programs, nonresident Fortran-IV cross assembler for 16-bit and larger minicomputers, and many ROM-based software packages. There is no general program library, but the factory can be consulted for specific program needs.

Important features of the software include compact instruction codes (60% of the instructions require just one byte), auto-incrementing and auto-decrementing are possible, register and memory pointers are available, the processor can perform relative addressing and all I/O instructions require a single byte.

Hardware support for the 3870 includes the F8 evaluation kit with 1024 bytes of RAM, a TTY monitor with breakpoint capability and a Fortran cross assembler. An assembler, editor and debug routine are also available on the company's SDB-50/70

Specifications

Data word size:	8 bits
Address bus size:	11 bits (internal)
Direct addressing range:	2048 words
Instruction word size:	8,16, or 32 bits
Number of basic instructions:	76
Shortest instruction/time (Register reference):	2 μs
Longest instruction/time (Subroutine call):	13 μs
Clock frequency (min/max):	1/4 MHz
Clock phases/voltage swing:	Internal
Dedicated I/O control lines:	32 I/O lines plus two control lines
Package:	40-pin DIP
Power requirements:	5 V/70 mA

Hardware

Model	Description	Price (100 qty)
MK3870	8-bit microcomputer	$19.00
MK3850N	F8 CPU	10.75
MK3853N	Static memory interface	9.50
MK3871N	Parallel I/O and timer	9.50

8-bit microcomputer, PMOS

Series 8000

General Instrument Corp.
600 West John Street
Hicksville, NY 11802
(516) 733-3000

Alternate Sources: AEG Telefunken and SGS-ATES.

The Series 8000 logic processor system is a multiple-chip set—the LP8000 processor chip, the LP6000 control memory and the LP1030 clock generator. Able to access 16 kwords over its all-MOS-level buses the Series 8000 system offers 24 bidirectional I/O lines. There are 48 general-purpose 8-bit registers on the LP8000 as well as an 8-bit bidirectional I/O port. The LP6000 control memory contains 16 lines of bidirectional I/O in addition to the 1 k $\times$ 8 control program.

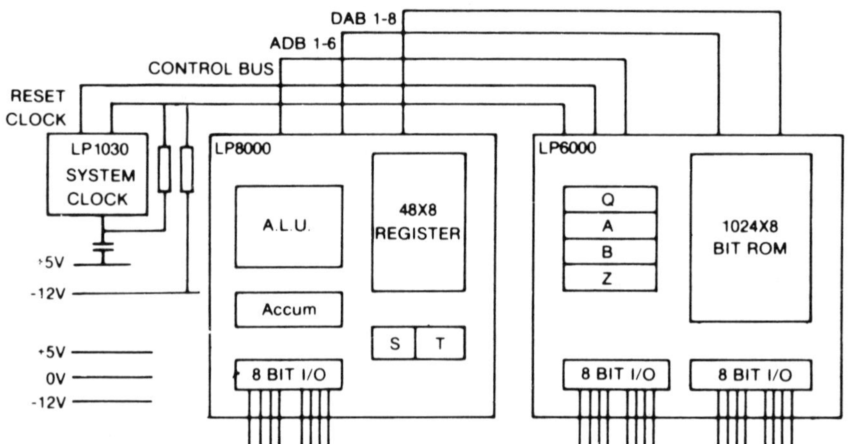

The architecture of the Series 8000 is based on a three-chip set—the CPU, ROM and clock generator. In the processor is an 8-bit ALU, a 48 $\times$ 8 register file, a four-word address stack and eight bidirectional I/O lines. The 8-bit data bus and 6-bit control bus combine to provide a 14-bit memory address.

Comments

The instruction set consists of 48 basic commands that are divided as follows: 11 register operations, nine jump instructions and 31 accumulator operations (including Binary and BCD Add, logic OR, AND and Exclusive-OR, and Compare).

Software support for the Series 8000 is composed of a Fortran IV cross assembler and simulator that can run on many minicomputer systems or is available from various time-sharing vendors. There is no program library available.

Special features of the software include the many accumulator operations and the multiple position bit shifts possible when handling BCD arithmetic.

Hardware support consists of several modules that permit ROM or PROM to be used to develop the software. There is also a prototyping system available—the GIC 8000—that has resident hardware and software debug aids.

Specifications

Data word size:	8 bits
Address bus size:	Internal
Direct addressing range:	16,384 bytes
Instruction word size:	8 bits
Number of basic instructions	51
Shortest instruction/time (many):	5 μs
Longest instruction/time (Load accumulator from module indirect)	15 μs
Clock frequency (min/max):	500/800 kHz
Clock phases/voltage swing:	1/11 V
Dedicated I/O control lines:	24 (3-chip syst.)
Package:	40-pin DIP
Power requirements:	5 V/30 mA −12 V/70 mA (LP8000 only)

Hardware

Model	Description	Price* (100 qty)
LP8000	8-bit processor chip	$10.00
LP6000	1 k $\times$ 8 ROM & 16 I/O lines	10.00
LP1000	Memory interface	8.50
LP1010	I/O buffer	7.50
LP1030	800 kHz clock generator	2.50
	*Main market emphasis is in Europe.	

16-bit microcomputer, NMOS

TMS 9940

Texas Instruments Inc.
P. O. Box 5012, M/S 308
Dallas, TX 75222
(214) 238-2011

Alternate sources: None.

A 16-bit CPU, with RAM, EPROM and I/O circuitry contained in a single 40-pin package. The TMS 9940 also contains a timer/event counter, a flag register, and reconfigurable I/O. Instructions are compatible with the TMS 9900 and, in addition, include two new instructions for manipulating BCD data and a single LIIM instruction to load an interrupt mask. Memory-to-memory architecture features multiple register files, in RAM, for faster response to interrupts and greater programming flexibility. The processor implements four levels of interrupts including the internal decrementer, which can be programmed as a timer or event counter.

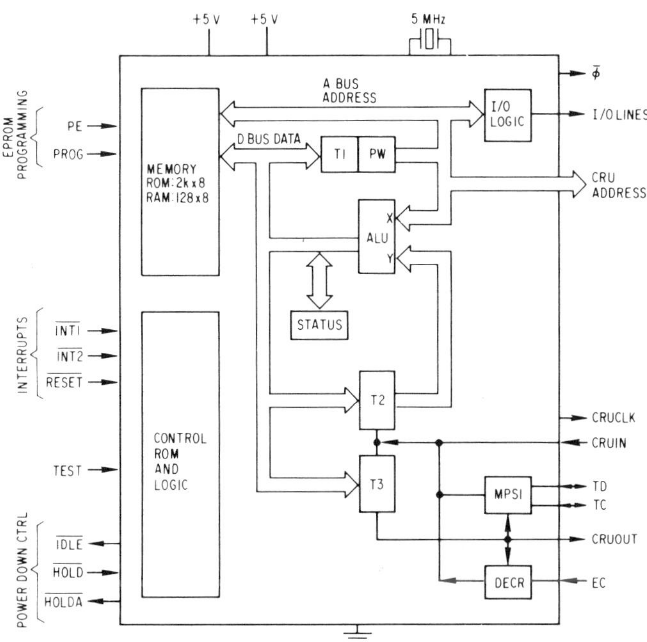

The TMS 9940 is a complete 16-bit computer system on a single chip. On the chip are 2048 bytes of ROM or UV PROM, 128 bytes of RAM, as well as an event counter/timer, a flag register and up to sixteen reconfigurable I/O lines. Even the clock generator is included on the chip. All lines are TTL compatible and the I/O lines are software configurable as either inputs or outputs.

Comments

Software for the TMS 9940 consists of all the instructions available on the TMS/SBP 9900 except for four commands that aren't applicable to the all-in-one configuration. Also, three new instructions have been added to simplify the manipulation of BCD coded data and to simplify masking operations. The 9940 can handle four levels of interrupt, and includes an internal decrementer that can be programmed as a timer or event counter.

Support software for the TMS 9940 consists of assemblers, editors, simulators and debuggers. High-level languages will also be available shortly. There is also a program library available since most

software is code compatible with the company's 990 series of minicomputers.

The most outstanding features of the software include the multiple register file capability and the flexibility it offers. The processor makes use of the minicomputer instruction set of the 990 series, including hardware multiply and divide commands. The software controllable counter/timer also provides a handy capability to implement timing loops.

Hardware support for the TMS 9940 includes all the support for the 9900—the TM 990 microcomputer modules, the PX 990 cassette-based prototyping system, and AMPL, a floppy-disc based development system. And, since most of the software is 990 code compatible, all the mini hardware is also at the designer's disposal.

Specifications

Data word size:	16 bits
Address bus size:	15 bits
Direct addressing range:	32,768 words
Instruction word size:	16 to 48 bits
Number of basic instructions:	68
Shortest instruction/time (Jump):	2 μs
Longest instruction/time (Divide):	45.2 μs
Clock frequency (min/max):	Dc/5 MHz
Clock phases/voltage swing:	1/TTL
Dedicated I/O control lines:	16
Package:	40-pin DIP
Power requirements:	5 V/160 mA

Hardware

Model	Description	Price (100 qty)
TMS 9940	16-bit all-in-one CPU	N/A
TMS 9901	Programmable interface	$8.75
TMS 9902	Asynchronous interface	7.50
TMS 9905	8:1 multiplexer	1.26
TMS 9906	8-bit latch	1.55
TMS 9907	8:3 priority encoder	1.01
TMS 9908	8:3 priority encoder	1.01

4-bit microcontroller, PMOS

CR1872

Alternate sources: None.

Western Digital
3128 Red Hill Ave.
P.O. Box 2180
Newport Beach, CA 92663
(714) 557-3550

A low-cost 4-bit microcontroller for dedicated control applications, the CR1872 includes a direct interface for keyboard or thumbwheel switches and decoded LED segment driver outputs. The on-chip ROM holds 512 × 10 bits, and the on-chip RAM is 32 × 4 bits.

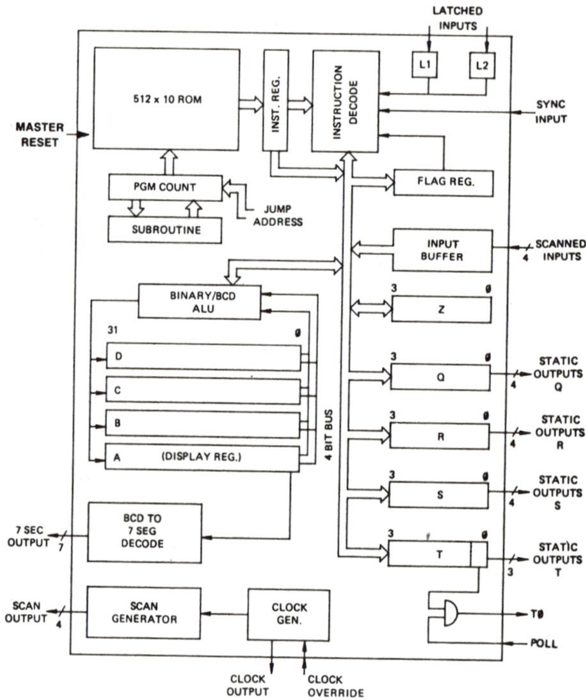

The stand-alone processor has scanned inputs and decoded outputs: seven input lines, 16 output lines, and LED segment driver outputs. All lines are compatible with TTL or CMOS logic families. In addition to the 512 × 10 bit on chip ROM, the 1872 has a 32 × 4 bit scratchpad RAM and on-board clock generator.

Comments

The instructions set is broken into four groups: program control (6), conditions (14), I/O (5), and ALU (9). All instructions are optimized for dedicated control applications and BCD data handling and display.

Software support consists of Assembler, Editor, and Simulator programs which can run on PDP-11 minicomputers.

The software set used by this processor is optimized for dedicated controller applications. A version of the processor pre-programmed as a timer is available for evaluation.

Hardware support includes a prototyping system that can be used in the SC/MP low-cost development system (LCDS) made by National Semiconductor. There is also a circuit card available that has a 64-pin version of the chip to permit external PROM connections for program development.

Specifications

Data word size:	4 bits
Address bus size:	None*
Direct addressing range:	None*
Instruction word size:	10 bits
Number of basic instructions:	34
Shortest instruction/time (Load Literal):	1 cycle
Longest instruction/time (BCD/ALU operations):	up to 32 cycles
Clock frequency (min/max):	5 kHz/150 kHz
Clock phases/voltage swing:	Internal or 1/5V
Dedicated I/O control lines:	30
Package:	40-pin DIP
Power requirements:	12 V/5 mA typ

*The address bus is internal so the direct addressing range is limited to the 512 words of on-board ROM.

Hardware

Model	Description	Price (100 qty)
CR1872	CPU No other support circuits available.	$11.00

4-bit microcontroller, PMOS

7150

Alternate sources: None.

ITT Semiconductors
74 Commerce Way
Woburn, MA 01801
(617) 935-7910

The 7150 microcontroller is designed for low-cost control of large appliances such as dishwashers and washing machines. It is a dedicated controller and does no calculations. There are 15 possible control input lines and 10 machine control output functions. The circuit is available in either an 18, 24 or 28-pin DIP, depending upon the number of control lines needed by the application. With the on-board ROMs, up to 10 machine control functions of up to 20 program steps each, can be defined.

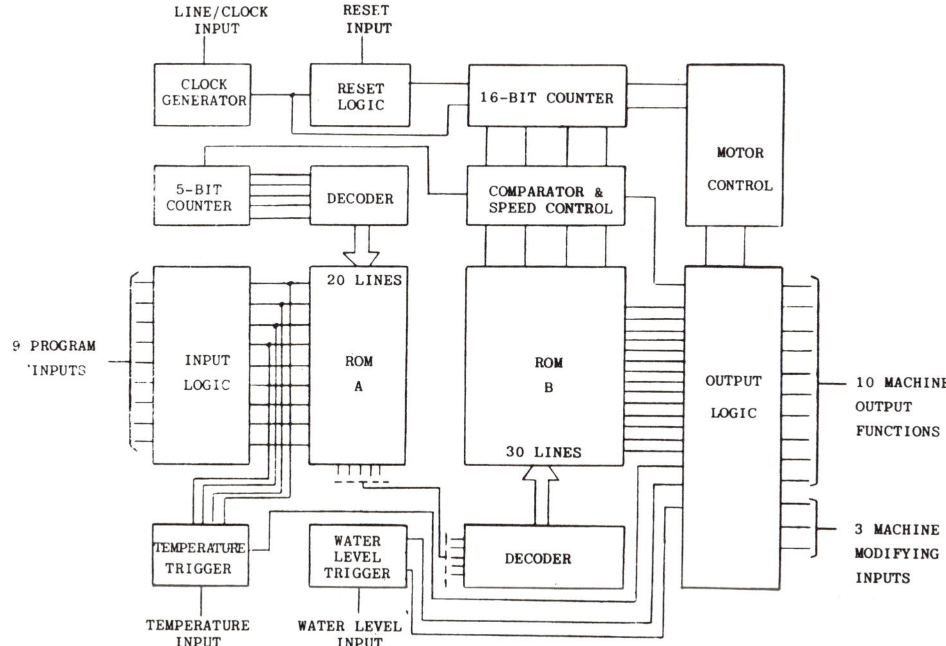

The architecture of the 7150 uses two ROMs to control the various output functions. There is no ALU since no data manipulation is required. However, there are two analog inputs to the processor that are used with an on-chip difference amplifier to form a temperature sensing circuit.

Specifications

Data word size:	Internal
Address bus size:	Internal
Direct addressing range:	Internal
Instruction word size:	Internal
Number of basic instructions:	N/A
Shortest instruction/time (Not applicable):	N/A
Longest instruction/time (Not applicable):	N/A
Clock frequency (min/max):	Dc/25 kHz
Clock phases/voltage swing:	1/10 V
Dedicated I/O control lines:	25 (max)
Package:	18, 24 or 28-pin DIP
Power requirements:	−15 V/30 mA

Comments

The Instruction set of the 7150 is strictly internal —all commands are predetermined by the manufacturer and the multiple program inputs determine the sequence of instruction execution.

Software support is nonexistent since the 7150 comes factory programmed.

Unusual software features include special subroutines and a capability to speed up programs by a factor of 64.

Hardware support is nonexistent. All that is available are the two support circuits for program position and numeric display.

Hardware

Model	Description	Price (100 qty)
7150	Microcontroller	N/A
7121	Program positioner	N/A
7122	Display driver	N/A

8-bit microcontroller, NMOS
8041/8741

Alternate sources: None.

Intel Corp.
3065 Bowers Ave.
Santa Clara, CA 95051
(408) 246-7501

The 8041/8741 Universal peripheral interface processors are designed to operate as slave microcomputers in 8080, 8085, 8048 or other 8-bit systems. They contain 1 kbyte of program memory (ROM or EPROM), I/O ports, an 8-bit CPU, clock and timer/counter in a 40-pin package. The interface processor also has a built-in single-step mode.

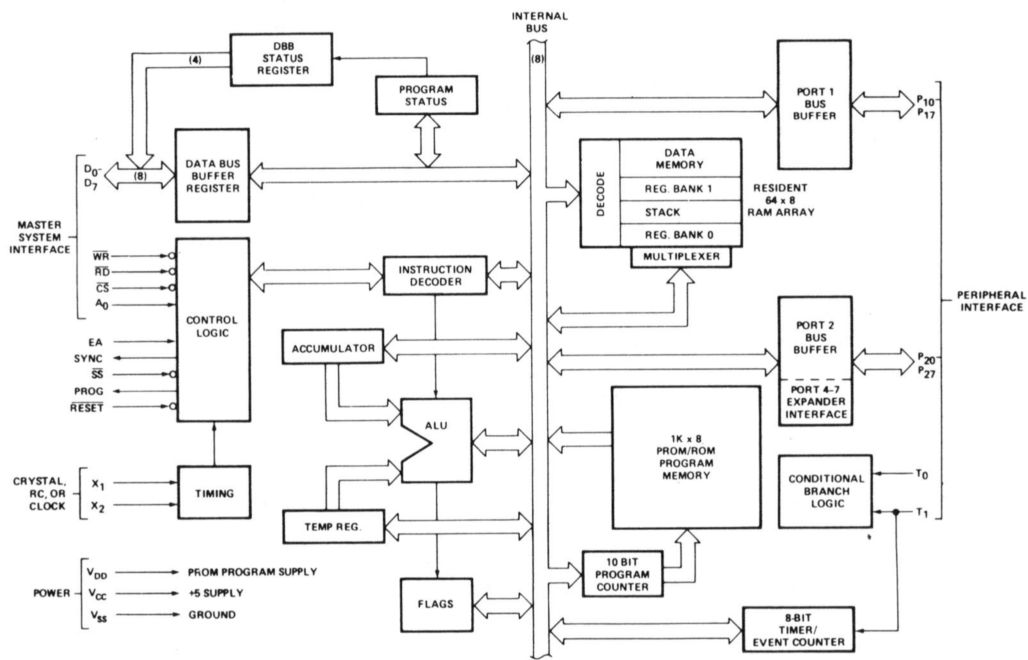

Since the device is a complete microcomputer, it can function as a stand alone unit. Of the 18 I/O lines, 2 are for input only, and 16 are input-output under program control. All I/O lines are TTL compatible and the bus port is three-state. An 8-bit timer/counter and a clock are on the chip.

Specifications

Data word size:	8 bits
Address bus size:	10 bits
Direct addressing range:	1024 words
Instruction word size:	8 bits
Number of basic instructions:	90
Shortest instruction/time (Many instructions*):	2.5 μs
Longest instruction/time (Many instructions):	5 μs
Clock frequency (min/max):	1 MHz/6 MHz
Clock phases/voltage swing:	1/TTL
Dedicated I/O control lines:	18
Package:	40-pin DIP
Power requirements:	5 V/65 mA

* The instruction set is divided about 50/50 between 2.5 and 5 μs instructions.

Comments

Included in the set of 90 instructions are 14 data moves, 28 accumulator and register operations, six flag, 20 branch and subroutine call, 12 timer and control and 10 I/O commands. All instructions are either one or two bytes and are executed in one or two machine cycles.

Support software consists of a macro assembler that can be used on the company's Intellec Microprocessor Development System.

Software features allow asynchronous data, commands and status to be transferred to an external (master) processor. Both 8-bit I/O ports are software configurable to act as inputs or outputs on a line by line basis. The internal counter/timer is software controllable.

Essentially the same hardware support offered for 8080 systems is used with the 8041/8741. This includes the Intellec Microcomputer Development System (MDS) and the ICE-41 in-circuit emulator. When used as a slave unit in an 8080 based system, the device can perform keyboard scanning, printer control and display multiplexing.

Hardware

Model	Description	Price (100 qty)
8041	ROM version of UPI	N/A
8741	UV PROM version of UPI	$156.
8243	I/O expander	

1-bit microprocessor, CMOS
MC14500B ICU

Alternate sources: None.

Motorola
5005 E. McDowell Rd.
Phoenix, AZ 85036
(602) 244-3716

Designed as a programmable logic controller, the single chip, 1-bit CMOS industrial control unit replaces multi-bit processors or hardwired logic in decision-oriented tasks. Housed in a 16-pin package, the device accepts 16 four-bit instructions. Each instruction performs logical operations on data appearing on a 1-bit bi-directional data line. The main attribute of the device is its simplicity in control system applications.

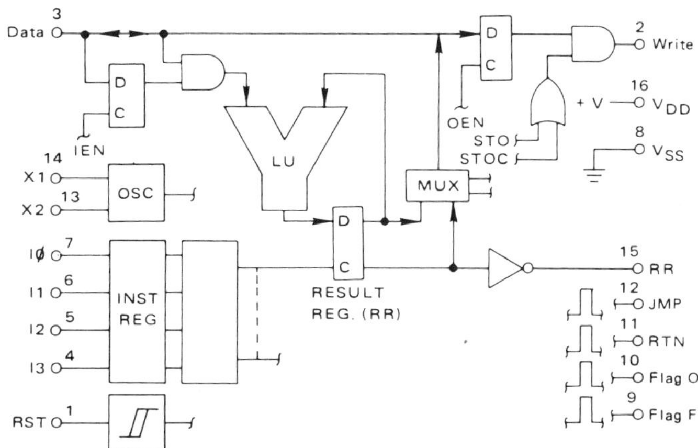

A minimum system consists of the processor, an external memory, program counter, 8-channel data selector and an 8-bit addressable latch. Instruction lines are TTL compatible and the 1-bit bi-directional data line has three-state capability. On-chip there are three 1-bit registers that are directly addressable, and the clock oscillator.

Comments

Sixteen 4-bit instructions comprise the entire set. There are seven logic instructions, five program control, two output and two no operation. All operations are performed at the bit level. Looping control structure is used, where the program counter feeding the external memory that inputs instructions to the processor wraps around after reaching its highest value and repeats the program.

The idea of this processor is not to require the use of any additional software support. Designed primarily as an industrial controller, the device is oriented towards a simple, repetitive control function.

Time invarient software is the important feature of this processor. This means that the processor can effect a conditional jump without parallel loading the program counter with the jump address. Whole blocks of instructions can be either turned on or off. This leads to the looping control structure in which the same sequence of commands are encountered with certain blocks of code being selectively enabled or disabled. In conventional systems the execution time of the program varies with the state of the input signals.

No prototyping hardware is available for this circuit. The design cycle for implementing a working sys-

tem is intended to be so short as not to require any additional hardware or software. Particular emphasis is made of the fact that this processor is much easier to use than 4, 8 or 16-bit models.

Specifications

Data word size:	1 bit
Address bus size:	Variable
Direct addressing range:	As determined by adress bus
Instruction word size:	4 bits
Number of basic instructions:	16
Shortest instruction/time (All are performed in same time):	1 μs
Clock frequency (min/max):	dc/1 MHz
Clock phases/voltage swing:	1/supply voltage
Dedicated I/O control lines:	4
Package:	16-pin DIP
Power requirements:	3 to 18 V/2 mA

Hardware

Model	Description	Price (100 qty)
MC14500B	1-bit processor	$4.88
MC14099	8-bit addressable latch	2.22
MC14599	8-bit read/write addressable latch with master reset	2.81
MC14512	8-channel data select	0.98

4-bit microprocessor, PMOS
MCS-40 (4004 and 4040)

Intel Corp.
3065 Bowers Ave.
Santa Clara, CA 95051
(408) 246-7501

Alternate sources: National Semiconductor.

The MCS-40 microcomputer family includes the 4040 and 4004 central processing circuits and a comprehensive line of support chips. Both circuits are PMOS and are instruction compatible, but the 4040 is an enhanced device, with 14 more instructions than the 4004 for a total of 60 commands. Other differences between the CPUs include a larger address stack in the 4040 (seven levels instead of three), a larger scratchpad in the 4040 (24 instead of 16), and the 4040 also has interrupt and single-step capability.

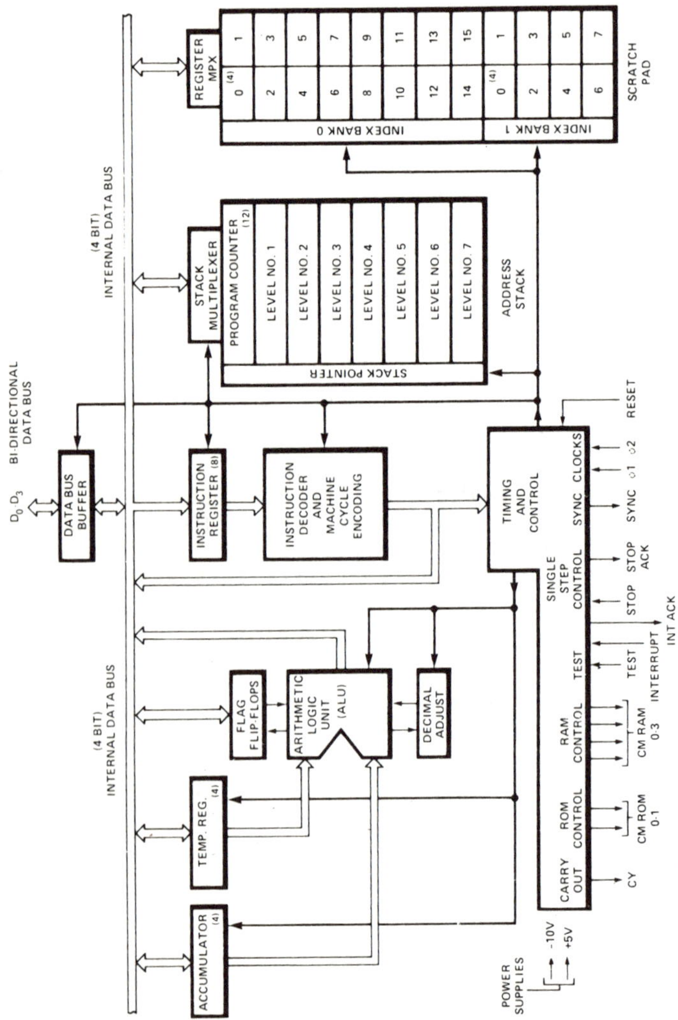

The architecture of the MCS-40 processors is almost identical except for the expanded stack and scratchpad areas of the 4040 as compared to the 4004. A minimal system typically requires three chips—the CPU, a clock generator and a memory circuit.

Comments

The instruction set of 60 commands for the 4040 and 46 instructions for the 4004 are compatible—all 4004 instructions can run on the 4040. Instructions are broken into three groups—basic operations, machine-only instructions, and I/O and RAM commands.

Software support for the MCS-40 family consists of the MAC40 cross assembler and a 4004/4040 cross simulator (Interp/40) that are available on time-sharing systems and for in-house computer systems. There is also a program library containing over 50 programs.

Important software features include the BCD adjust instruction for decimal arithmetic and a register bank switch command for data save operations.

Hardware support for the MCS-40 family consists of the Intellec 4/Mod 40 hardware and software development system, with PROM resident monitor and peripheral interfaces. Also available are RAM memory boards and a designers kit.

Specifications

Data word size:	4 bits
Address bus size:	12 bits
Direct addressing range:	8192 words
Instruction word size:	8 bits
Number of basic instructions:	60 (4004: 46)
Shortest instruction/time (Add):	10 μs
Longest instruction/time (Jump):	20 μs
Clock frequency (min/max):	0.5/0.75 MHz
Clock phases/voltage swing:	2/15 V
Dedicated I/O control lines:	8
Package:	24-pin DIP (4004: 16-pin DIP)
Power requirements:	15 V/40 mA

Hardware

Model	Description	Price (100 qty)
4004	4-bit CPU	$5.00
4040	Enhanced 4-bit CPU	5.50
4003	10-bit shift register	2.75
4265	Programmable general-purpose I/O	3.85
4269	Programmable kbd/disp.	7.75
4201A	Clock generator	3.25
4008/9	Memory interface ckts.	6.50 ea
4289	Standard memory interface	8.20
4002	320-bit RAM & 4 I/O lines	4.45
4001	256 × 8 ROM & I/O	10.00
4308	1024 × 8 ROM & I/O	8.50
4316	2048 × 8 ROM	16.90
4702A	256 × 8 EPROM	11.70

4-bit microprocessor, PMOS

PPS-4, PPS-4/2

Alternate sources: AEG Telefunken.

Rockwell International Microelectronic Devices
P.O. Box 3669
Anaheim, CA 92803
(714) 632-3729

Forming either a three or two-chip processor, the PPS-4 and PPS-4/2 central processor chips provide over 50 instructions and 12 dedicated I/O lines. The 4/2 CPU is a newer version of the 4 and can operate with an inexpensive 3.58 MHz crystal. The PPS-4 requires an external clock. Both processors, though, are totally instruction compatible and have 8-bit instruction/data buses and 11-bit address buses. The one major difference is that the PPS-4/2 CPU automatically floats all output lines when power is turned on; the PPS-4 doesn't. And, the 4/2 can directly drive low-power LED display segments.

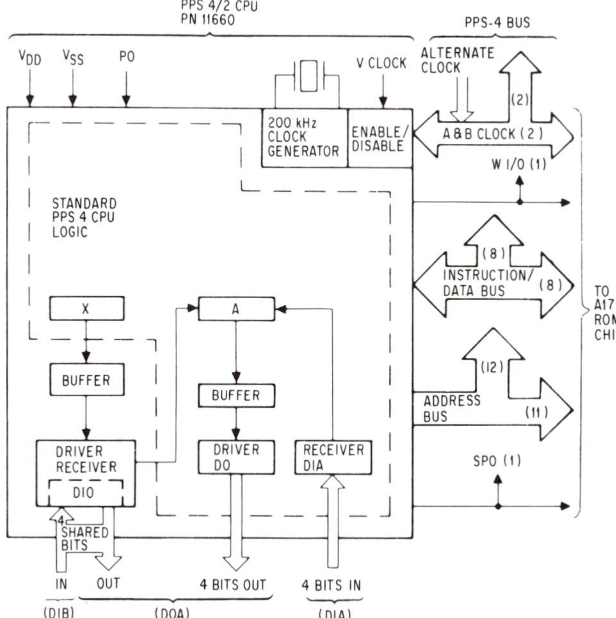

The straightforward architecture of the PPS-4 and 4/2 revolves around the 4-bit accumulator and the three four-bit I/O buses. All lines are designed for direct MOS-level interfaces so to connect to other logic families buffer circuits must be used. The PPS-4 requires an external clock while the 4/2 just needs an external crystal.

modification in addition to the basic data transfer instruction, and software controllable interrupts.

Hardware support for the PPS-4 and 4/2 starts with simple CPU modules designed to plug into the PPS MP Universal Assemulator. Other modules available as plug-ins include memory boards, I/O boards and prototyping modules.

Specifications

Data word size:	4 bits
Address bus size:	12 bits
Direct addressing range:	4096 words
Instruction word size:	8 bits
Number of basic instructions:	50
Shortest instruction/time (Transfer):	5 μs
Longest instruction/time (Load B long):	10 μs
Clock frequency (min/max):	199 kHz
Clock phases/voltage swing:	4/12 V (PPS-4); Internal (PPS-4/2)
Dedicated I/O control lines:	12
Package:	42-pin QUIL
Power requirements:	17 V/26 mA

Comments

The instruction set contains a total of 50 commands that can be grouped as follows: 10 arithmetic and logic, 24 data transfer, six transfer, five skip, four I/O and one special address generation instruction.

Software support for the PPS-4 and 4/2 includes a Fortran IV simulator and cross assembler for use on in-house computer systems and time-share networks as well as resident assemblers, supervisors, text editors and debug routines for use on the PPS MP Universal Assemulator hardware and software development system.

Special features of the software include the capability to perform an automatic memory address

Hardware

Model	Description	Price (100 qty)
PPS-4	CPU	$18.15*
PPS-4/2	CPU	10.00*
10706	Clock generator	7.45
10738	Bus interface	4.50
11049	Interval timer	8.50
10696	General purpose I/O	8.50
10930	Serial data controller	15.00

*Price as of Oct. 1. Peripheral chip prices were also cut on Oct. 1. Consult distributors for current cost.

8-bit microcontroller, bipolar (STTL)

8X300

Alternate sources: None.

Signetics
811 E. Arques Ave.
Sunnyvale, CA 94086
(408) 735-8055

Featuring control-oriented instructions, the 8X300 is a fixed instruction microcontroller. Each of the eight 16-bit control instructions can be executed in 250 ns. The single-chip device handles 8-bit data and can execute data formats of one to eight bits at equal speed. Processor timing can be set via an external crystal or clock source.

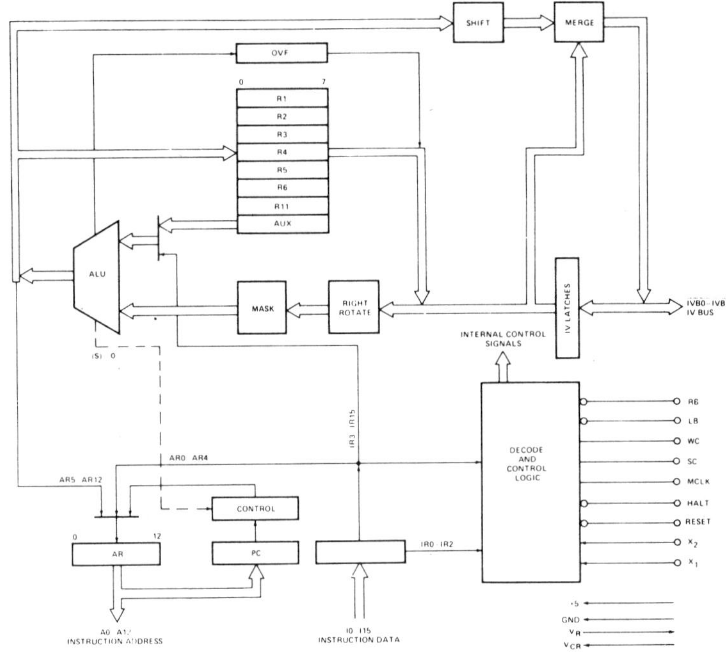

The architecture of the 8X300 is designed so that several operations can take place simultaneously —shift, merge, rotate and mask. A minimal system contains the 8X300, some memories and several 8-bit I/O ports. All lines are TTL compatible and the 8-bit interface bus has three-state capability.

Comments

The instruction set contains only eight instructions —Move, Add, AND, XOR, Execute, Nonzero transfer, Transmit and Jump. Input data can be rotated and masked while output data are shifted and merged —all within a 250 ns cycle time.

Software support for the 8X300 consists of a cross assembler. There is no program library available.

Unusual software features include the simplicity of operation and the identical 250 ns execution speed for each instruction. The circuit uses addressed I/O so the instructions can address up to 512 8-bit I/O ports directly from data bus.

Hardware support consists of the 8X300KT100SK, a designers kit and McSim, a development system produced by Scientific Microsystems, Mountain View, CA. McSim has an in-circuit emulation capability.

Specifications

Data word size:	8 bits
Address bus size:	13 bits
Direct addressing range:	8192 words
Instruction word size:	16 bits
Number of basic instructions:	8
Shortest instruction/time (All instructions):	250 ns
Clock frequency (min/max):	Dc/4 MHz
Clock phases/voltage swing:	Internal or external TTL
Dedicated I/O control lines:	8
Package:	50-pin DIP
Power requirements:	5 V/450 mA

Hardware

Model	Description	Price (100 qty)
8X300	8-bit microcontroller	$48.75
8T32	8-bit programmable I/O port	3.50
8T33	8-bit programmable I/O port	3.50
8T35	8-bit programmable I/O port	3.50
8T36	8-bit programmable I/O port	3.50
8T39	Bus extender	5.40

8-bit microprocessor, CMOS

CDP 1802

RCA Solid State Division
Box 3200
Somerville, NJ 08876
(201) 685-6731

Alternate sources: Hughes Solid State Products, Solid State Scientific Inc.

Fabricated using CMOS technology, the 1802 offers static operation, high noise immunity, wide voltage tolerances and speeds faster than possible with NMOS construction. The device's architecture features register orientation and on-chip direct memory access and clock to lower the cost of memory and systems. The 1802 is still the only 8-bit CMOS microprocessor available.

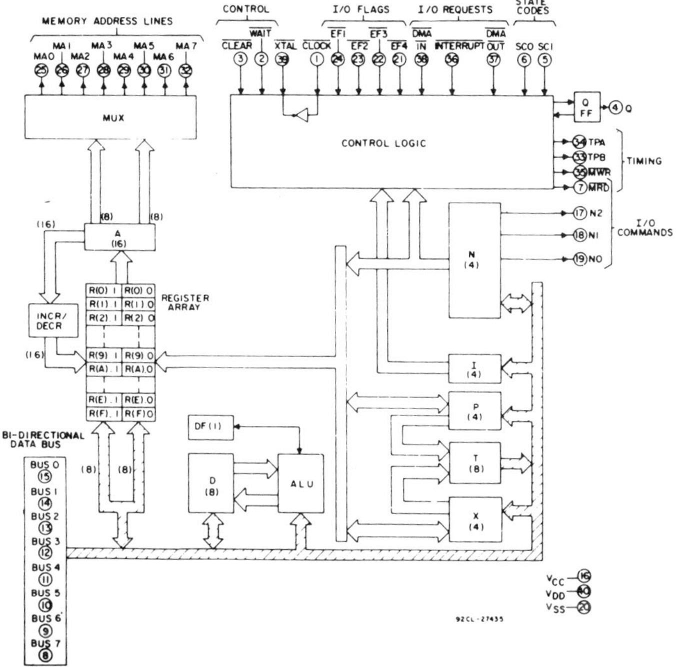

The architecture of the 1802 revolves around the 16 x 16 bit register file that is used to simplify addressing and memory reference commands. Because of the on-chip register file and the built-in clock, a minimal system can be built around the processor and a single ROM.

Comments

The 91 basic instructions include 10 for control, seven for memory reference, seven for register operation, 12 for logic operations, 12 for arithmetic operations, 20 short branch instructions, eight long branch instructions, nine skip instructions, and 14 I/O instructions. On-chip program storage includes a 16 × 16-bit scratchpad RAM.

Software support includes arithmetic, resident editor and assembler, cross assembler/simulator, and firmware debug packages as well as a full floppy-disc based program development system. Also available is a high-level interpretive language.

Features of the software include simple 1, 2, or 3-byte instructions and simple timing loops for debug-

ging. There is also a wide variety of branch and skip instructions from which to choose to permit rapid selection of a subroutine or program jump. A programmable serial port is also included on the chip to permit simple serial I/O without any specialized communications circuits.

Hardware support includes the Microtutor II learning tool, the COSMAC Development System for software development, and an evaluation kit for prototyping and breadboarding.

Specifications

Data word size:	8 bits
Address bus size:	16 bits
Direct addressing range:	65,536 words
Instruction word size:	1 to 3 bytes
Number of basic instructions	91
Shortest instruction/time (Most):	2.5 μs
Longest instruction/time (Long Branch):	3.75 μs
Clock frequency (min/max):	Dc/6.4 MHz
Clock phases/voltage swing:	1/supply voltage
Dedicated I/O control lines:	9
Package:	40-pin DIP
Power requirements:	4 to 12 V/1.6 mA (5 V)

Hardware

Model	Description	Price (100 qty)
1802	Commercial CPU	$15.90
	Industrial CPU	19.50
1852	8-bit I/O port	6.50
1853	N-bit decoder	
1854	UART	10.55
1856/57	Memory & I/O bus Buffers/separators	4.25
1858/59	Memory latches decoders	4.45
1861	TV interface	N/A

8-bit microprocessor, NMOS

3850

Fairchild Semiconductor
464 Ellis St.
Mountain View, CA 94042
(415) 962-3816

Alternate sources: Mostek, Motorola and SGS-ATES.

The multichip F8 microcomputer family is designed to handle I/O intensive applications. The minimal system typically consists of the 3850 CPU and one or more 3851, 56 or 57 program storage units, which can hold up to 2048 bytes of instructions and provide I/O lines and a programmable timer.

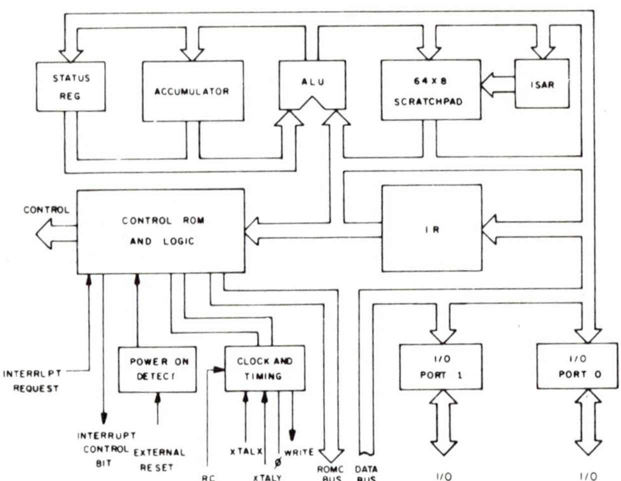

The architecture of the 3850 CPU provides a distributed format, thus permitting simple system expansions. The processor contains a 64 byte scratchpad RAM and 16 I/O lines. Any program storage unit added to the system brings 16 I/O lines, a counter/timer and other features depending on the version. All I/O lines are TTL compatible and the data and address buses have three-state capability.

Comments

The instruction set contains a total of 76 basic instructions split as follows: 15 accumulator reference, eight memory reference, 12 branch and jump, 13 address modification, 15 scratchpad register reference and 13 control instructions.

Software support is available in many forms; there is a Fortran IV cross assembler that can run on 16-bit minicomputers, there are editor, assembler and debugger routines in the resident development system and ROM based programs, such as Fairbug, which has load, dump, display and store features.

Outstanding software features start with the fact that 60% of the instructions are one byte, thus providing compact code. I/O instructions are only one byte and both register and memory locations can be automatically incremented or decremented by some instructions.

Hardware support starts with the F8 evaluation kit that contains 1024 bytes of RAM, a TTY monitor routine with breakpoint capability and a Fortran cross assembler. Other hardware includes the SDB-50/70 software development board that has, in ROM, an editor, assembler and debugger. For in-circuit emulation the AIM-S1 system provides complete real-time device emulation.

Specifications

Data word size:	8 bits
Address bus size:	16 bits
Direct addressing range:	65,536 bytes
Instruction word size:	1 to 3 bytes
Number of basic instructions:	76
Shortest instruction/time (Add from scratchpad):	2 µs
Longest instruction/time (Call to subroutine):	13 µs
Clock frequency (min/max):	0.1/2 MHz
Clock phases/voltage swing:	Internal
Dedicated I/O control lines:	16
Package:	40-pin DIP
Power requirements:	5 V/80 mA
	12 V/25 mA

Hardware

Model	Description	Price (100 qty)
F3850	CPU, Commercial	$9.95
F3850	CPU, Industrial	12.95
F3850	CPU, Military	40.00
F3851	1 k ROM, I/O & timer	9.95
F3852	Dynamic memory interface	7.45
F3853	Static memory interface, I/O and timer	7.45
F3854	Direct memory interface	5.95
F3856	2 k version 3851	14.95
F3857	2 k ROM plus F3851	14.95
F3861	Peripheral I/O with timer	6.45
F3871	Same as 3861 but also does pulse width measurement	9.50

8-bit microprocessor, NMOS
MCS-80 (8080A)

Intel Corp.
3065 Bowers Ave.
Santa Clara, CA 95051
(408) 246-7501

Alternate sources: Advanced Micro Devices, Mitsubishi, National Semiconductor, NEC Microcomputers, Siemens, Signetics (Philips) and Texas Instruments.

The 8080A is an 8-bit parallel processor designed for use in general-purpose computing applications. Fabricated with silicon-gate NMOS technology, the 8080A contains six general-purpose 8-bit registers, and 8-bit accumulator, four testable flag bits, an 8-bit parallel-processing arithmetic and logic unit, a 16-bit stack pointer and a 16-bit program counter. The processor can handle vectored interrupts and can directly address up to 512 I/O ports. Arithmetic and logic instructions can set or reset four flags and a fifth flag is used for decimal arithmetic only.

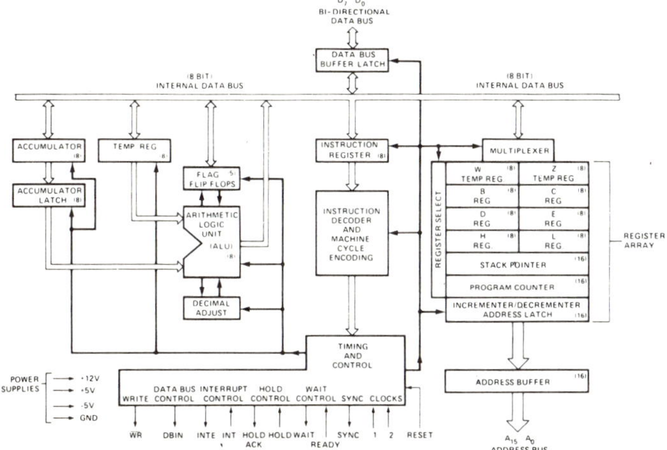

The typical 8080A system consists of a processor, a clock, a bus controller, some memory and a memory decoder. Both the data and address buses are TTL compatible and have three-state capability. All but the clock lines are TTL-compatible.

Comments

The 8080A has 78 basic instructions divided into five groups: Data transfer, Arithmetic, Logic, Branch and Stack, and I/O and Machine control. There are also four addressing modes—direct, indirect, register and immediate. The move, load and store instruction groups can transfer either 8 or 16 bit data words between memory, the six working registers and the accumulator.

Software support for the 8080A includes a relocating macroassembler, a text editor and PL/M—all available on the company's own development system. There is also a program library (Insite) available to Intel customers that contains well over 200 programs submitted by users.

The basic software of the 8080A is designed for rapid stack manipulation and flexible jumps from the main program to subroutines. The ability to increment or decrement memory locations, the six general-purpose registers or the accumulator as well as register pairs or the stack pointer provides simple program looping capability.

Hardware support is available in several forms— from the low cost SDK-80 prototyping kit to the larger Microprocessor Development Systems in the Intellec family. Also available is a large range of 8080A-based computer boards from general-purpose CPU boards to multichannel analog-input boards. The large prototyping and development system, the Intellec-MDS offers the most flexibility— the system comes with a CPU, 16 k of RAM, 2 k of ROM, and software and hardware interfaces for terminals, printers and other equipment.

Specifications

Data word size:	8 bits
Address bus size:	16 bits
Direct addressing range:	65,536 words
Instruction word size:	8 to 24 bits
Number of basic instructions:	78
Shortest instruction/time (Add reg. to accum.):	$2\mu s$, typ.
Longest instruction/time (Swap H&L with top of stack):	$9\mu s$, typ.
Clock frequency (min/max):	0.5/3 MHz
Clock phases/voltage swing:	2/9 V
Dedicated I/O control lines:	None
Package:	40-pin DIP
Power requirements:	12 V/40 mA
	5 V/60 mA
	−5 V/10 μA

Hardware

Model	Description	Price (100 qty)
8080A	CPU (commercial)	$13.10
8080A	CPU (MIL level C)	31.60
8205	1-of-8 decoder	2.80
8212	8-bit latch/buffer	2.90
8214	Priority Interrupt controller	4.65
8216	4-bit bidirectional bus driver	2.75
8224	Clock driver	
8226	Inverting version, 8216	2.75
8228	Bus controller	
8251	USART	
8253	Counter/timer	17.55
8255	Parallel I/O	7.40
8257	DMA controller	
8259	Interrupt controller	17.20
8279	Keyboard/disp. control	14.10

8-bit microprocessor, NMOS

MCS-85 (8085)

Intel Corp.
3065 Bowers Ave.
Santa Clara, CA 95051
(408) 246-7501

Alternate sources: Siemens, NEC and Advanced Micro Devices all by mask exchange.

The 8085 processor is a software-compatible upgrade of the 8080A processor. It offers two more instructions and has many of the peripheral circuits originally needed built right onto the same chip as the processor. With five levels of vectored interrupt, a serial I/O line and a clock speed of 3 MHz, the 8085 offers 8080A users a simple way to upgrade existing systems without loosing any software. And, since the clock is on chip, all signal lines are TTL compatible, with the address and data buses having three-state capability.

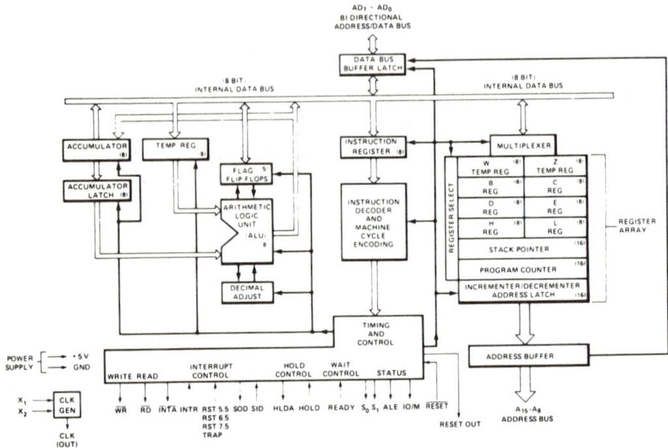

The basic architecture of the 8085 is the same as that of the 8080A. The only differences are the built-in clock generator, the built-in system control circuit and the multiplexed address/date bus structure to make available several pins for additional control.

Comments

The instruction set of the 8085 contains all of the 8080A's instructions plus two more—RIM (read interrupt mask) and SIM (set interrupt mask)—for a total of 80 basic commands. The RIM and SIM instructions are used in conjunction with the interrupt capability built into the 8085 to provide four vectored interrupts, three of which are maskable.

Available software support for the 8085 includes all the existing 8080A software available through Insite—the company's user's software program library—and the many companies and private organizations that offer 8080A and 8085 software. An 8085 macroassembler can also be purchased, as well as PL/M when an MDS system with floppy disc is used.

Special features of the two new instructions permit the 8085 to handle serial inputs and outputs, and set up special masking bits to set or reset flags for the levels of vectored interrupts. Otherwise, all 8080A instructions can run on the 8085 without modification. The only adjustment that may have to be made is in any timing loops that use the 2 MHz clock frequency of the 8080A to compensate for the new 3 MHz clock.

Hardware support for the 8085 includes the ICE-85, an in-circuit emulator; the SDK-85 low-cost prototyping system; and the UPP 855 and EPROM programmer. Also, most of the development hardware available for the 8080A can be used to develop 8085 circuits and programs. The entire Intellec MDS microprocessor development system can be used, with just a few changes.

Specifications

Data word size:	8 bits
Address bus size:	16 bits*
Direct addressing range:	65,536 bytes
Instruction word size:	8 bits
Number of basic instructions:	80
Shortest instruction/time (Move data):	1.3 μs
Longest instruction/time (Double add):	5.2 μs
Clock frequency (min/max):	0.5/3 MHz
Clock phases/voltage swing:	1/TTL
Dedicated I/O control lines:	None
Package:	40-pin DIP
Power requirements:	5 V/170 mA

* 8085 uses partially multiplexed address bus—eight lines are direct and eight are shared with the data bus.

Hardware

Model	Description	Price (100 qty)
P8085	CPU (commercial temp)	$19.00
D8085	CPU (industrial temp)	24.00
P8155	256 byte RAM, I/O & timer	18.00
P8156	Same as 8155	18.00
P8355	2 kbyte ROM & 16 line I/O	consult factory
P8755-8	2 k UV EPROM & 16 line I/O	125.00
8205	1 of 8 binary decoder	2.80
8212	8-bit I/O port	2.90
8214	Priority interrupt	4.65
8216	Bidirectional bus driver	2.75
8226	Inverting version, 8216	2.75
8253	Programmable timer	17.55
8259	Interrupt controller	17.20
8279	Kbd/display interface	14.10

8-bit microprocessor, NMOS
MCS 650X, 651X

MOS Technology
950 Rittenhouse Rd.
Norristown, PA 19401
(215) 666-7950

Alternate sources: Rockwell Microelectronic Devices and Synertek.

The 8-bit pipelined microprocessor is available in nine variants (10 from Rockwell). The 6502 family has an on-board one-phase clock while the 6512 family works with an external two-phase clock (for systems that need maximum timing control). Both families include models that can address 4, 8, and 65 kbytes (6502, 6515). Maximum operating frequencies are 1 MHz or 2 MHz (suffix A).

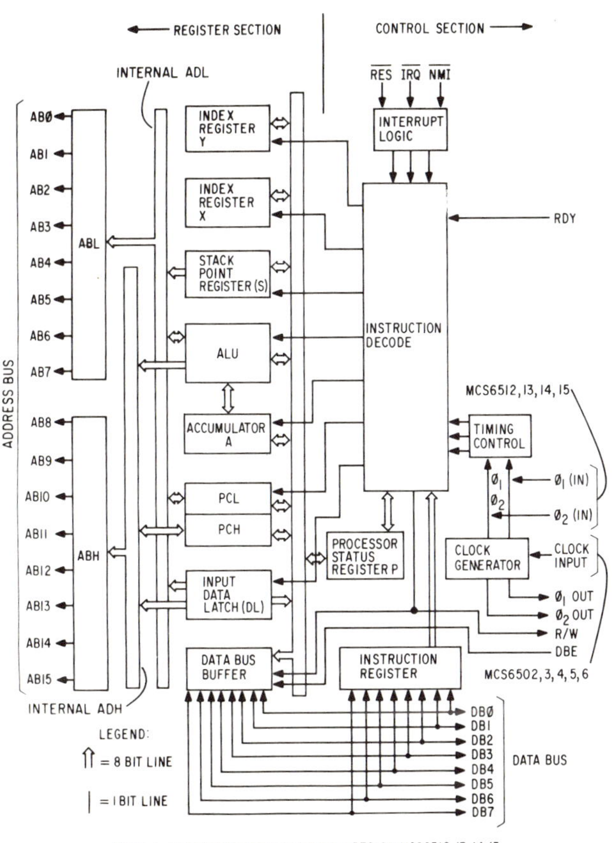

The architecture of the MCS6500 permits all registers to accept data from the data bus and transfer data back and forth since they are all connected to the same internal bus. A minimal system consists of the CPU and some memory (for a 651X system you also need a clock generator).

Comments

The instruction set is memory-oriented with emphasis on convenient addressing of data in memory tables. The 56 instructions have the following addressing modes: accumulator immediate and absolute addressing, zero page indexed zero page, and indexed absolute addressing; implied and relative addressing; indexed indirect, indirect indexed, and absolute indirect addressing.

Software support includes a cross-assembler for PDP-8, 10, 11; a text editor, a debugger, a resident assembler, a math package, a Fortran compiler, a cross-emulator and Basic (cross and host).

Outstanding software features include: add and subtract in decimal mode with automatic correction, powerful addressing modes (indexed indirect and indirect indexed) and a Basic interpreter.

Hardware support consists of the KIM-1 board (including a μP, hex keyboard, 6-digit display, 1 k × 8 RAM, 16 I/O lines and control program); KIM-2 (4 k RAM expansion); KIM-3 (8 k RAM expansion); KIM-4 (motherboard), TIM (a 6530 with monitor software for interfacing serial terminals). Also available is the MDT 650 development terminal.

Specifications

Data word size:	8 bits
Address bus size:	16 bits
Direct addressing range:	65,536 bytes
Instruction word size:	8 to 24 bits
Number of basic instructions:	56
Shortest instruction/time (Decrement register):	1 μs
Longest instruction/time (Rotate memory):	3 μs
Clock frequency (min/max):	20 kHz/2 MHz
Clock phases/voltage swing:	1/TTL or 2/5 V
Dedicated I/O control lines:	3
Package:	28 or 40-pin DIP
Power requirements:	5 V/140 mA

Hardware

Model	Description	Price (100 qty)
6502	On-bd clock, 65 k, 40 pin μP	$10.90
6503	On-bd clock, 4 k, 28 pin	8.50
6504	On-bd clock, 8 k, 28 pin	8.50
6505	On-bd clock, 4 k, 28 pin	8.50
6506	On-bd clock, 4 k, 28 pin	8.50
6507	Rockw. only, 8 k, 28 pin	9.65
6512	Ext. clock, 65 k, 40 pin	10.90
6513	Ext. clock, 4 k, 28 pin	8.50
6514	Ext. clock, 8 k, 28 pin	8.50
6515	Ext. clock, 4 k, 28 pin	8.50
6520	Peripheral interface adaptor (40-pin)	6.55
6522	6520 plus 2 timers (16-bit)	6.75
6530	16 I/O, 8 k ROM, 65 × 8 RAM, timer	13.00
6532	like 6530, but 128 × 8 static RAM	$12.75

8-bit microprocessor, NMOS

MC6800

Motorola, IC Div.
3501 Ed Bluestein Blvd.
Austin, TX 78721
(512) 928-2600

Alternate sources: American Microsystems, Fairchild, Fujitsu, Hitachi and Sescosem/Thomson CSF.

Designed as a general-purpose central processor, the MC6800 provides 8-bit computational capability with an instruction set of 72 commands. The processor has a bidirectional data bus, a full 16-bit address bus and can operate from a 5 V supply. There are three versions of the MC6800 available—the original MC6800 with a 1 MHz clock rate, the MC68A00 with a 1.5 MHz clock, and the MC68B00 with a 2 MHz clock. All versions are pin compatible.

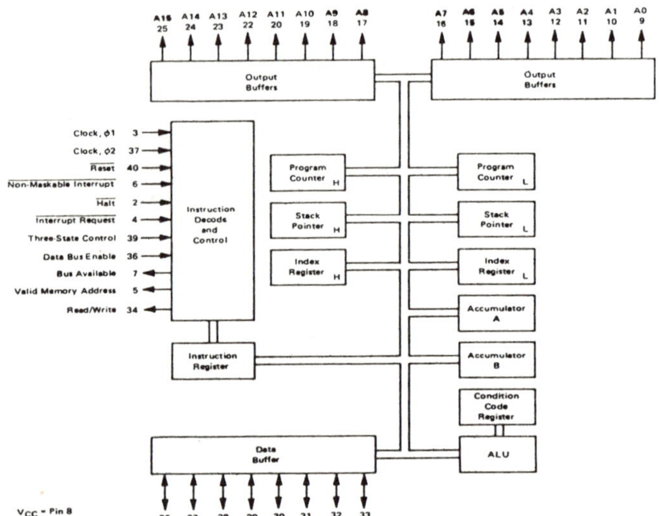

A minimum system for the MC6800 will typically consist of the processor, some ROM and RAM, a clock circuit and some I/O circuits. All lines except the clock lines are TTL compatible and the address bus, data bus and R/W line also have three-state capability. The 6800 has two accumulators, but all stack space is in the user-supplied RAM—there are no auxiliary registers on the processor chip.

and the alternate sources. And, for the program development engineer, the EXORciser system, consisting of a CPU board, a 2-k static RAM board, a 16-k dynamic RAM board, a baud-rate board, serial and parallel interfaces, a PROM programmer and a PROM/EPROM board can be used with the floppy-disc operating system. Also available is a user system evaluator (USE) that can help with the early prototyping efforts.

Specifications

Data word size:	8 bits
Address bus size:	16 bits
Direct addressing range:	65,536 words
Instruction word size:	8 bits
Number of basic instructions:	72
Shortest instruction/time (Load accumulator A):	1 μs
Longest instruction/time (Software interrupt):	6 μs
Clock frequency (min/max):	Dc/2 MHz
Clock phases/voltage swing:	2/ Vcc− 0.6 to Vss+ 0.4 V
Dedicated I/O control lines:	9
Package:	40-pin DIP
Power requirements:	5 V/100 mA

Comments

The basic instruction set consists of 72 commands that contain binary and decimal arithmetic operations, logic instructions shift and rotate functions, branch and stack manipulation commands and memory transfer operations. I/O commands are stored in the memory address space. Most instructions operate on both the ALU and memory.

The basic software support includes an assembler, editor, macro-assembler, a disc-based operating system and several high-level languages—Basic and Fortran. The user program library contains more than 65 programs.

Software features include direct page memory addressing and relative branches that allow position independent code to be written. A read/modify/write instruction can be used to modify the contents of a memory location without bringing the contents into the accumulator.

Hardware support for the MC6800 comes in several forms. For the circuit designer there are several evaluation board systems available from Motorola

Hardware

Model	Description	Price (100 qty)
MC6800	CPU (commercial), 25-up	$17.95
MC6800	CPU (industrial), 25-up	49.00
MC6800	CPU (military), 25-up	76.00
MC6820	Peripheral interface adapter	6.60
MC6840	Programmable timer	13.00
MC6850	Asynchronous communications adapter	7.80
MC6854	Data link controller	17.00
MC6860	600 bps modem	8.00
MC6862	2400 bps demodulator	13.15
MC68488	General purpose interface adapter	14.00
MC6843	Floppy-disc controller, 25-up	25.00
MC6844	DMA controller, 25-up	23.50
MC6845	CRT controller, 25-up	25.00

8-bit microprocessor, NMOS

MC6802

Alternate sources: Fairchild and Hitachi.

Motorola, Inc.
Integrated Circuit Div.
3501 Ed Bluestein Blvd.
Austin, TX 78721
(512) 928-2600

A general-purpose central processor for the M6800 family, the MC6802 includes a crystal-controlled clock oscillator and 128 bytes of on-chip RAM, 32 bytes of which can be retained during power-off by using battery backup. Like the earlier MC6800, it operates from a 5-V supply, and has a bidirectional data bus, a 16-bit address bus and 72 instructions. Maximum clock rate is 4 MHz.

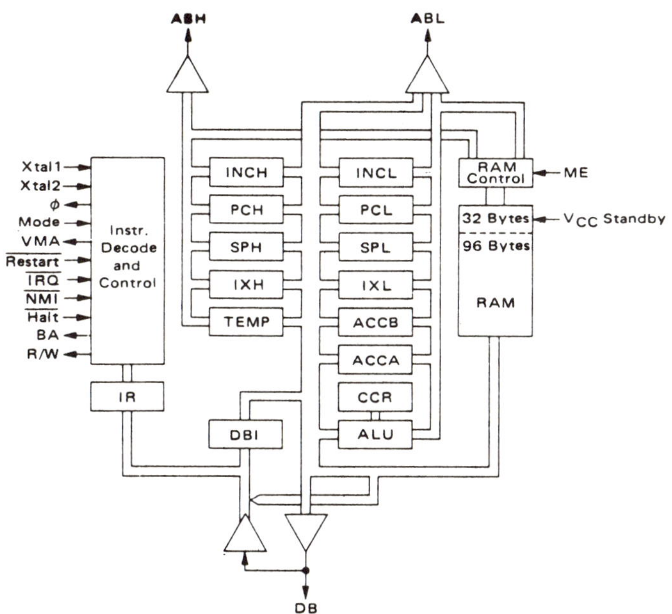

The architecture of the MC6802 resembles that of the MC6800 except that the 6802 includes the stack and the clock oscillator on the chip. A minimum system requires just two chips—the MC6802 MPU and the MC6846, a combination ROM and I/O timer.

ment, the EXORciser system can be used with a floppy-disc operating system. The EXORciser system includes a CPU board, a 2-k static RAM board, a 16-k dynamic RAM board, a baud-rate board, serial and parallel interfaces, a PROM programmer and a PROM/EPROM board.

Specifications

Data word size:	8 bits
Address bus size:	16 bits
Direct addressing range:	65,536 words
Instruction word size:	8, 16 or 24 bits
Number of basic instructions:	72
Shortest instruction/time (Load accumulator A):	2 μs
Longest instruction/time (Software interrupt):	12 μs
Clock frequency (min/max):	1 MHz/4 MHz
Clock phases/voltage swing:	Internal
Dedicated I/O control lines:	9
Package:	40-pin DIP
Power requirements:	5 V

Comments

The instruction set contains 72 commands, including binary and decimal arithmetic operations, logic instructions, shift and rotate functions, branching commands and memory transfer operations. I/O commands are stored in the memory address space.

Software support offered includes an assembler, editor, macro assembler, a disc-based operating system and several high-level languages such as Basic and Fortran. The user program library contains over 65 programs.

Software features include direct page addressing of memory for shorter coding, and relative branches that allow position-independent coding. Read/modify/write instructions operate on memory without passing data through an accumulator.

Hardware support comes in several forms. Several evaluation-board systems are available from Motorola and other sources. A user system evaluator (USE) can aid prototyping. For program develop-

Hardware

Model	Description	Price (100 qty)
MC6802	CPU (commercial), 25-up	$22.00
MC6802	CPU (industrial), 25-up	45.00
MC6846	Combined ROM/timer	N/A
MC6820	Peripheral interface adapter	6.60
MC6840	Programmable timer	13.00
MC6850	Asynchronous communications adapter	7.80
MC6854	Data link controller	17.00
MC6860	600-bps modem	8.00
MC6862	2400-bps demodulator	13.15
MC68488	General purpose interface adapter	14.00
MC6843	Floppy-disc controller, 25-up	25.00
MC6844	DMA controller, 25-up	23.50
MC6845	CRT controller, 25-up	25.00

8-bit microprocessor, NMOS
2650

Alternate sources: Advanced Memory Systems and National Semi-conductor.

Signetics
811 East Arques Ave.
Sunnyvale, CA 94086
(408) 739-7700

The 2650 family of microprocessors contains general-purpose devices that can address up to 32 kbytes of memory. There are several versions of the processor available—all pin and software compatible, but differing in clock speed. The 2650 has a maximum clock of 1.25 MHz, the 2650A a max of 1.5 MHz and the 2650A-1 a max of 2 MHz. Variable length instructions, seven general-purpose registers and three-state buses are among the processor's features.

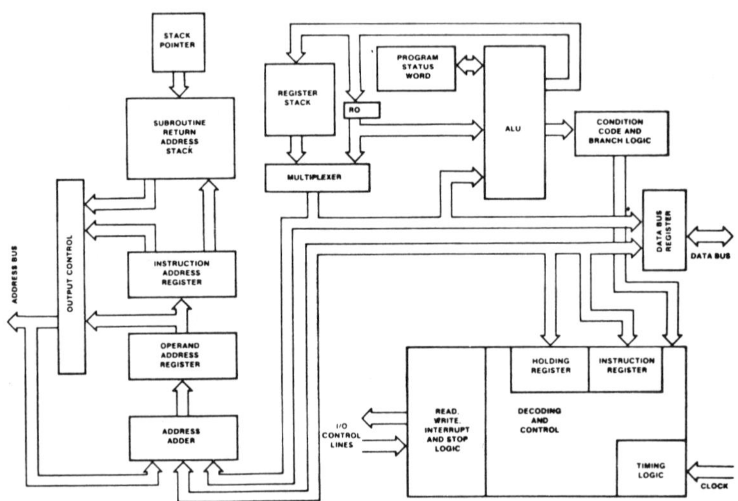

The architecture of the 2650 is centered about the 8-bit ALU and a seven-word register stack. There is also another register stack on the chip to hold subroutine return addresses (it can hold up to eight 15-bit addresses). The 2650 has a single level of interrupt, requires a single-phase external clock and is TTL compatible on all lines.

Comments

The instruction set for the 2650 family contains 75 commands, which are divided into 1, 2 and 3 bytes long operations. Instructions can be grouped as follows: 26 arithmetic and logic operations, 22 branch commands and another 26 that are I/O, program status and load/store instructions.

Software support for the 2650 processor family consists of a ROM-based editor and loader (PIP-BUG) and several cross Fortran IV programs for assembly and simulation that run on 16 or 32 bit computers. There is also a high-level language, PLus, that permits PL-type programming.

Strong points of the software set include auto incrementing or decrementing of the index register for arithmetic indexed instructions, all of the branch commands except for indexed branching can be conditional and the I/O instructions are either one or two-byte commands.

Hardware support for the 2650 family consists of a prototyping kit, a pre-assembled processor card and the Twin, a dual-microprocessor hardware and software development system.

Specifications

Data word size:	8 bits
Address bus size:	15 bits
Direct addressing range:	32,768 bytes
Instruction word size:	1 to 3 bytes
Number of basic instructions:	75
Shortest instruction/time (No operation):	0.5 μs (A-1)
Longest instruction/time (Add absolute):	2 μs (A-1)
Clock frequency (min/max):	Dc/2 MHz
Clock phases/voltage swing:	1/TTL
Dedicated I/O control lines:	9
Package:	40-pin DIP
Power requirements:	5 V/100 mA

Hardware

Model	Description	Price (100 qty)
2650	8-bit CPU, 1.25 MHz	N/A
2650A	8-bit CPU, 1.5 MHz	13.50
2650A-1	8-bit CPU, 2 MHz	N/A
2651	Programmable communication interface	13.70
2652	Multiprotocol communications controller	24.90
2655	Programmable peripheral interface	12.60
2656	System memory interface	19.70

8-bit microprocessor, NMOS

Z80-CPU

Alternate sources: Mostek, NEC and Sharp.

Zilog Inc.
10460 Bubb Rd.
Cupertino, CA 95014
(408) 446-4666

Based on the architecture of the 8080, the Z80 can perform the 78 instructions of that processor plus 80 additional instructions. The ion-implanted NMOS device is offered in two versions — the Z80 with 2.8 MHz maximum clock and the Z80A with a 4.5 MHz clock. Operating from a single 5-V supply and a single-phase external clock, the processor contains 17 internal registers and built-in dynamic RAM refresh circuitry and has three modes of interrupt response.

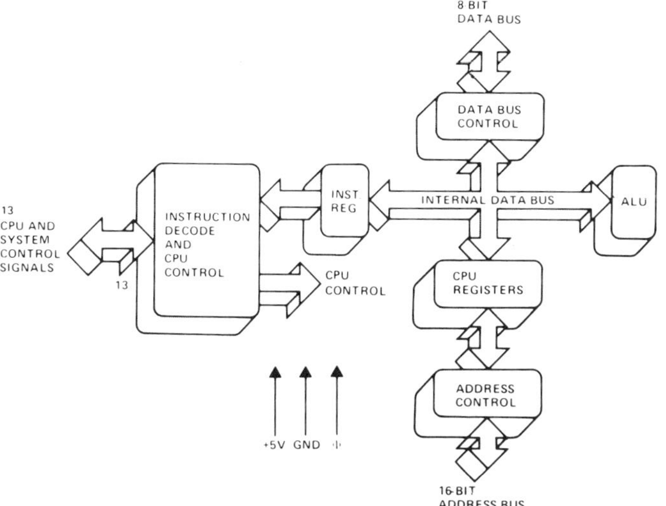

The architecture of the Z80 resembles that of the 8080A, except that there is a second bank of eight 8-bit registers that mirrors the eight registers in the 8080A. All timing generation is on the processor chip except the oscillator, and the Address bus is structured so that refresh addresses appear on the lower half of the bus to refresh dynamic RAMs. A minimal system consists of the processor, a clock source and some memory.

Comments

The instruction set of the Z80 contains all 78 op codes of the 8080A's instruction set as well as another 80 codes. Of the 158 total instructions, there are 21 8-bit Load commands, 20 16-bit Load commands, 14 Exchange, Block transfer and Search instructions, 17 Arithmetic and Logic commands for 8-bit operations, 11 instructions for 16-bit arithmetic and logic operations, 12 general-purpose arithmetic commands, 16 shift and rotate functions, nine Bit set, Reset and Test commands, 11 Jump instructions, seven Call/Return directives and 12 I/O operations.

Software support includes a macroassembler that can generate relocatable code, a linker that can link together program modules and generate a load module with absolute addresses, and several high-level languages—PL/M, PL/Z and Basic. Also available is a text editor and a file maintenance and debug routine that supports the floppy-disc based program development system.

Special features of the instruction set include the block-move operations that permit large sections of data held in memory to automatically be relocated.

Hardware support provided for the Z80 includes a development system with in-circuit emulation capability, real-time debug and program storage modules. The system has a dual floppy-disc operating system and can be expanded to handle up to 64 kbytes of RAM and many interface options for terminals and printers.

Specifications

Data word size:	8 bits
Address bus size:	16 bits
Direct addressing range:	65,536 words
Instruction word size:	One to three bytes
Number of basic instructions:	158
Shortest instruction/time (Load register to register):	1 μs
Longest instruction/time (Set bit at address IX+d):	5.75 μs
Clock frequency (min/max):	5 kHz/4.5 MHz
Clock phases/voltage swing:	1/5 V
Dedicated I/O control lines:	5
Package:	40-pin DIP
Power requirements:	5 V/90 mA (Z80A)
	5 V/60 mA (Z80)

Hardware

Model	Description	Price (100 qty)
Z80	CPU (commercial)	$ 24.50
Z80	CPU (military)	165.00
Z80A	8-bit-commercial	29.50
Z80A	8-bit-Mil	N/A
Z80-PIO	2-port parallel I/O	10.00
Z80A-PIO	Higher speed version	14.00
Z80-CTC	Quad counter/timer	16.00
Z80A-CTC	Higher speed version	20.00
Z80-DMA	Two port direct memory access	38.00
Z80A-DMA	Higher speed version	N/A
Z80-SIO	Dual full-duplex serial I/O channels	N/A
Z80A-SIO	Higher speed version	N/A

8-bit microprocessor, PMOS

8008, 8008-1

Intel Corp.
3065 Bowers Ave.
Santa Clara, CA 95051
(408) 246-7501

Alternate sources: None.
Not recommended for new designs.

The 8008 and 8008-1 were the first 8-bit single-chip microprocessors. There are currently just the two versions available—the 8008 has a 20 μs instruction time while the 8008-1 has a 12.5 μs cycle time. Either unit is a complete 8-bit parallel processor that can address up to 16 kbytes of memory, handle up to seven levels of subroutine nesting and respond to external interrupts. Most of the 48 instructions are oriented for data handling although addition, subtraction and logic operations are available.

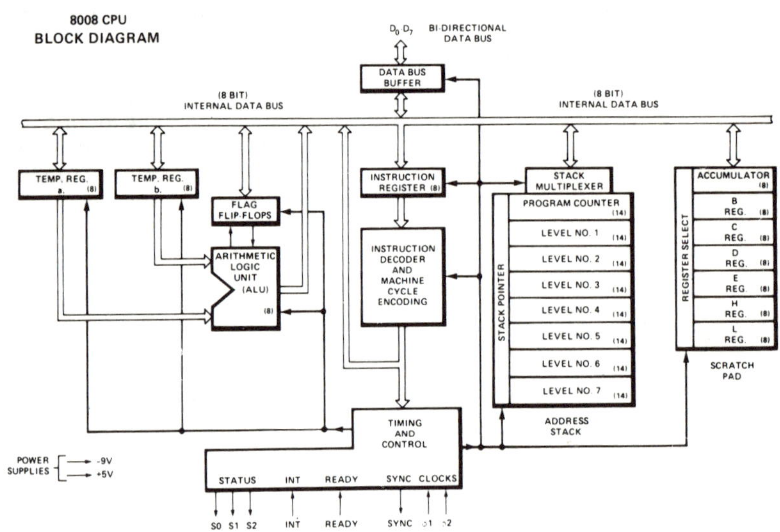

The architecture of the 8008 family parts is similar to the 8080 which has superseded it. On the 8008 chip are a 7-word × 14-bit stack register, a 6-word x 8-bit scratchpad register and a parallel 8-bit ALU. An external clock is required along with some RAM or ROM to form a minimal operating system.

Comments

The instruction set for the 8008 family has 48 basic instructions that can be divided as follows: seven index register commands, 12 accumulator directions, 16 arithmetic, logic and shift commands, and 13 program counter, stack, I/O and machine instructions.

Software support for the 8008 family consists of the MCS-8 cross assembler, which is written in Fortran IV and can run on most 32-bit computer systems. Also available is an 8008 simulator that is written in Fortran IV.

Software features include the ability to access up to 16 kbytes of RAM or ROM with just an 8-bit data bus, the ability to handle up to seven nesting levels of subroutines and the capability to respond to externally generated interrupts.

Hardware support for the 8008 family is nonexistent since it is not recommended for new designs.

Specifications

Data word size:	8 bits
Address bus size:	Multiplexed (8 bits and 6 bits)
Direct addressing range:	16,384 bytes
Instruction word size:	1, 2 or 3 bytes
Number of basic instructions:	48
Shortest instruction/time (Return):	1.25 μs (8008-1)
Longest instruction/time (Call):	37.5 μs (8008-1)
Clock frequency (min/max):	333/500 kHz
Clock phases/voltage swing:	2/11 V
Dedicated I/O control lines:	4
Package:	18-pin DIP
Power requirements:	5 V/20 mA −9 V/40 mA

Hardware

Model	Description	Price (100 qty)
8008	8-bit microprocessor	$24.25
8008-1	8-bit microprocessor	26.90

8-bit microprocessor, PMOS (SC/MP) or NMOS (SC/MP II)

SC/MP and SC/MP II

National Semiconductor
2900 Semiconductor Drive
Santa Clara, CA 95051
(408) 737-5000

Alternate sources: Rockwell, Signetics and Western Digital for SC/MP II, none for SC/MP.

Both the SC/MP and SC/MP II are low cost 8-bit microprocessors intended primarily for simple control applications. The PMOS SC/MP costs under $10 but is limited to a 1-MHz maximum clock rate. The higher performance SC/MP II can operate at 4-MHz clock rates. Both versions have on-chip clock oscillators and timing generators.

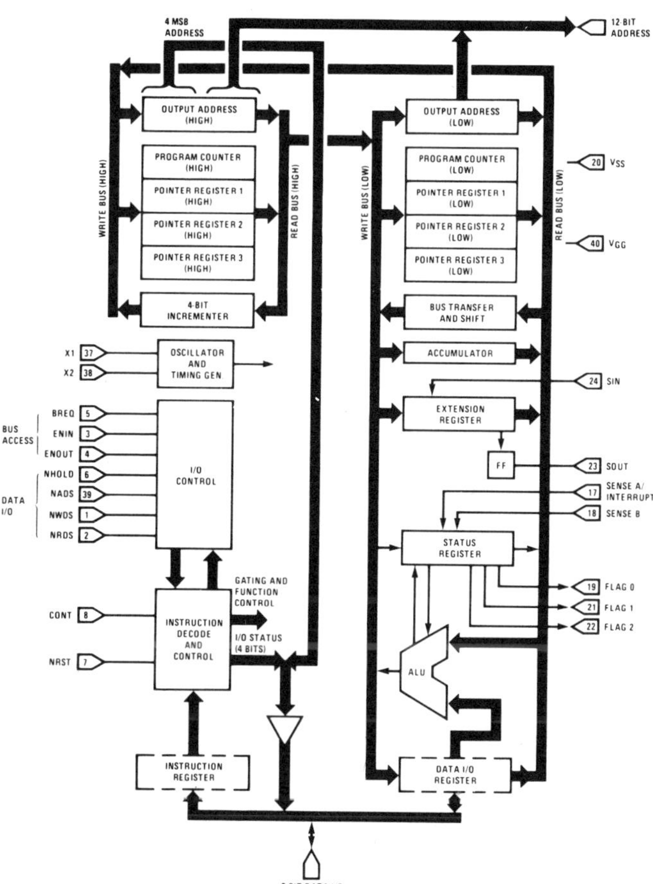

Software features include the ability to directly address up to 65 kwords with a 12-bit address bus and four bits siphoned from the data bus. SC/MP chips can be cascaded to simplify multiprocessing.

Hardware support for the SC/MPs comes in several forms. For low cost, the SC/MP kit provides a minimal system with a TTY interface. A portable terminal, the SC/MP keyboard kit, permits simple program entry and development. More extensive support comes from application cards (CPU, RAM and ROM/PROM) and a complete stand-alone development system (LCDS).

Specifications

Data word size:	8 bits
Address bus size:	12 bits
Direct addressing range:	65,536 words
Instruction word size:	8 and 16 bits
Number of basic instructions:	46
Shortest instruction/time (Shift, rotate, I/O):	5 μs (NMOS)*
Longest instruction/time (Decimal add):	23 μs (NMOS)*
Clock frequency (min/max):	Dc/1 MHz (PMOS); dc/4 MHz (NMOS)
Clock phases/voltage swing:	Internal
Dedicated I/O control lines:	14
Package:	40-pin DIP
Power requirements:	5 V/125 mA
*PMOS version requires double the time.	−7 V/135 mA

The architecture of the SC/MP provides the processor with DMA capability as well as a simple cascadable structure that is handy for multiprocessing applications. On the chip is the clock circuit to simplify the timing requirements.

Comments

The instruction set of 46 commands breaks down into 24 single-byte instructions and 22 double-byte instructions. Single-byte instructions include those for an extension register, the pointer register, and for shift, rotate and serial I/O. Double byte instructions include all memory operations.

Software support offered includes a high-level interpretive language, NIBL, written especially for the industrial user. Also available are conversational cross-assemblers that run on minicomputers. A Fortran cross-assembler is available on GE and National CSS time-sharing networks.

Hardware

Model	Description	Price (100 qty)
SC/MP	8-bit CPU (PMOS)	$9.00
SC/MP II	8-bit CPU (NMOS)	N/A
DM8334	8-bit bit-addressable latch	3.20
DM8131	6-bit unified bus comparator	2.56
DM8546	Three-state, 8-bit, I/O shift register	3.84
MM5307	Baud-rate generator/ programmable real-time clock	12.00
DS8692, 8693, 8694	Seiko-printer interface set	N/A

8-bit microprocessor, PMOS

PPS-8, PPS-8/2 (P/N 11806)

Rockwell International
P.O. Box 3669
Anaheim, CA 92803
(714) 632-3729

Alternate sources: AEG Telefunken.

Eight-bit parallel processing systems, the PPS-8 and PPS-8/2 form minimum micro-computers with five and two-chip sets, respectively, and are software compatible. The CPU chip can handle both prioritized interrupts and direct memory accesses.

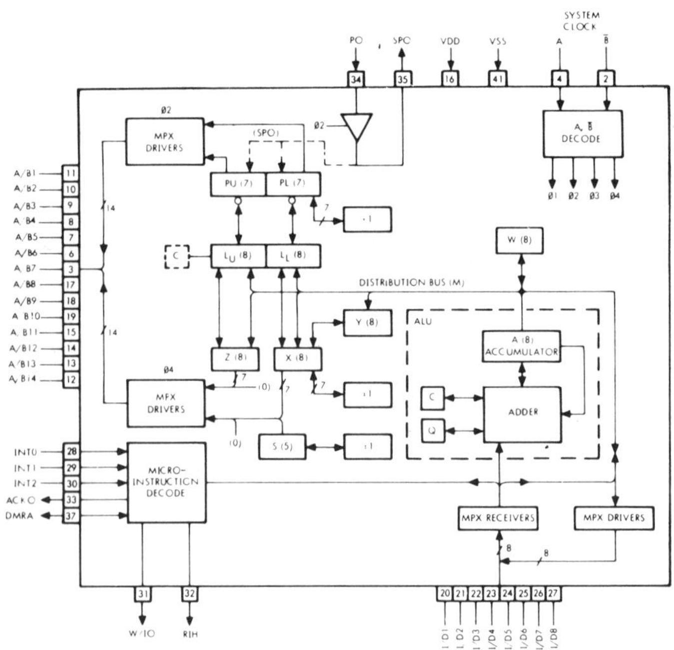

controlled DMA transfers of up to eight prioritized channels at 256 kbytes/s are possible. There is also a 5-bit stack pointer available to address the sub-routine stack.

Hardware support includes a floppy-disc based program/hardware development system, the PPS MP Universal Assemulator. There are also many peripheral interface cards and memory support products available.

The architecture of the PPS-8 processor is designed to handle both binary and BCD arithmetic. An external two-phase clock must be used, but inside the chip the clock is expanded into four-phase dynamic logic. A minimal system configuration consists of the CPU, a clock and the necessary memory and I/O circuits.

Specifications

Data word size:	8 bits
Address bus size:	14 bits
Direct addressing range:	16,384 bytes
Instruction word size:	8, 16, 24 bits
Number of basic instructions:	109
Shortest instruction/time (Many):	4 μs
Longest instruction/time (Some):	15 μs
Clock frequency (min/max):	199/256 kHz
Clock phases/voltage swing:	2/MOS
Dedicated I/O control lines:	15
Package:	42-pin QUIL
Power requirements:	17 V/35 mA

Comments

The instruction set of the PPS-8 family consists of 24 data transfer commands, 10 stack operations, 13 arithmetic and logic instructions, six increment/decrement operations, 23 branch/skip commands, 21 register operations, four I/O instructions and eight bit-manipulation directions.

Software support for the PPS-8 family consists of a Fortran IV cross assembler and a Fortran IV simulator. There is also a software development system, the PPS MP Universal Assemulator, that does program assembly, debug, emulation and even incoming device testing.

Software features include BCD arithmetic capability as well as dedicated I/O instructions. Software

Hardware

Model	Description	Price (100 qty)
PPS-8	CPU	$20.00*
PPS-8/2	CPU	$11.25*
10706	Clock generator	$ 7.45
10738	Bus interface	$ 4.50
11049	Interval timer	$ 8.50
10817	DMA controller	$18.75
10453	Parallel data controller	$15.00
10936	Floppy disc controller	$40.00
10696	General purpose I/O	$ 8.50
10930	Serial data controller	$15.00

*Price as of Oct. 1. Peripheral circuit prices have been cut as well. Consult distributors.

12-bit microprocessor, CMOS

IM 6100

Alternate sources: Harris Semiconductor.

Intersil, Inc.
10900 N. Tantau Ave.
Cupertino, CA 95014
(408) 996-5000

Able to emulate the Digital Equipment Corp. PDP-8 minicomputer's instruction set, the IM 6100 processor provides the user with a wealth of readily available software. The CMOS processor can also operate from a single supply and, since it draws only about 2 mA (at 5 V and 4 MHz) it is ideal for portable equipment design. The processor's architecture is also very similar to that of the PDP-8, with the only major difference in the bus—the IM 6100 doesn't use the DEC patented Unibus structure and timing.

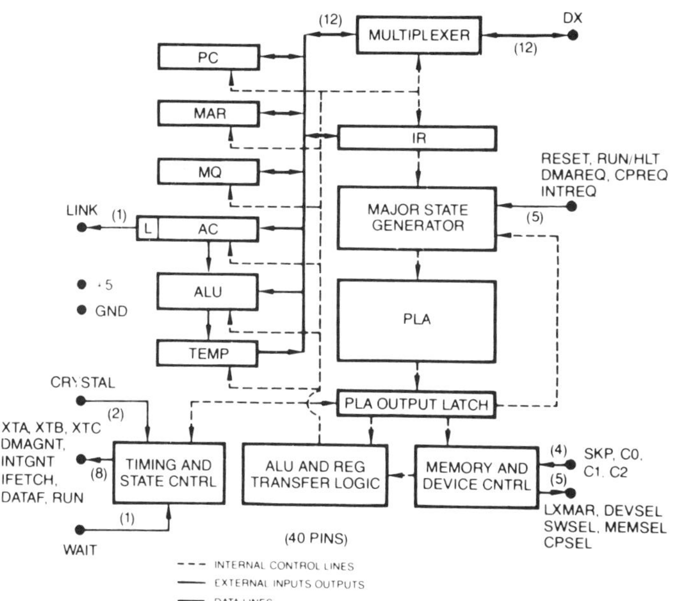

The architecture of the IM 6100 resembles that of the PDP-8 minicomputer. Signals are available that can help create a front panel so that the processor can be manually controlled. The processor's on-board crystal-controlled clock can be driven by an external source.

a dual floppy-disc based development system—the Intercept. Plug-in boards, including 1 k RAM, 2 k PROM, Serial I/O, cassette interface, and parallel I/O circuits are available.

Specifications

Data word size:	12 bits
Address bus size:	12 bits
Direct addressing range:	256 words
Instruction word size:	12 bits
Number of basic instructions:	80
Shortest instruction/time (AND, OR, Jump, etc.):	2.5 μs
Longest instruction/time (Autoindexed increment and skip if zero):	5.5 μs
Clock frequency (min/max):	Dc/8 MHz (10 V)
Clock phases/voltage swing:	1/CMOS or TTL
Dedicated I/O control lines:	24
Package:	40-pin DIP
Power requirements:	5 V/2.5 mA or 10 V/10 mA

Comments

The instruction set of the IM 6100 is divided into three groups—Memory reference instructions, Operate instructions, and Output transfer instructions. There are six memory reference instructions, with three addressing modes each. Another 62 commands are Operate instructions and the remaining 12 instructions are I/O transfer commands.

Software support offered includes an extended software package containing loaders, editors, assemblers, debuggers and a floating point arithmetic program. Also available is FOPAL, a Fortran cross assembler, FOCAL, a high-level interpreter and the DECUS program library with over 1000 programs.

The most important software features include the code-compatibility with the PDP-8 and the flexible addressing modes. And, some of the Operate instructions can be combined with other Operate commands to make multifunction instructions.

Hardware support for the IM 6100 ranges from a single-board learning system—the Intercept Jr.—to

Hardware

Model	Description	Price (100 qty)
IM 6100	12-bit CPU (commercial)	$15.00
IM 6100	Industrial grade CPU	16.50
IM 6100	Military grade CPU	52.80
IM 6101	Programmable parallel interface element	8.65
IM 6102	Memory extender/DMA controller/timer	15.00
IM 6103	Multimode latched port	10.00
IM 6402	CMOS UART (16x clock)	4.00
IM 6403	CMOS UART (xtal clock)	4.00
IM 6312	1 k x 12 mask ROM	27.90
IM 6512	64 x 12 CMOS RAM	5.00
IM 6603	1 k x 4 CMOS UV EPROM	25.00

12-bit microprocessor, PMOS

T3190

Alternate sources: None.

Toshiba Transistor Works
1 Komukai Toshiba-cho Kawasaki-shi
Kanagawa-ken, Japan
044-511-3111

The 12-bit microprogrammed parallel processor has machine instructions such as multiply and divide. Other features include asynchronous read/write, DMA capability, eight-level prioritized interrupt and seven addressing modes.

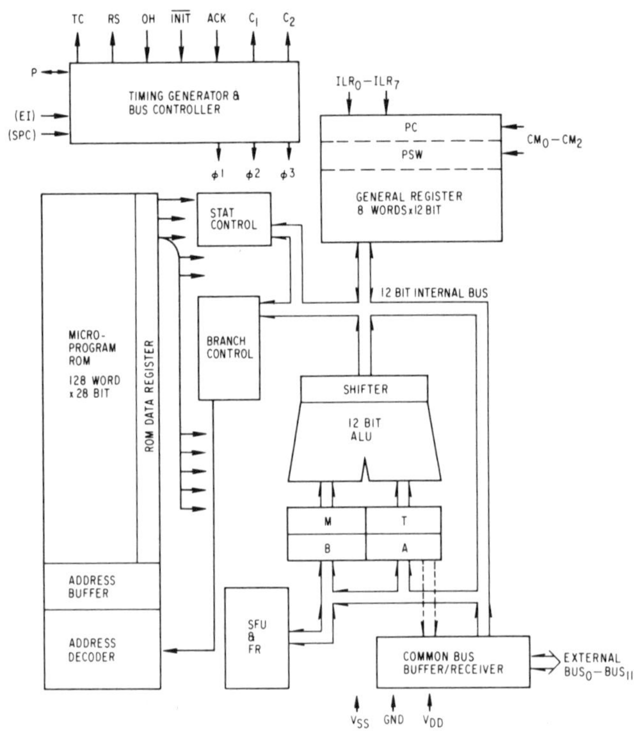

The T3190 has a three-state data/address bus and an eight-word register stack. The minimum system requires a processor, the MM111C RAM, TMM121C PROM, T3416 memory control unit, T3418 I/O control unit, and a 3220 general-purpose I/O register.

Comments

The instruction set consists of three data transfer instructions, nine logical instructions, seven arithmetic instructions including multiply and divide, and two branch instructions.

Software support consists of a cross-assembler and simulator written in Fortran VI, a self-assembler and a software package including debug and PROM program. Floating-point arithmetic package and over 50 other programs are available.

Software features of the T3190 include hardware multiply and divide capability as well as multi-bit rotates.

Hardware support includes EX-0 (a single-board computer containing 512 words of RAM, 3.5 kwords of PROM and a control panel); EX-1 (a single board with 4 k RAM or PROM, TTY interface and a control panel); EX-12/5 (a single board with 2 k of RAM, 2 k of PROM and a control panel); and EX-12/10 (a single board with 2 k of RAM, 2 k of PROM, a TTY interface, a DMA controller and a control panel).

Specifications

Data word size:	12 bits
Address bus size:	12 bits
Direct addressing range:	4096 words
Instruction word size:	12 bits
Number of basic instructions:	21
Shortest instruction/time (Load register):	6.6 μs
Longest instruction/time (Divide):	104 μs
Clock frequency (min/max):	0.63/2 MHz
Clock phases/voltage swing:	3/Internal
Dedicated I/O control lines:	None
Package:	36-pin DIP
Power requirements:	5 V/140 mA
	−5 V/35 mA

Hardware

Model	Description	Price (100 qty)
T3190	12-bit μP	$47.00
T3219	Interrupt latch unit	13.00
T3220	Gen-purp. I/O register	15.00
T3269	Bidirectional driver	12.00
T3416	Memory control unit	16.00
T3418	I/O control unit	13.00
T3445	DMA control unit	28.00
TMM111C	128 × 4 static RAM	8.50

16-bit microprocessor, bipolar

F100-L

Alternate sources: None.

Ferranti Limited
Western Road, Bracknell
Berkshire RG12 1RA, England
(0344)3232

The F100-L and its support chips use bipolar CDI technology and was developed to meet defense specifications and operate over the full MIL temp range. Its features include an 8 MHz cycle speed via a single-phase clock; multiple direct memory access capability; vectored priority interrupts; and the ability to call external hardware, such as a multiply/divide chip (under development). The 29 basic instructions yield 110 variants.

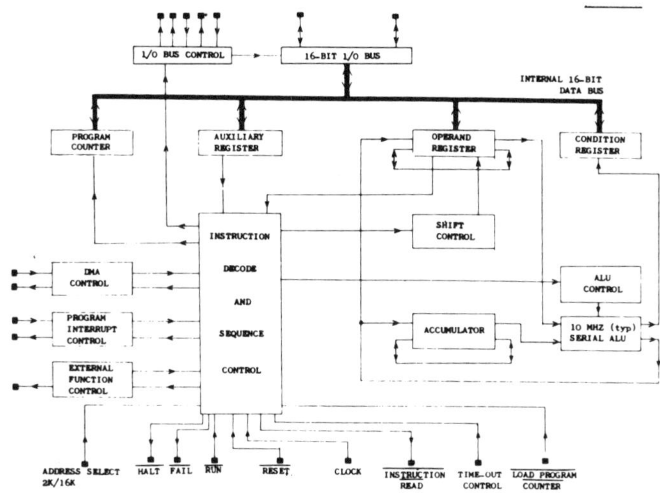

The architecture of the F100-L uses a multiplexed data and address bus. However, to simplify the handling of data many of the bus control functions are handled by support chips. The processor performs all of its ALU operations in a serial mode—the ALU is only 1 bit wide. An external clock is required and a clock rate of up to 20 MHz is possible. All lines are TTL compatible.

Comments

The instruction set of the F100-L contains 29 commands that are divided into the following groups: load and store (2), arithmetic and logic (7), shifts (6), bit manipulation (2), jumps (10), and machine control (2). The processor also has four addressing modes—direct, pointer indirect, immediate data and immediate indirect.

Software support for the F100-L is available on many levels. Programs can be written in F100-L assembly language or in a real-time high-level language called Coral 66. There are several cross-software products—a simulator, an assembler and a linking editor—all written in Fortran IV and available on time-sharing networks or for in-house use.

Special features of the software include the ability to transfer control to another "slave" processing chip, individual bit set and reset instructions and the indirect addressing modes.

Hardware support consists of several chips to simplify direct memory accesses and control of peripheral devices. There are also some micro-computer systems available that can be used for prototyping or the final system. Available are a 13-slot card cage with power supply, a processor card, RAM cards, ROM cards, specialized interfaces and prototyping cards.

Specifications

Data word size:	16 bits
Address bus size:	16 bits
Direct addressing range:	32,796 words
Instruction word size:	16 bits
Number of basic instructions:	29
Shortest instruction/time (Uncond. jump):	0.94 μs
Longest instruction/time (Jump using stack):	5.75 μs
Clock frequency (min/max):	Dc/8 MHz
Clock phases/voltage swing:	1/TTL
Dedicated I/O control lines:	10
Package:	40-pin DIP
Power requirements:	5 V/75 mA

Hardware

Model	Description	Price
F100-L	Microprocessor (MIL temp range)	N/A
F111-L	Control interface	N/A
F112-L	Data interface	N/A
F101-L	Multiply-divide (under development)	N/A

16-bit microprocessor, I³L

9440

Alternate sources: None.

Fairchild Camera and Instrument Corp.
464 Ellis Street
Mountain View, CA 94042
(415) 962-5011

The 9440 is a 16-bit microprocessor fabricated with the company's proprietary Isoplanar I²L process (I³L). Housed in a 40-pin DIP, the processor requires less than a watt. All of the 9440's software is instruction compatible with the Nova minicomputer series made by Data General Corp. Up to 63 peripheral I/O devices can be serviced via the programmed or interrupt driven I/O.

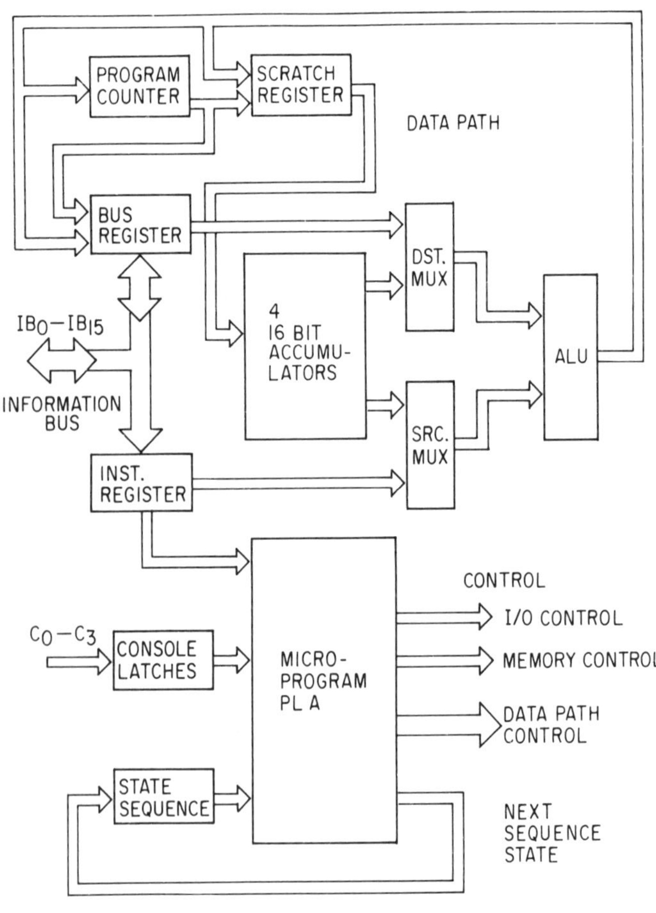

high-level languages such as Basic and Fortran, and stand-alone software. There is no program library available from Fairchild, but many companies offer code-compatible Nova software.

Special features of the software include the various addressing modes—absolute addressing of page zero, and three relative addressing modes using one of the multiple accumulators or program counter.

Hardware support for the 9440 has not yet been defined. However, expected aids will consist of full development systems and hardware debugging tools. Many companies offer Nova hardware.

Specifications

Data word size:	16 bits
Address bus size:	15 bits
Direct addressing range:	32,768
Instruction word size:	16 bits
Number of basic instructions:	
Shortest instruction/time (Jump to subroutine):	1.12 μs
Longest instruction/time (Increment and skip if zero):	3 μs
Clock frequency (min/max):	Dc/10 MHz
Clock phases/voltage swing:	1/TTL
Dedicated I/O control lines:	4
Package:	40-pin DIP
Power requirements:	5 V/150 mA 1 V/200 mA

The architecture of the 9440 varies considerably from that of the Nova although the μP can perform the same instructions. The 9440 uses a 4-bit ALU to process data and has an on-board clock generator that just needs an external crystal. Three-state outputs are included on the data/address bus, otherwise all lines are TTL compatible.

Comments

The instruction set of the 9440 contains all the Nova 1200 minicomputer commands. Basic operations include arithmetic and logic commands, memory reference operations, flag or bit test directions, I/O instructions and branch operations.

Software support includes resident diagnostics, assemblers, compilers, editors, operating systems,

Hardware

Model	Description	Price (100 qty)
9440	16-bit microprocessor There are currently no special support circuits available.	N/A
9441	Memory control unit	N/A
9442	I/O control unit	N/A
9443	Hardware multi- ply/divide	N/A

16-bit microprocessor, NMOS

mN601 (microNova)

Alternate sources: None.

Data General Corp.
Route 9
Southboro, MA 01772
(617) 485-9100

Full Nova minicomputer 16-bit architecture and instruction set is included in a single 40-pin silicon-gate NMOS chip. Subroutine calls can be handled with Save and Return instructions. The processor performs 16-bit hardware multiply and divide, and is provided with hardware stack and frame pointers with stack overflow protection. System memory support can control up to 32 kwords of RAM/PROM, with integral hidden refresh and control logic for dynamic RAMs.

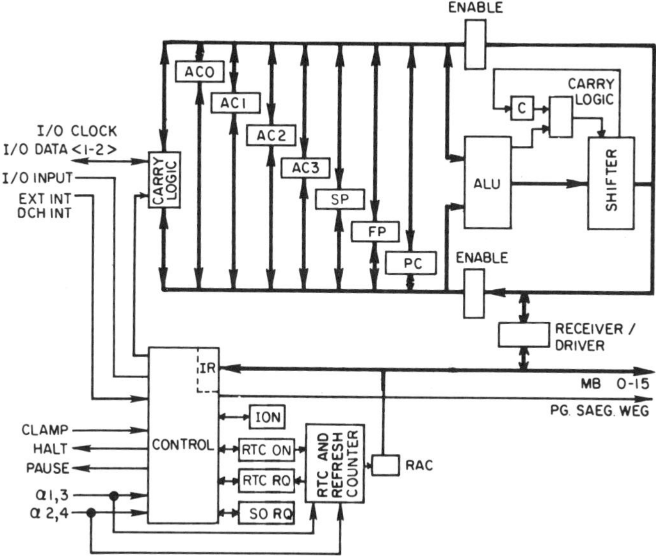

Included in the basic chip set are the mN601 microprocessor, mN640 clock driver and the mN629 I/O transceiver. All I/O lines are decoded for I/O interfacing and are not available for control purposes. The lines are open-collector TTL compatible. Four 16-bit registers in the CPU can act as source or destination accumulator.

Comments

There are 72 basic instructions that are broken into six groups: Memory-reference, six instructions; Arithmetic and logic, 10 instructions; Input/output, 11 instructions; Stack manipulation, 12 instructions and Central processor control, nine instructions. The microNova instructions are code-compatible with existing Nova minicomputers, thus permitting simple processor upgrades.

The choice of available software is very wide since most Nova software will run on microNova systems. For program development, assemblers, text editors, library file editors and relocatable loaders are available. For disc-based development systems, high-level languages such as Basic and Fortran IV are available in addition to the disc-operating system. Most disc-based systems come with a program library that includes logarithmic, exponential, trig, array handling and character-formatting routines.

Software features include 16-level interrupt and Save and Return instructions for subroutine calls,

and 16-bit hardware multiply and divide. Stack capability control is handled with hardware stack and frame pointer registers. The processor can also handle direct memory accesses via a control line.

Memory support hardware is provided by the following units: Models 8567 to 8570, PROM boards (512 to 4 kwords); Model 8572 (4 k RAM); and Model 8573 (8 k RAM). A PROM programmer board, Model 8574 is also available. Diskette subsystems include the single-drive Model 6038 and the dual-drive Model 6039. Interfacing is provided by the 4210 general purpose interface board and the 4207 asynchronous interface board.

Specifications

Data word size:	16 bits
Address bus size:	15 bits
Direct addressing range:	32,768 words
Instruction word size:	16 bits
Number of basic instructions:	72
Shortest instruction/time (Add):	2.4 μs
Longest instruction/time (Divide):	59.04 μs
Clock frequency (min/max):	dc/8.3 MHz
Clock phases/voltage swing:	2/14 V
Dedicated I/O control lines:	None
Package:	40-pin DIP
Power requirements:	5 V/20 mA
	10 V/60 mA
	14 V/30 mA
	4.25 V/0.25 mA

Hardware

Model	Description	Price (100 qty)
mN601	CPU	$114.95
mN603	I/O controller	$70.00
mN606	4-k dynamic RAM	$13.00
mN629	CPU I/O Transceiver	$30.00
mN634	Octal bus transceiver	$10.00
mN506	Quad sense amp	$12.00
mN636	I/O controller transceiver	$10.00
mN638	Memory clock driver	$7.00
mN640	I/O & CPU clock driver	$7.00

16-bit microprocessor, NMOS
CP1600, CP1610

General Instrument Corp.
600 W. John Street
Hicksville, NY 11802
(516) 733-3000

Alternate sources: EM&M Semiconductor and ITT Semiconductor.

The CP1600 and 1610 are 16-bit NMOS microprocessors that use a multiplexed data and address bus. Both circuits are pin and instruction compatible and only differ in package and operating frequency. The 1600 comes in a ceramic DIP and operates at clock frequencies to 5 MHz, while the 1610 comes in a plastic DIP and operates to 2 MHz. Either processor can do conditional branching on status word or 16 external conditions as well as handle almost unlimited program interrupts and DMA requests.

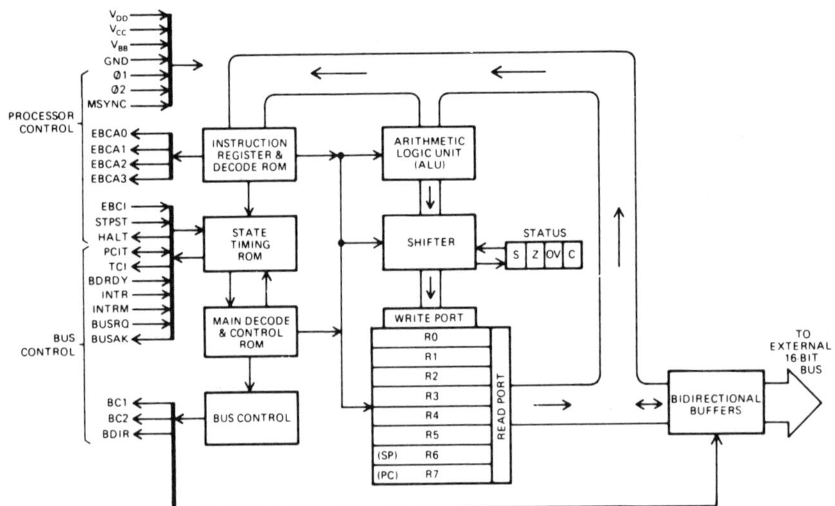

The architecture of the CP1600 family processors starts with a 16-bit parallel ALU and an eight-word general-purpose register file that is directly accessible by the processor. All lines are TTL compatible except for the clock lines, and the 16-line bus has three-state capability.

Comments

The instruction set for the CP1600 and 1610 contains 87 commands that provide four addressing modes and conditional branching on the contents of the status word. Instructions include: 20 arithmetic and logic operations, eight I/O instructions (also including all four addressing modes), 18 conditional branch commands, six Jump operations, 28 internal register operations and seven control instructions.

Software support for the CP1600 family consists of an assembler, a "super assembler," a text editor, a relocating linking loader, diagnostic routines, an object module linker, and a cross software package written in Fortran IV. There is also an extensive program library available.

Strong points of the software include the large number of conditional branches possible as well as unlimited interrupt capability.

Hardware support consists of a wide array of circuit boards, cage assemblies and even complete systems. Memory, interface, I/O, CPU and console modules are available for the Gimini microcomputer.

Specifications

Data word size:	16 bits
Address bus size:	16 bits
Direct addressing range:	65,536 words
Instruction word size:	10 bits
Number of basic instructions:	87
Shortest instruction/time (Control group):	1.6 μs (5 MHz)
Longest instruction/time (Jump group):	4.8 μs (5 MHz)
Clock frequency (min/max):	Dc/5 MHz
Clock phases/voltage swing:	2/10 V (nominal)
Dedicated I/O control lines:	10
Package:	40-pin DIP
Power requirements:	5 V/12 mA
	12 V/70 mA
	−3 V/0.2 mA

Hardware

Model	Description	Price (100 qty)
CP1600	16-bit CPU, 3.3 MHz	$38.50*
CP1600A	16-bit CPU, 5 MHz	N/A
CP1610	16-bit CPU, 2 MHz	$8.00
DAC1610	Dual d/a converter	4.00
IOB1610	Input/output buffer	4.60
MUX1610	18-channel analog mux	2.95
RO-3-5120	512×10 bit ROM	8.17*
RO-3-20480	2048×10 bit ROM	16.50
	* 1000 qty price	

16-bit microprocessor, NMOS or PMOS

INS8900, PACE

Alternate sources: None.

National Semiconductor
2900 Semiconductor Dr.
Santa Clara, CA 95051
(408) 737-5000

Architecturally similar to the PACE PMOS microprocessor, the INS8900 is intended to supersede the PACE. The 16-bit word size and flexible instruction set give the processor minicomputer-like computational power. Features include an on-chip 10 word stack, indirect addressing, a choice of 8 or 16-bit word operation and memory-mapped I/O.

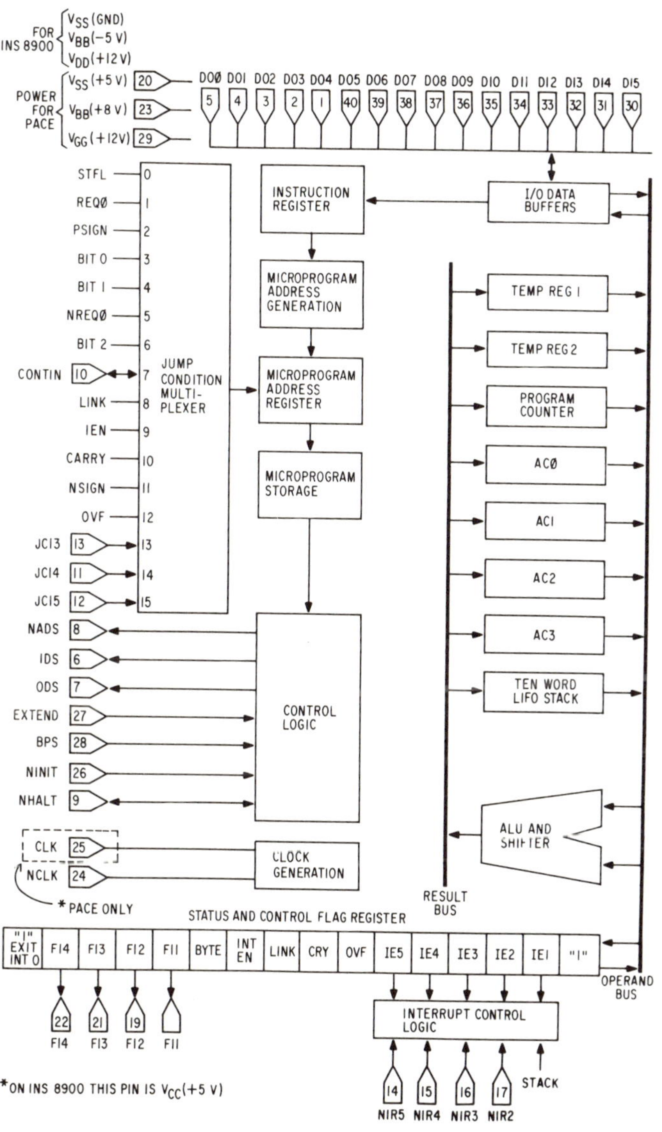

and logic operations, 10 memory reference commands, 13 branch and skip instructions and 10 register operations.

Software support for the INS8900 includes conversational assemblers, a Fortran cross assembler, a Basic interpreter and a floppy-disc operating system. There is also a user's group that has a library of over 50 programs.

Software features include multilevel priority interrupts, four separate flag outputs, three jump inputs and simple stack manipulation commands. Software also determines whether the processor performs the operations on either 8 or 16-bit data.

Hardware support for the INS8900 includes CPU card, a floppy-disc operating system, a low-cost development system and an in-circuit emulator to simplify hardware debugging.

Specifications

Data word size:	8 or 16 bits
Address bus size:	16 bits
Direct addressing range:	65,536
Instruction word size:	8 or 16 bits
Number of basic instructions:	45
Shortest instruction/time (Load and store):	8 μs
Longest instruction/time (Decrement and skip if zero):	16 μs
Clock frequency (min/max):	1.5/2 MHz
Clock phases/voltage swing:	1/12 V
Dedicated I/O control lines:	7
Package:	40
Power requirements: for INS8900	5 V/10 mA
	12 V/50 mA
	−5 V/0.2 mA
for PACE:	−12 V/40 mA
	−8 V/0.1 mA
	5 V/85 μA

The architecture of the INS8900 and the PACE provides a 10-word stack as well as four general-purpose registers and an independent 16-bit status and control flag register. There is also a six-level vectored priority interrupt system built into the chip. However, an external single-phase clock must be supplied. A minimal system consists of the CPU, a clock and some memory.

Comments

The instruction set of the INS8900 contains 45 commands that can be divided into 12 arithmetic

Hardware

Model	Description	Price (100 qty)
INS8900	Microprocessor	$19.95
PACE	Microprocessor	19.95
	There are no specially designed interface circuits.	

16-bit microprocessor, NMOS
MN1610

Panafacom
6-17-15 Shinbashi Minatoku
Tokyo, Japan
03-438-0311

Alternate sources: None.

A high-speed 16-bit parallel processor, the MN1610 has 33 basic instructions. Also included are five arithmetic registers, two of which may be used as index registers. The processor has six addressing modes, a three-level multi-interrupt control, and a bus priority control function for DMA.

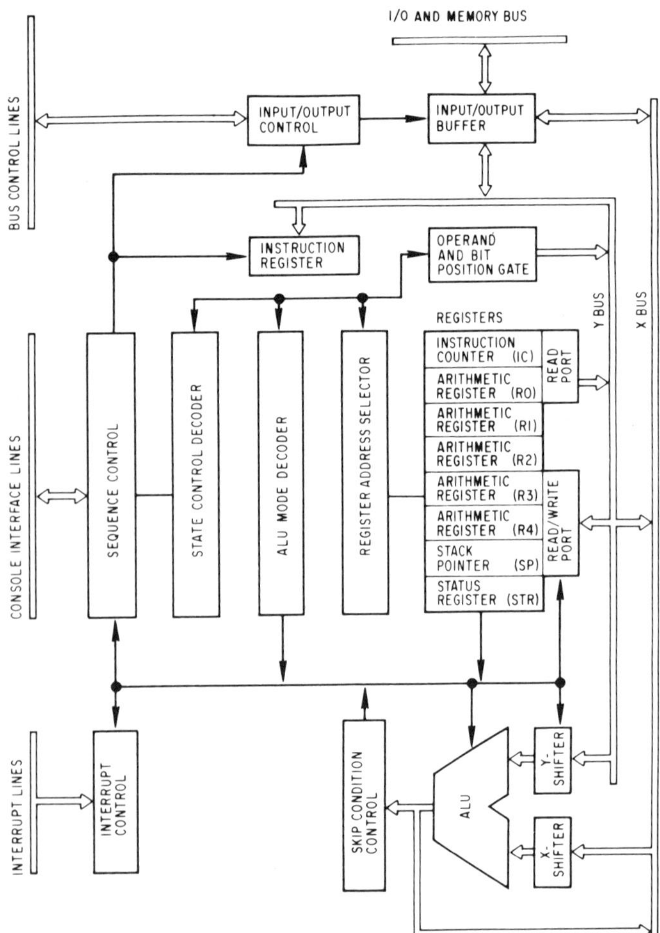

Included in the basic chip set are the MN1610 CPU, the MN1640 real-time controller, and memory—typically 4 kbits of RAM and 8 kbits of ROM. The six I/O lines include four that are output-only and 2 that are input-only. All lines are TTL compatible except the clock input, which is MOS, and the 16 bidirectional data/address bus lines are three-state.

Comments

The 33 basic instructions built into the processor include six register-to-memory commands, 12 register-to-register commands, 12 register change operations and three I/O and register command instructions. Over 345 possible operation codes are possible using combinations of the addressing modes with various operands. I/O addressing is used, thus permitting up to 256 I/O addresses.

Support software packages include Assembler language processors, Linkage Loaders, and utilities such as Editors, Tracer, and self-debugger. Simulator, ROM support, and channel connection sup-

port software programs are also available. Also available are many cross-software programs that can run on large mainframe systems.

Software features include five addressing modes that provide the processors with a flexible programming structure. There are also three levels of multiple interrupt possible by using information held in the program status word. The register to register operations permit many byte manipulation and byte comparison operations. And, bit manipulation instructions permit individual bits in a word to be set, reset or tested.

Hardware support for the MN1610 ranges from small circuit cards that contain the processor, memory and I/O functions to full blown minicomputer-like systems with front panels and complete machine control. Also available are memory cards, I/O cards, Process control cards, and DMA control cards. The complete system with programmers panel, the L-16A, is available in a 6 or 12-card cabinet.

Specifications

Data word size:	16 bits
Address bus size:	16 bits
Direct addressing range:	65,536 words
Instruction word size:	16 bits
Number of basic instructions:	33
Shortest instruction/time (Add):	3 μs
Longest instruction/time (Increment memory and skip):	12 μs
Clock frequency (min/max):	100 kHz/2 MHz
Clock phases/voltage swing:	2/12 V
Dedicated I/O control lines:	6
Package:	40-pin DIP
Power requirements:	5 V/60 mA
	12 V/55 mA
	−3 V/200 mA

Hardware

Model	Description	Price (100 qty)
MN1610	CPU	$35.00
MN1630	8-bit subchannel adapter	15.00
MN1640	Real-time controller	15.00
MN1650	DMA channel controller	20.00

16-bit microprocessor, NMOS
16-bit microprocessor, I²L (bipolar)

For NMOS version:
Texas Instruments
P.O. Box 1443, MS-653
Houston, TX 77001
(713) 494-5115

For I²L version:
Texas Instruments
P.O. Box 5012, MS-308
Dallas, TX 75222
(214) 238-2011

TMS-9900/SBP-9900

Alternate sources: American Microsystems for the TMS-9900, none for the SBP-9900.

Both the TMS-9900 and SBP-9900 are 16-bit microprocessors with separate data and address buses. The TMS version is a silicon-gate NMOS device that can operate at speeds of up to 3 MHz and requires a four-phase clock input. It's twin, the SBP unit, is an I²L equivalent that can operate at 2 MHz clock rates, but it requires just a single-phase clock input. The I²L unit also permits the supply current to be adjusted so that power consumption can be reduced in noncritical applications.

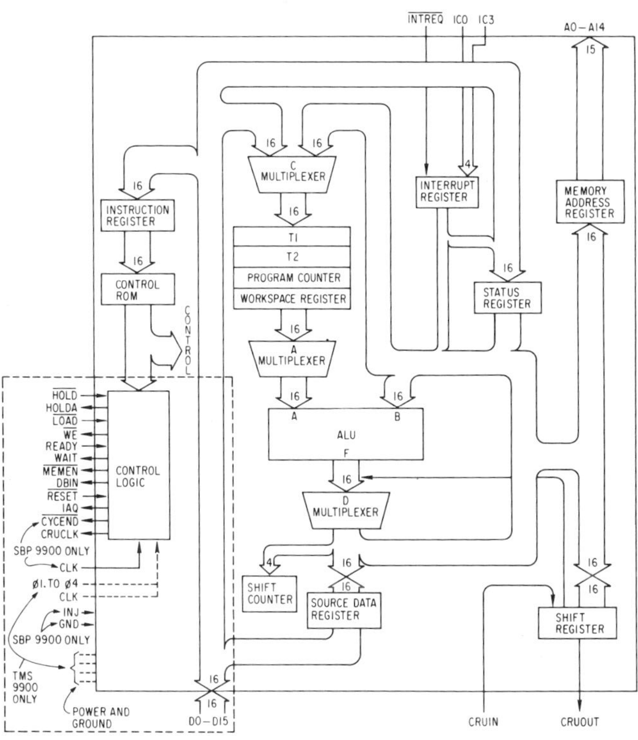

The 16-bit memory-to-memory architecture of the 9900 μPs permits flexible register files to be set up in memory. A minimal system consists of the CPU, a clock generator and the necessary memory.

The most outstanding features of the software include the multiple register file capability and the flexibility offered by the dual bus structure. The processors use addressed I/O and has three software controlled lines—a Hold/Hold Acknowledge, a Ready/Wait, and an Interrupt line.

Hardware support for the processors includes a series of 990 modules containing central processor cards and memory cards, the PX990 cassette-based development system and AMPL, a floppy-disc based software and hardware development system.

Specifications

Data word size:	16 bits
Address bus size:	15 bits
Direct addressing range:	32,768 words
Instruction word size:	16 to 48 bits
Number of basic instructions:	69
Shortest instruction/time (Branch):	2 μs
Longest instruction/time (Divide):	31 μs
Clock frequency (min/max):	0.5/4 MHz
Clock phases/voltage swing:	4/12 V or 1/TTL
Dedicated I/O control lines:	3
Package:	64-pin DIP
Power requirements:	5 V/75 mA
	−5 V/0.1 mA
	12 V/40 mA
	or variable for I²L version

Comments

The minicomputer-like instruction set of 69 commands provides 26 arithmetic, logic and data manipulation instructions; 14 internal register to memory operations; five data transfer commands; and 24 control functions. Instructions include binary multiply and divide as well as provisions for 16 prioritized interrupts and programmed and DMA I/O capability.

Support software for the 9900-series μPs includes assemblers, editors, simulators, debuggers and high-level languages such as PL/9900, Basic and Fortran. There is also a program library available since all software is code compatible with the larger 990 minicomputer systems.

Hardware

Model	Description	Price (100 qty)
TMS9900	16-bit CPU (NMOS)	$70.58
SBP9900	EJ version (−40 to +84 C range)	193.00
SBP9900	MJ version (−55 to +125 C range)	386.00
SBP9900	NJ version (MIL 883)	424.60
TMS9901	Programmable interface	8.75
TMS9902	Asynchronous interface	7.50
TMS9904	Clock driver	5.42

16-bit microprocessor, NMOS
TMS 9980

Alternate sources: None.

Texas Instruments Inc.
P.O. Box 5012, M/S 308
Dallas, TX 75222
(214) 238-2011

Software compatible with the TMS 9900 series of microprocessors, the 9980 incorporates a 16-bit CPU with an 8-bit data bus and an on-chip clock in a single 40-pin package. The separate bus structure simplifies system designs, and memory-to-memory architecture features multiple register files, in memory, for faster response to interrupts. Adding memory forms a working minimum system.

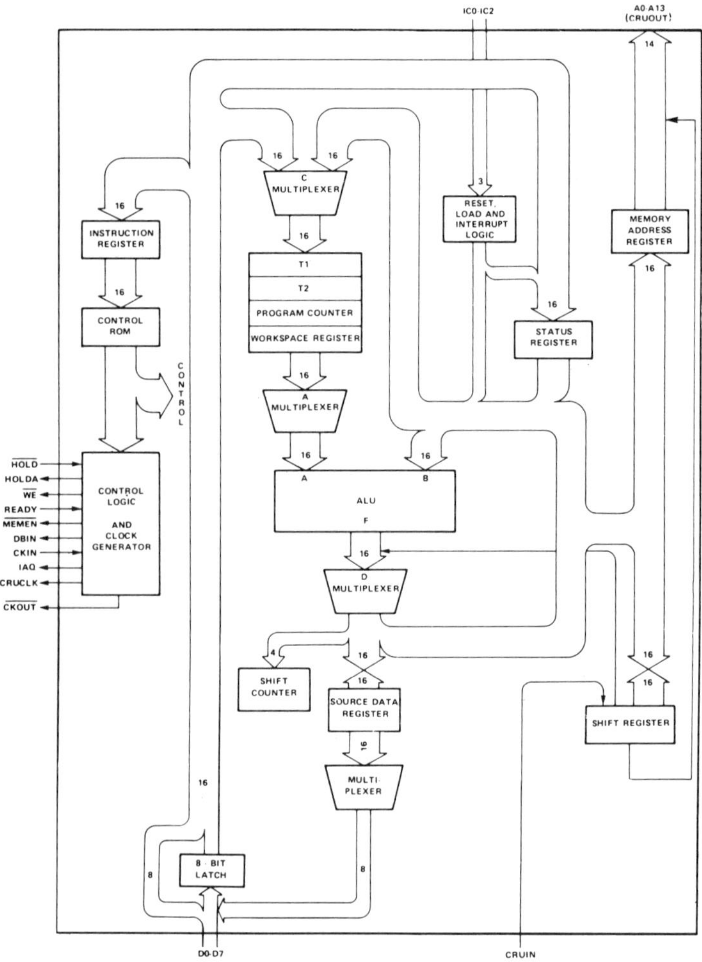

The TMS 9980 is almost identical in architecture to the TMS/SBP 9900. The only difference is that the 9980 uses an 8-bit data bus instead of a 16-bit, a 14-bit address bus instead of a 15 bit and has fewer levels of prioritized interrupt. And, the 9980 has its clock generator built onto the same chip .

Comments

The minicomputer-like instruction set of the TMS 9980 is identical to that of the TMS/SBP 9900 processors. Included are 26 arithmetic, logic and data manipulation instructions, 14 internal register to memory operations, five data transfer commands and 24 control functions. Instructions include binary multiple and divide as well as provisions for four levels of prioritized interrupt. The processor also has programmed DMA and I/O capability.

Software support for the TMS 9980 consists of assemblers, editors, simulators, debuggers and high-level languages such as PL/9900, Basic and Fortran. There is also a program library available.

The most outstanding features of the software include the multiple register file capability and the flexibility offered by the dual bus structure. The processor uses addressed I/O and has several lines that control I/O operations—the Hold, Hold Acknowledge, Ready, Wait, Interrupt Control and Control Register lines.

Hardware support for TMS 9980 development includes all the support for the 9900—the TM 990 microcomputer modules, the PX 990 cassette-based prototyping system and AMPL, a floppy-disc based development system.

Specifications

Data word size:	16 bits*
Address bus size:	14 bits
Direct addressing range:	8192 words
Instruction word size:	16 to 48 bits
Number of basic instructions:	69
Shortest instruction/time (Branch):	4.8 μs
Longest instruction/time (Divide):	54.4 μs
Clock frequency (min/max):	1 MHz/2.5 MHz
Clock phases/voltage swing:	1/TTL
Dedicated I/O control lines:	11
Package:	40-pin DIP
Power requirements:	12 V/50 mA
	5 V/50 mA

*Memory is organized in byte format; two sequential bytes form one data word.

Hardware

Model	Description	Price (100 qty)
TMS 9980	CPU	$30.62
TMS 9901	Programmable interface	8.75
TMS 9902	Asynchronous interface	7.50
TMS 9905	8:1 multiplexer	1.26
TMS 9906	8-bit latch	1.55
TMS 9907	8:3 priority encoder	1.01
TMS 9908	8:3 priority encoder	1.01

16-bit processor set, NMOS

MCP-1600/WD-16

Alternate sources: None.

Western Digital Corp.
3128 Red Hill Ave., Box 2180
Newport Beach, CA 92663
(714) 557-3550

Available as either an unprogrammed chip set (MCP-1600) or as a preprogrammed processor (WD-16), the multiple-chip processor can perform either 8 or 16-bit operations. Both sets consist of a data-processing circuit (CP1611B), a control circuit (CP1621B), and several microprogram-control ROMs (CP1631Bs). The programmed chip set resembles the LSI-11 minicomputer made by Digital Equipment Corp. in both architecture and instruction set.

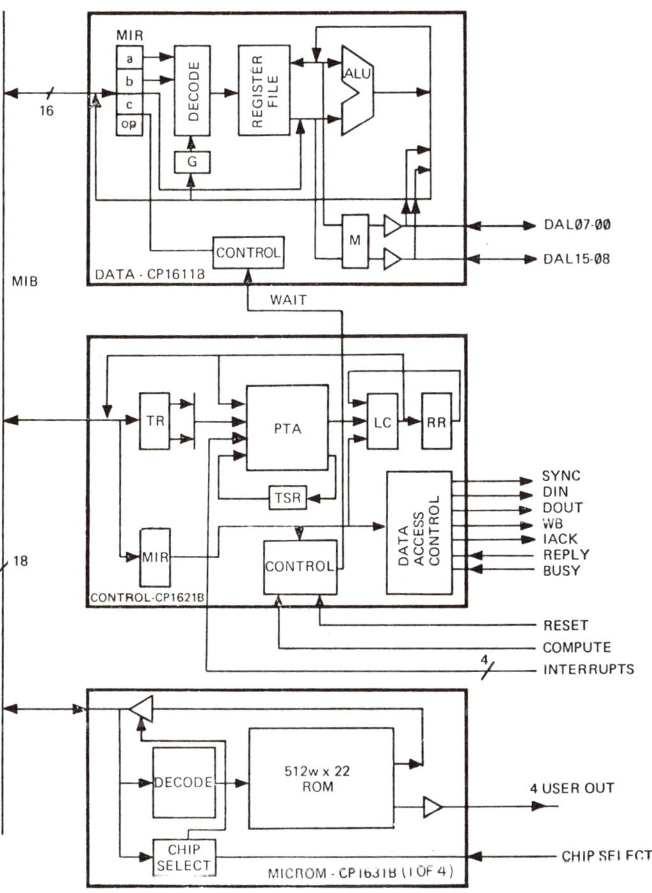

The basic chip set consists of a data-manipulation chip containing an 8-bit ALU and 26 8-bit registers. The 16 registers can be set up to act as program counter, stack pointer, accumulator and general-purpose 8 or 16-bit registers. A typical minimal system consists of a data chip, a control chip, two to four ROM chips, a clock generator and buffers.

Comments

The WD-16 instruction set consists of 16 branch commands, 16 register-only operations, five floating-point arithmetic instructions, eight block-move directions, three supervisory commands, 16 single-operand word operations, 16 single-operand byte operations, 12 double-operand instructions word and byte), and eight different addressing modes. There are no dedicated I/O instructions since the processor uses memory-mapped I/O. Software includes vectored interrupts with a 16-bit priority mask, hardware multiply/divide, floating-point arithmetic and up to 16 Mbyte addressing.

Available software includes an assembler, editor, simulator, and debugger that are intended to run on a disc-based PDP-11/05 system from DEC. Single-user software, floppy-disc based, without higher-level languages, is available in source form.

Software features include hardware register-save/restore, vectored-interrupt overhead consisting of two op codes, and program-counter-relative addressing. Supervisory calls automatically save registers or do a tabled jump. The floating-point format uses an 8-bit exponent and a 40-bit mantissa.

Prototyping hardware includes a two-board CPU set that is S-100 bus compatible, as well as a single-board floppy-disc controller (also S-100 bus compatible) that has on-board PROM-based software and a DMA controller. A microprogramming development system consisting of a CPU, writable control store and memory boards is available.

Specifications

Data word size:	8 or 16 bits
Address bus size:	16 bits
Direct addressing range:	65,536 words
Instruction word size:	2 to 6 bytes
Number of basic instructions:	116*
Shortest instruction/time (load condition codes):	2.1 μs
Longest instruction/time (Floating point div.):	780 μs
Clock frequency (min/max):	2/3.3 MHz
Clock phases/voltage swing:	4/12 V
Dedicated I/O control lines:	None
Package:	40-pin DIP
Power requirements:	5 V/50 mA
*Or 99 in the programmed version	-5 V/0.5 mA
	12 V/35 mA

Hardware

Model	Description	Price (100 qty)
WD-16	CPU chip set	N/A
FD1771	Floppy-disc controller	$60.00
TR1602	UART	7.00
TR1863	UART (5-V only)	8.55
BR1941L	Baud-rate generator	7.50
UC1671	Astro (mux'd address)	30.00
UC1971	Astro (chip select)	N/A
TR1953	USART (Intel 8251 equiv)	10.00
TR1923	BOART (async only)	8.00
SD1933	Synchronous data-link controller (1 to 9)	55.00
DM1883	DMA controller	N/A
FR1502	FIFO buffer (40 x 9)	16.00
CG1921J	Clock generator (4 ϕ)	7.50

2-bit processor slice, Schottky-TTL

Series 3000

Alternate sources: Signetics.

Intel Corp.
3065 Bower Ave.
Santa Clara, CA 95051
(408) 246-7501

The Series 3000 bipolar bit slices are two-bit microprogrammable processor sections that contain a multifunction arithmetic and logic unit, some working registers and the necessary control logic. The processor chip, the 3002, can be cascaded to form an n x 2 bit system. The multiple buses that act as inputs and outputs make the processor readily adaptable to many high-speed controller applications.

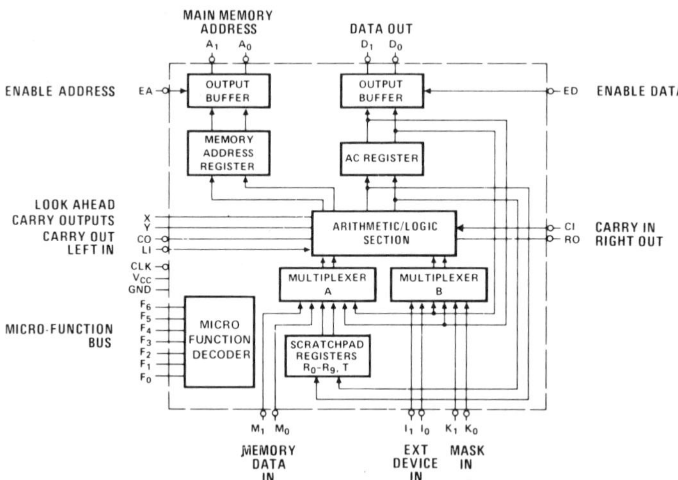

A minimal system for the Series 3000 is hard to define since the user determines the processor word length and the amount of microprogram storage needed. A typical 16-bit machine application, though, might require about 25 to 35 devices. The processor's architecture revolves about the ALU and 11 general-purpose registers. All operations are controlled by the function bus, which accepts the microprogram control words and selects both operands and the ALU operation to be performed.

Comments

The instruction set of the 3002 central processing element consists of over 40 Boolean and binary operations, all controlled by the 7-bit input to the function bus. Each 3002 has five independent two-line buses that accept data from external memory (M bus), transfers data from an I/O device (I bus), function as a microprogrammed mask (K bus), act as a memory address bus (A bus) and function as a data bus (D bus).

Software support for the Series 3000 consists of CROMIS, a cross microassembler written in Fortran IV and available for use on a 16-bit or larger computer system. There is no general program library available for the family.

Software features put the various I/O buses to good use. For instance, output buses A and D often present address and data to external main memory during the same microcycle. Also, operations such as byte swapping can be done in fewer cycles than with other processors by taking advantage of the D and M bus manipulation commands.

Hardware support for the series 3000 consists of the Intellec MDS 800 system with the following options: ICE 30, an in-circuit emulator; ROM SIM, a ROM simulator; and a PROM programmer. There is also a chip set available for the designer to begin breadboarding his circuit.

Specifications

Data word size:	2 bits
Address bus size:	On microprogram controller
Direct addressing range:	512 words on 3001
Instruction word size:	7 bits
Number of basic instructions:	Over 40
Basic ALU instruction execution time:	150 ns
Clock frequency (min/max):	Dc/6.67 MHz
Clock phases/voltage swing:	1/TTL
Dedicated I/O control lines:	User defined
Package:	28-pin DIP
Power requirements:	5 V/190 mA

Hardware

Model	Description	Price (qty.)
D3002	2-bit processor slice	$13.35
D3002M	MIL version of slice	48.15
D3001	Microprogram controller	8.80
D3001	MIL version	26.75
D3003	Look-ahead carry gen.	6.60
P3212	Hex buffer	2.90
P3214	interrupt controller	4.65
P3216	Hex bus driver	2.75
P3226	Hex bus driver	2.75

4-bit processor slice, CMOS or STTL

Macrologic (9405A, or 34705)

Fairchild Camera and Instrument Corp.
464 Ellis Street
Mountain View, CA 94042
(415) 962-3955

Alternate sources: Signetics.

The Macrologic 4-bit processor slice is available in either CMOS or Schottky-TTL technologies. The ALU sections, 9405A for STTL and 34705 for CMOS, can be cascaded and then microprogrammed to form a complete digital processor. Containing an eight instruction ALU and an 8 × 4 bit RAM bank, the processor slice can operate at micro-instruction rates of 10 MHz. A total of 64 microinstructions are possible via the six instruction code lines. The processor comes in a 24-pin "skinny" DIP (400 mils wide).

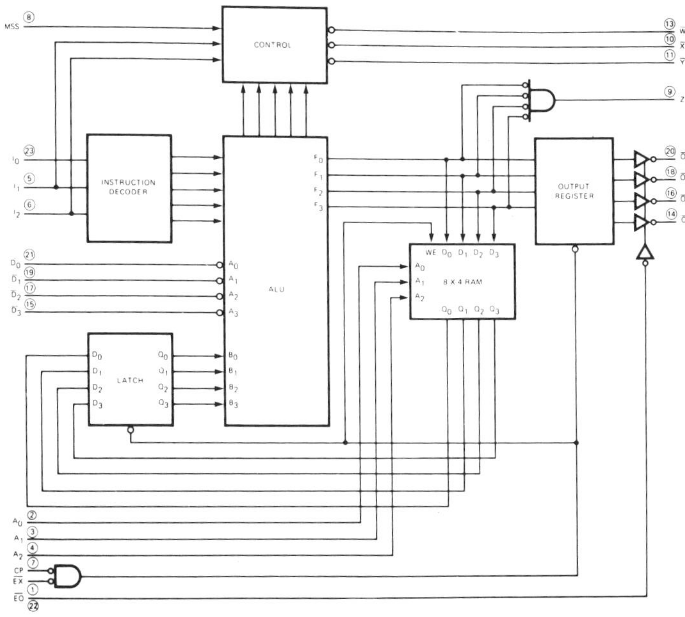

Outstanding features of the software include the relatively simple instruction organization and the addressing flexibility of the on-chip 8 x 4 bit RAM.

Hardware support for the processor slice is practically nonexistent. The only support is the availability of the circuits such as the CRC checker/generator, the program sequencer and specialized memory devices.

Specifications

Data word size:	4 bits
Address bus size:	4-bit expandable
Direct addressing range:	User defined
Instruction word size:	6 bits (ALU)
Number of basic instructions:	8 (ALU only)
Shortest instruction/time (any microinstruction):	100 ns
Clock frequency (min/max):	Dc/12 MHz
Clock phases/voltage swing:	1/TTL
Dedicated I/O control lines:	User defined
Package:	24-pin DIP
Power requirements:	5 V/160 mA

The architecture of the Macrologic slices is such that the chips can be cascaded to make an n × 4 bit processor. Carry outputs are provided for carry-lookahead operation and three status signals are also available—accumulator zero, negative or overflow. The four data output lines have three-state capability. A minimal system is hard to define, but a typical organization might use 30 to 50 chips.

Hardware

Model	Description	Price (100 qty)
9405A	4-bit processor slice from—	$12.00
34705	CMOS version of 9405A	15.31
9401	Cyclic redundancy check generator	7.80
9403	16 x 4 FIFO	13.00
9404	Data path switch	3.90
9406	Program stack	12.00
9407	Data access register	8.75
9408	Microprogram sequencer	34.75
9410	16 x 4 register file	5.50
9423	64 x 4 FIFO	N/A

Comments

The microinstruction set for the Macrologic processor slice contains only eight basic ALU operations—Add, Add and increment, AND, OR, Exclusive-OR, Load, Output, and Load complement. When combined with the eight address instruction inputs, the processor's instructions increase to 64.

Software support for the processor slice consists of microprogram assemblers written in APL and Fortran that are available either on time-sharing networks or for direct purchase.

4-bit processor slice, Schottky TTL

Am2901A

Alternate sources: Fairchild, Monolithic Memories, Motorola, National Semiconductor, Raytheon, Sescosem, and Signetics

Advanced Micro Devices
901 Thompson Place
Sunnyvale, CA 94086
(408) 732-2400

The Am2901A has become the "industry standard" 4-bit bipolar processor slice. It consists of a 16 word × 4 bit two-port RAM, a high-speed arithmetic and logic unit and the necessary shifting, decoding and multiplexing circuitry. Any number of 2901A slices can be cascaded to make a processor with a word length of n × 4. There are many support circuits available, and also the widest number of second sources for any bit-slice device. *Coming soon from AMD is an enhanced version of the 4-bit slice, the 2903, which will have additional instructions such as multiply and divide.

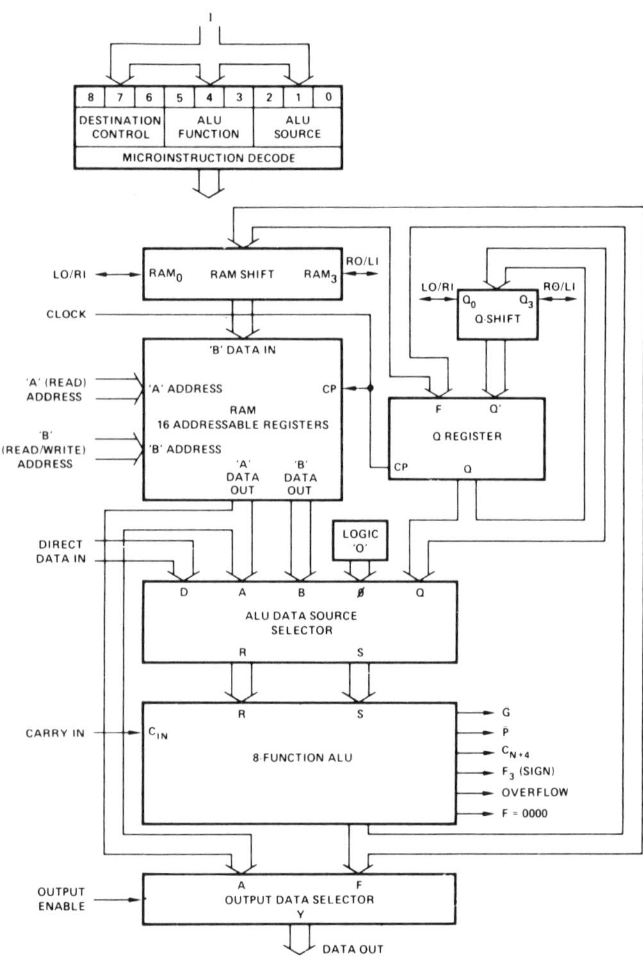

A minimal system is hard to pin down since the word size can be set to any size. However a typical number of circuits would be between 40 and 60. The high-speed ALU in the 2901A can perform its operations on two 4-bit input words, one from a two-input multiplexer and the other from a three-input mux.

Comments

The instruction set of the 2901A bit slice permits many variations, as determined by the way the nine-bit instruction word is set up. The ALU itself only has eight possible basic operations, but there are also eight source operands and another eight destination codes, for 256 operations.

Software support for the 2901A bit slice consists of three programs—AMDASM/TS, a time-shared microprogram assembler; AMDASM/80, a micro-program assembler that can run on the Intel Microprocessor development system; and AMDASM/29, a resident assembler for the System 29 microprogram development system made by AMD.

Software features include the two register organization of the 2901A, making possible a wide number of instruction combinations. There are four status flags—carry, overflow, zero and sign—that can function as outputs and there is also a left or right shift operation available that is independent of the ALU.

Development hardware includes the Am2900K1, a learning and evaluation kit. Also available is the System 29 microprogramming system.

Specifications

Data word size:	4 bits
Address bus size:	User defined
Direct addressing range:	User defined
Instruction word size:	9 bits
Number of basic instructions:	8
Basic ALU instruction execution time:	110 ns typ.
Clock frequency (min/max):	dc/15 MHz
Clock phases/voltage swing:	1/TTL
Dedicated I/O control lines:	4 flag lines
Package:	40-pin DIP
Power requirements:	5 V/160 mA

Hardware

Model	Description	Price (100 qty)
Am2901A	4-bit processor slice	$14.70
Am2901A	MIL version	71.40
Am2902	Carry look-ahead	2.65
Am2905	Bus interface ckt. O.C.	5.40
Am2906	Bus interface ckt. O.C.	7.45
Am2907	Bus interface ckt. O.C.	4.75
Am2909	Microprogram sequencer	5.95
Am2910	Microprogram controller	N/A
Am2911	Microprogram sequencer mini version	3.95
Am2913	Interrupt expander	2.53
Am2914	Vectored interrupt controller	29.95
Am2918	One-by-two-port register	3.08
Am29LS18	Low power Am2918	2.60
Am2919	Another version, 2918	3.10
Am2930, 31 & 32	Program control units	N/A
Am29803	16-way branch control	4.95
Am29811	Instruction controller	3.25

4-bit processor slice, bipolar (STTL)

5701/6701

Alternate sources: ITT Semiconductor.

Monolithic Memories, Inc.
1165 E. Arques Ave.
Sunnyvale, CA 94086
(408) 739-3535

A 4-bit slice of a digital processor on a single chip, the 5701/6701 provides 36 instructions and has 16 directly addressable, two-port accumulators, a separate scratchpad register bank and a 175 ns cycle time. The slices can be cascaded with full carry look-ahead and they have a low fan-in input bus and a three-state output bus.

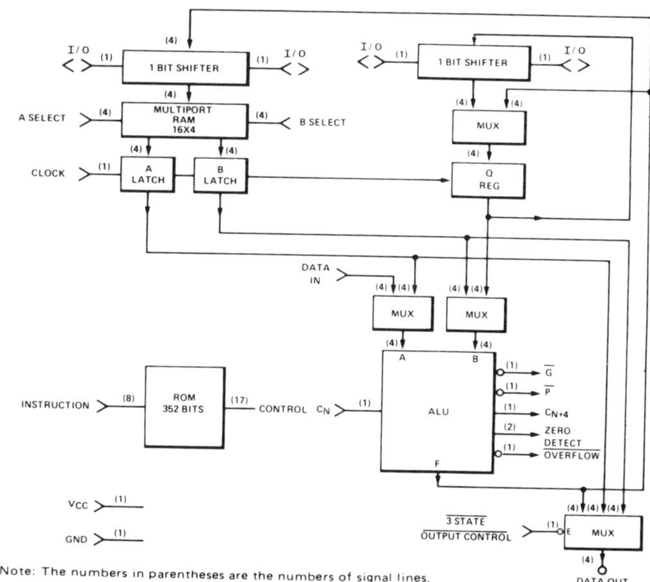

Note: The numbers in parentheses are the numbers of signal lines.

The architecture of the 5701/6701 bit slice includes a 16 word x 4 bit dual-port RAM as well as a 36 instruction ALU and a single 4-bit working register that can be used as a second accumulator or as an extension to permit an 8-bit result. On the chip are also some microprogrammed ROMs that determine the operation of the ALU for each incoming instruction.

Specifications

Data word size:	4 bits
Address bus size:	User defined
Direct addressing range:	User defined
Instruction word size:	8 bits (internal)
Number of basic instructions:	36
Shortest instruction/time (5701 or 6701):	175 or 230 ns
Clock frequency (min/max):	Dc/5.2 MHz
Clock phases/voltage swing:	1/TTL
Dedicated I/O control lines:	User defined
Package:	40-pin DIP
Power requirements:	5 V/280 mA

Comments

The microprogram instruction set of the 5701/6701 processor slices contains 36 instructions. The instructions include addition, subtraction, transfer or decrement or increment, AND, OR, Exclusive-OR, Invert and 2's complement, all with various combinations of internal registers.

Software support consists of a Fortran IV cross assembler that is designed to run on 16 and 32-bit minicomputers and mainframes. There is no program library available.

Special features of the software include overflow detection and the logic shifting capability. The slices can perform multiple nanosecond instructions such as subtract, shift and store in just one clock cycle.

Hardware support for the processor is minimal—the only products are the microprogram controller, which can address 512 words of microprogram storage, and standard memory circuits such as PROMs and multiport RAMs.

Hardware

Model	Description	Price (100 qty)
5701	4-bit slice (MIL)	$ 56.50
6701	4-bit slice (commercial)	26.15
57110	Microprogram controller (MIL version)	28.00
67110	Microprogram controller (commercial version)	14.00

4-bit processor slice, ECL
MC10800

Motorola Semiconductor
5005 E. McDowell Rd.
Phoenix, AZ 85036
(602) 244-6900

Alternate sources: None.

The MC10800 family of ECL processor circuits offers the highest speed processing of digital data in LSI form. With a full family of support devices and ECL logic elements, high-performance digital processors with n × 4 bit word lengths can be designed around the family of parts. Most of the devices in the family are housed in a special 48-pin quad in-line package to get the density desired without using large packages.

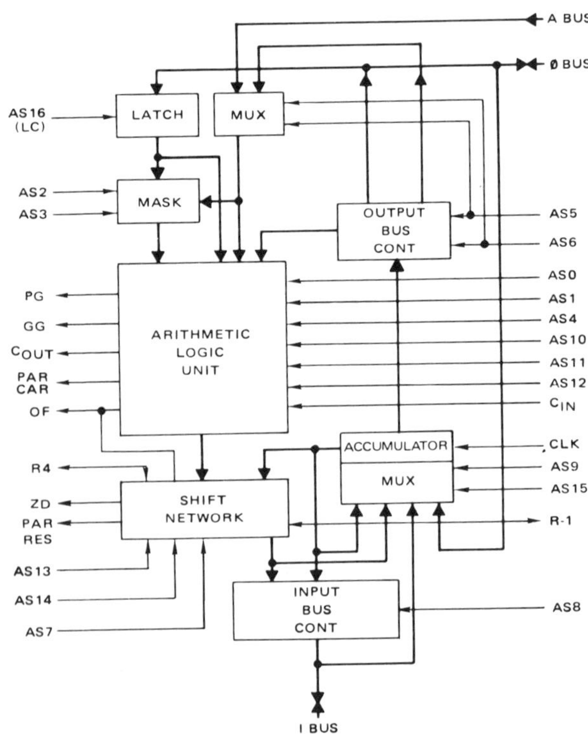

A minimal system using the 10800 family of circuits is difficult to specify since the word size and memory requirements are determined by the user. However, a typical system for a 16-bit machine might require 25 to 40 devices. Architecture of the 10800 slice is very straightforward. Three buses are used to feed information into and out of the processor's ALU— the A bus, the Ø bus and the I bus—of which the A bus is input only. And, there are no on chip registers aside from the accumulator and latches for the Ø bus, so external registers must be used.

Comments

The instruction set of the 10800 processor chip can perform logic operations, binary arithmetic, and BCD arithmetic on combinations of one, two or three variables. These variables are the A bus, the output bus latch and the accumulator. Various select lines on the processor also control the routing of data within the chip. Simple instructions typically execute in 25 to 50 ns—about twice as fast as the other available bit-slice processors.
At this time there is no support software for the 10800 family except for a programming handbook that shows how to develop a microprogram. And, there is no library of user programs yet available.
The 10800 family of bit slice processors is the only one to include BCD arithmetic capability as well

as normal binary. It also includes a 9's complement circuit to simplify the BCD calculations. The overall instruction set of the 10800 bit slice has so many variations since the 10 basic ALU operations can be performed on combinations of one, two or three inputs, that the total number of possible instructions is more than 1000 variations.

At this time there are no prototyping systems or program development aids available for use with the 10800 family. However, boards compatible with the company's EXORciser (the M6800 microprocessor development system) will be available shortly.

Specifications

Data word size:	4 bits
Address bus size:	User determined
Direct addressing range:	User determined
Instruction word size:	User determined
Number of basic instructions:	About 10*
Basic ALU instruction execution time:	30 to 50 ns
Clock frequency (min/max):	Dc/10 MHz
Clock phases/voltage swing:	2/MECL 10,000
Dedicated I/O control lines:	User determined
Package:	48-pin QUIL
Power requirements:	−5.2 V/ 240 mA
	−2 V/199 mA

*for ALU only

Hardware

Model	Description	Price (100 qty)
MC10800	4-bit processor slice	$30.00
MC10801	Microprogram controller	50.00
MC10802	Multiphase clock source	15.00
MC10803	Memory interface circuit	40.00
MC10804	4-bit ECL/TTL shifter	4.00
MC10805	5-bit ECL/TTL shifter	4.75
MC10806	32 × 9 bit register	62.00
MC10808	16-bit programmable shifter	25.00

4-bit processor slice, bipolar (I²L)

SBP0400A, 0401A

Alternate sources: None.

Texas Instruments
P.O. Box 5012, M/S 308
Dallas, TX 75222
(214) 238-2011

The SBP0400A or 0401A 4-bit processor slice can be microprogrammed and configured to build any size digital processor. Integrated injection logic technology permits the user to define the speed/power consumption by adjusting the injector current. The difference between the 0400A and 0401A is slight—the 0400A has an on-chip pipeline register to help speed up processing while the 0401A requires an external register.

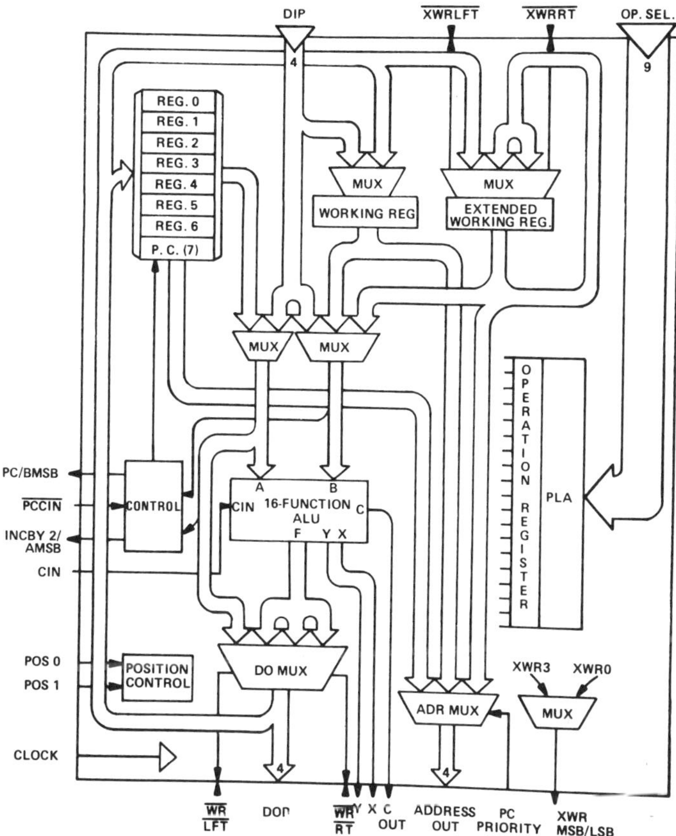

The architecture of the processor slice provides separate data in, data out, address out and control ports, as well as a 16 function ALU. On the chip are an eight-word general register file, two 4-bit working registers, dual scaled-shifters (with on chip handling of end conditions) and a factory programmable logic array that generates on-chip control signals. A minimal system is hard to specify since it depends on word size and control options. A typical system might contain 30 to 50 chips.

Comments

The micro-instruction set of the SBP0400A/0401A can execute any of the 512 possible micro-instructions within a single clock cycle. Operand modifications or combinations via eight arithmetic or logic operations are possible in the ALU as well as combinations of ALU instructions with other commands.

Software support is practically nonexistant. The only material available as an aid to programming is the "Bipolar Microcomputer Components Data-Book," in which SBP0400A/0401A programming is explained. There is no program library available.

Outstanding software features include the availability of pipelined or unpipelined architecture to suit the design. The slices have an independent program counter with unjammable access controls and a relative position control to define the slice rank in n-bit applications.

Hardware support for the SBP0400A/0401A consists of the LCM-1000 series of microprogrammable prototyping modules as well as standard TTL and MOS circuits.

Specifications

Data word size:	4 bits
Address bus size:	4 bits (expandable)
Direct addressing range:	N.A.*
Instruction word size:	13
Number of basic instructions:	16 (ALU)
Shortest instruction/time (All):	350 ns
Clock frequency (min/max):	Dc/3.3 MHz
Clock phases/voltage swing:	1/TTL
Dedicated I/O control lines:	5
Package:	40-pin DIP
Power requirements:	5 V/40 mA (typical)

*Depends on the number of cascaded slices

Hardware

Model	Description	Price (100 qty)
SBP0400A	4-bit slice (pipelined)	$14.62
SBP0400A	MIL temp version	43.85
SBP0401A	4 bit slice (unpipelined)	14.62
SBP0401A	MIL version	43.85
	No special interface circuits are needed	

4 bit processor slice, bipolar (STTL)

SN74S481

Alternate sources: None.

Texas Instruments
P.O. Box 5012
Dallas, TX 75222
(214) 238-2011

The SN74S481 4-bit microprogrammable processor slice is available in either Schottky-TTL or low-power Schottky-TTL technology. It can be used to build a processor with almost any word size. Both versions have fully parallel I/O ports and memory address ports as well as on-chip circuits that define the slice rank and perform sign-bit protection and fill in.

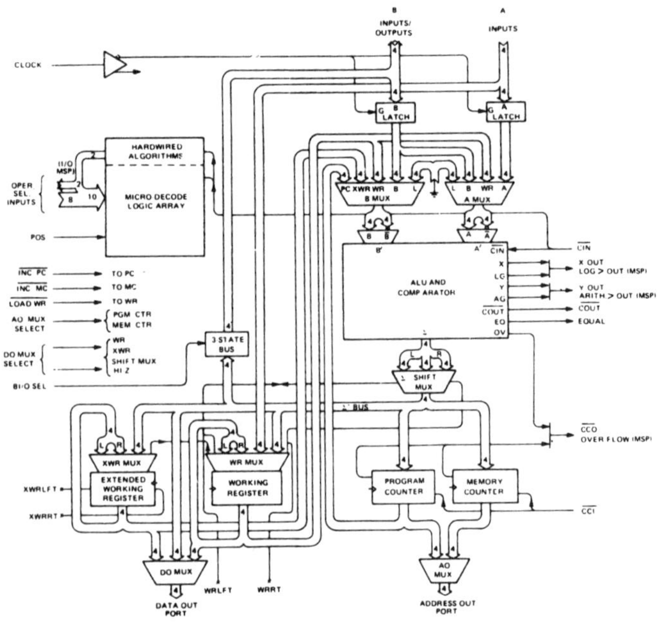

Architecture features of the 74S481 include fully parallel dual input and output ports, a full function ALU with look-ahead carry, magnitude and overflow decision capabilities, a double-length accumulator and dual memory address generators on chip. A typical system consists of 30 to 50 circuits.

Comments

The instruction set of the processor's ALU consists of only 16 arithmetic and logic commands. But also included in the chip are macroprogrammable multiply and divide algorithms and multidirectional data flow control. There are 24,780 unique operations possible, including automatic CRC update.

Software support for the 74S481 family is minimal. There are no programming languages or aids to the designer except for the company's "Bipolar Micro-computer Components Data Book," which describes how to work with the processor slices.

Important software features include the preprogrammed multiply and divide operations for double precision signed or unsigned numbers, cyclic redundancy character accumulation instructions to

help in error prevention, and simultaneous one clock compound operations.

Hardware support is minimal at present. In 1978, evaluation processor modules that duplicate the TI 990 minicomputer's instruction set will be available.

Specifications

Data word size:	4 bits
Address bus size	4 bits (expandable)
Direct addressing range:	N.A.*
Instruction word size:	N.A.
Number of basic instructions:	16 (ALU)
Shortest instruction/time (microinstruction):	67 ns
Longest instruction/time (signed integer divide):	200 to 250 ns
Clock frequency (min/max):	Dc/15 MHz
Clock phases/voltage swing:	1/TTL
Dedicated I/O control lines:	8
Package:	48-pin QUIL
Power requirements:	5 V/200 mA

*Depends on the number of cascaded slices.

Hardware

Model	Description	Price (100 qty)
74S481	4-bit slice (plastic)	$19.60
74S481	4-bit slice (ceramic)	29.25
74S481	4-bit slice (MIL)	87.75
SN74S482N	4-bit controller	6.30
SN74S330N	12-In, 50-Term, 6-Out FPLA	9.00
SN74S225N	16-word-by-5-bit FIFO	4.50
SN74S226N	Quad bus transceiver	2.25
SN74S182N	Carry look-ahead	2.91
SN74S240N	Octal inv/buffer	4.20
SN74S241N	Octal buffer/driver	4.20
SN74S373N	Octal transparent latch	4.72
SN74S374N	Octal D-type register	4.72

4-bit processor slice, PMOS

IMP-8, 16 (00A/520)

National Semiconductor
2900 Semiconductor Drive
Santa Clara, CA 95051
(408) 737-5000

Alternate sources: None.

The IMP series of 4, 8 and 16-bit processors is built around a 4-bit PMOS slice (P/N 00A/520) that can be cascaded. The slice, called a register and arithmetic unit (RALU), combines with control ROM circuits (CROMs) to form a complete microcomputer. Contained in the RALU are a seven-word × 4-bit general register bank, a status register, and a 16-word × 4-bit last-in first-out stack, as well as a multifunction ALU.

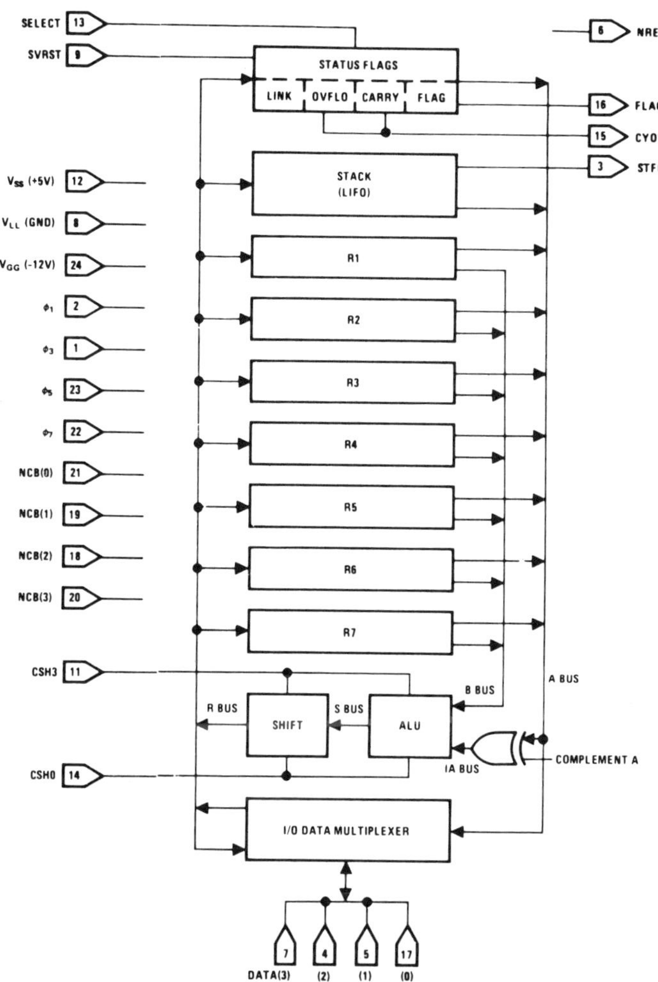

Software support for the IMP family consists of resident and cross assemblers. Resident software can run on any of the IMP systems since all processors share the same set of commands. The cross software is written in Fortran IV and can run on many 32-bit computers. Also available are diagnostic, loader and debug programs.

Software features include the compatibility of instructions from the smaller processors to the largest and the flexibility of defining your own instruction set by the control program in the CROM.

Hardware support for the IMP processor family consists of several processor cards built around the RALU and CROMs as well as full microcomputer systems—the IMP-16L or IMP-16P. Memory cards, I/O cards and card cages are available.

Specifications

Data word size:	4 bits (ALU)
Address bus size:	4, 8 or 16 bits
Direct addressing range:	Up to 65,536 words
Instruction word size:	23 bits (CROM)
Number of basic instructions:	42
Shortest instruction/time (nonmemory reference):	12 μs (average)
Longest instruction/time (memory reference):	20 μs (average)
Clock frequency:	5.17 MHz max.
Clock phases/voltage swing:	4/16 V
Dedicated I/O control lines:	4
Package:	24-pin DIP (RALU)
Power requirements:	5 V/40 mA
	−12 V/40 mA

The architecture of the IMP processor family is split into three basic chips. On the RALU are all the RAM registers, counters and control logic (including the ALU). The CROM holds the microprogram for the macroinstructions while the interface logic circuit provides the flags, condition-jump controller, program counter and program-counter stack. All circuits interface directly via MOS level buses and require a four-phase nonoverlapping clock.

Comments

The macroinstruction set of the IMP processor slice contains 42 commands including 16 register operations, two flag instructions, 13 memory reference operations, five branch commands and six increment/decrement and I/O instructions. The IMP-16L processor has 17 optional instructions including multiply and divide and bit operations.

Hardware

Model	Description	Price (100 qty)
00A/520	4-bit RALU	$22.00
8A/521D	8-bit wide control CROM	40.00
16A/521D	16-bit wide control CROM	27.50
IMP-16A/523D	Power I/O CROM (25-up)	40.50
IMP-16A/524D	Arithmetic CROM (25-up)	40.50

Focus on Floppy-Disc Drives

DAVE BARNES
Electronic Design

In a floppy-disc drive, the medium spins while the head stays put. But dive into the specs on the 30 available models, and your head may end up spinning.

To select the right floppy drive for your job, you have to choose from a wide range of capacities and transfer rates, decide on a hard-sectored or soft-sectored format, satisfy yourself of the reliability of the unit you choose, and match it with an appropriate controller, interface, and software. You also must consider your company's requirements for tomorrow.

You face a choice between 8-in. and 5-1/4-in. diskettes, single and double density, single and double-sided recording, tunnel or straddle erase, and (soon) single and double-track density. You have to pick a head that's crowned or flat, ceramic or ferrite, single or double, and that's moved by a voice coil, a traditional lead screw or the newer metal band.

Is your head spinning yet? You're still not out of the woods. There are many conflicting manufacturer's claims to evaluate. You may find three "fastest" actuators, four "best" heads, maybe eight "smartest" door interlock systems.

Then come the not-so-technical headaches. Keeping in mind cost and vendor reliability. Second-guessing the next IBM move and its impact on what's available. Comparing drive mechanical details: "If this snap-action switch got designed *out* of two other brands after a few months of field use, do I want it in mine? Does it really harm the diskette envelope? Why did two manufacturers replace the switch with a LED-photodiode assembly?"

With so many different floppy designs, the performance picture hasn't stabilized by a long shot. For example, a half-dozen vendors have followed Shugart with two-headed standard floppies that double the on-line capacity of their units. More changes can be expected as soon as IBM tips its hand on double-track density.

Right now, many drives have built-in provisions for double track. They use two (in one case, three) stepper increments to do a one-track move. There is no guarantee that this will completely satisfy the new IBM format. But there's hope. Although many drives are used to record non-IBM-compatible formats, IBM compatibility is still the watchword for factors as basic as the track geometry itself.

As if waiting for double-track standards weren't enough, rumor now has it that IBM will soon bring out a 3-1/2-in. micro-sized floppy. Indeed, *no* part of floppy-disc technology is standing still. Look at the

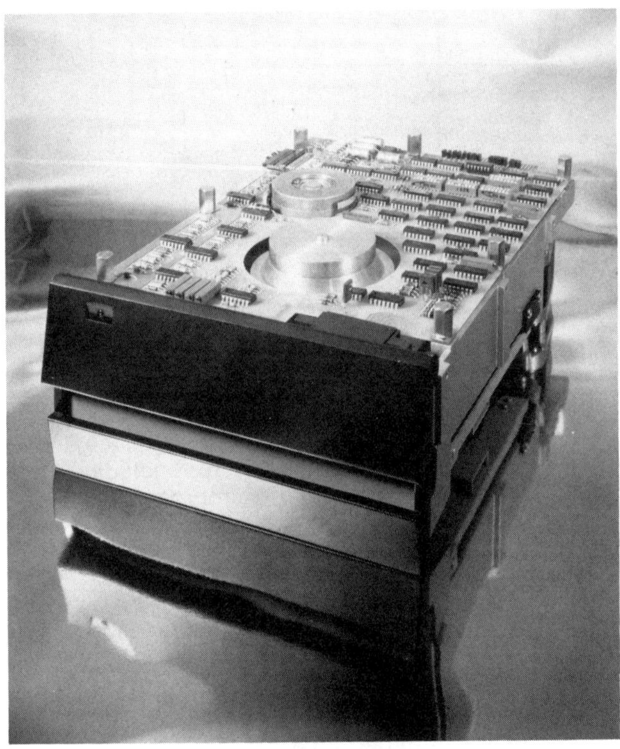

This double-sided, double-density IBM-compatible Mayflower 700 from MFE measures 30% smaller than competition, and multiplies media life by four. Dc-motored 750 version claims a high 10,000-h MTBF and low power—30 W. The 700 and the 750 are the first floppy products of MFE, an established cassette builder.

frame—a component that few electronic designers normally consider very exciting. Manufacturers have been stamping them out of aluminum or steel for years —drilling a few holes, and going on from there.

Now Memorex has introduced a plastic chassis. It's molded in one piece of extra-rugged fiberglass-reinforced polyester (FRP), which gives you lighter weight and tolerances that may be unachievable with aluminum or steel.

FRP can also save money, since the molding process incorporates a large number of inserts, holes, bosses and gussets without any per-unit labor expense.

But along with the new benefits, are there any new problems? Will the electrical shielding of the old metal chassis be missed? Or the magnetic shielding of the steel one?

The floppy disc field is only five years old. But the typical design you'll look at is one or two years old at the most, and may have been redone to correct the faults or limitations of the first-generation design.

A child of diversity

But aren't all floppy drives based on an IBM standard format, and therefore alike? In format, yes. In construction, dependability, and performance, no.

Innovations and variations in design have come from a dozen noncaptive manufacturers, which are still manufacturing floppy drives for OEM use, from three or four that have stopped manufacturing floppies, and from suppliers like IBM, Burroughs and Sycor, which build floppies for only their own products.

What was a single, well-defined product five years ago has been superseded by a broad spectrum of competing products, each bringing something a little different to your search party. Tables 1, 2, and 3 tell the growth story.

Before you can simply run a finger down the charts and pick a winner, you have to examine the whole range of available products. You should also be aware of spec tricks and be ready to visit and grill every prospective supplier.

Table 1 shows the tremendous range of floppy-disc drives with integration levels defined along the horizontal axis of the chart, and data capacities along the vertical axis. At the right-hand side of the chart are some of the quasistandard specs for most of the products in each capacity level. The arrow at the left reminds you that it all began with the standard floppy, from which came the smaller-capacity minifloppy as well as the larger-capacity combinations of double-density, double-head, and (soon) double-track.

Examine the integration levels. No doubt if you're designing for volume production, you will end up buying basic floppy-disc drives with read-write and motion-control electronics and little else (level 1 or 2). These days, you'll probably evaluate several existing controllers before seriously thinking about building your own.

The light, rigid chassis of the Model 550 from Memorex, molded from fiberglass-reinforced polyester, meets tight tolerances that steel and aluminum can't. Its design permits factory upgrading to the recently introduced dual-head 552 version.

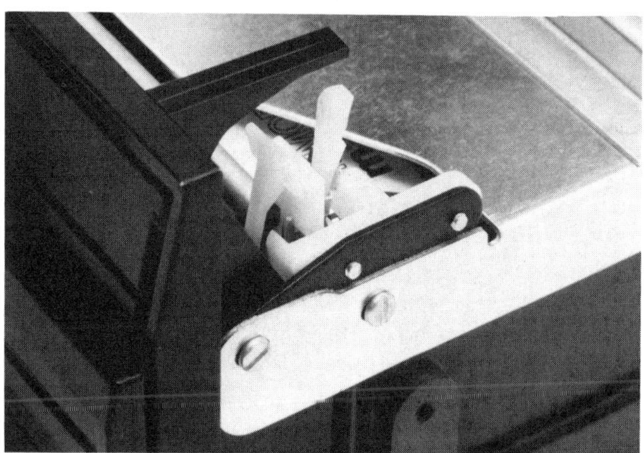

To reduce the usual disc-damage problems, Memorex 550/552 drives use a "balanced-velocity" clamping design (top) that cuts slippage during diskette engagement, and a door-controlled latch/eject mechanism (bottom) that pops media in and out and is interlocked to prevent the door from closing on a diskette that's not fully in.

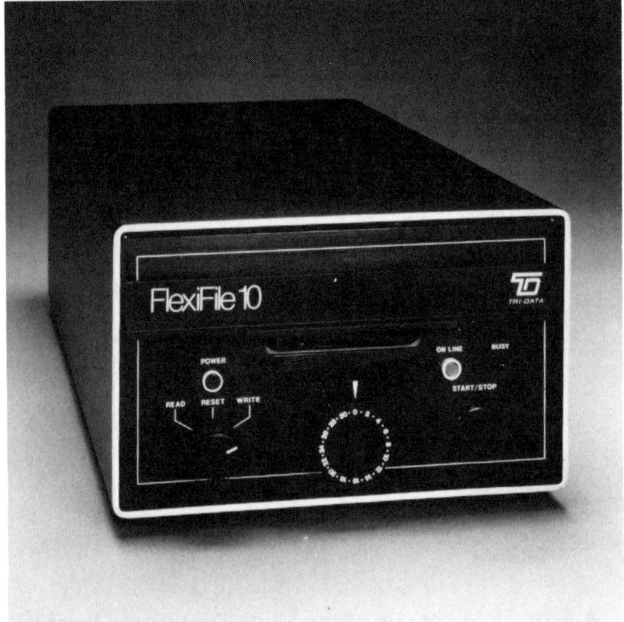

Seeking guaranteed interchangeability of diskette media, Tri Data departs from industry standards with its floppy drives for the Flexifile 10 (left) and 11 (right). Track width is triple the industry standard, though the 8-in. medium affords only 32 tracks, 98 kbytes of storage and 40 kbytes/s transfer with 100-rpm operation.

Dual-index and file-protect sensors permit recording of data on both sides of a microdiskette on the Wangco Model 82 Micro-Floppy. Up to four units can be daisy-chained on a single bus.

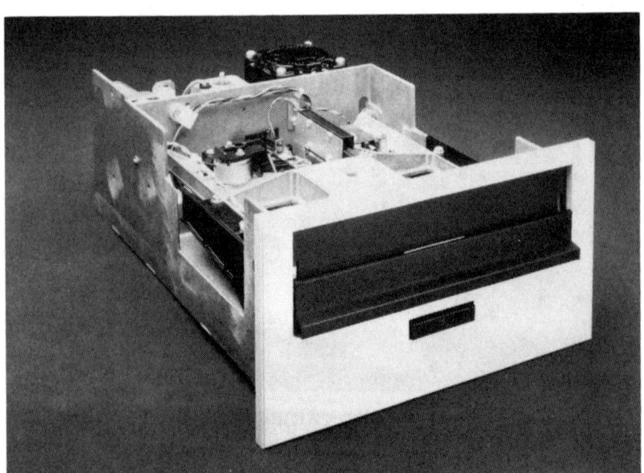

A double-sided, double-density floppy-disc drive, the SA 850 from Shugart Associates is plug-compatible with the company's standard 800.

Perhaps, however, you can get your project off the ground six months sooner by buying a complete ready-to-go floppy-storage subsystem. It can "front" for you in system-level tests, while you engineer your production version to be functionally similar but much more cost-effective. To determine if this two-pronged approach makes sense, you may want to look at complete, packaged floppy subsystems as well as bare drives. Talk with the system builders. They're old hands at evaluating and comparing basic drives.

Use Tables 2 and 3 to complete the overview of available products. Get in touch with vendors early in the design and stay plugged in on spec changes and new product announcements.

Now to the specs.

Digging into the data sheets

One question you'll surely ask: How long do diskettes last? Most manufacturers specify track life as 3-million to 5-million passes (rotations) per track, and their accompanying literature smoothly assures you that the early problems with media life have been solved for the most part.

But once you do the arithmetic and discover that even a low diskette speed of 360 rpm (low compared with the 1800 to 3600 rpm of fixed-head discs) translates to more than a half-million passes per day, you don't feel so assured.

A track can wear out in as little as six 24-hour days.

No problem, if the wear is distributed among the 77 tracks of a standard floppy, and if no diskette spends too much time on the system, and if the heads aren't loaded against the medium when data aren't being accessed.

Table 1. What's available in floppies

	Integration Levels					
	Diskette media only	Drive with electronics	Dual with electronics	Level 1 or 2 drive, plus controller	Level 3 drive, plus interface	Level 4 hardware, plus software
	Level 0	Level 1	Level 2	Level 3	Level 4	Level 5
Double-sided & double-density floppy disk (Level 4)	See "Need More Info (Media)"	See Table 2	Example: PerSci 277 and 297 dual drives are comparable in size to most single drives; four 2-diskette duals fit vertically across 19" rack.	Available from many vendors, Tables 2, 3.	Available from some vendors of each group	See "Need More Info (Systems)"
"Flippy"® or double-sided floppy disk (Level 3)						
Single-sided double-density floppy disk (Level 2)						
Standard floppy disk (Level 1)						
Mini-floppy® or Micro-floppy® disk (Level 0)		See Table 3.	N.A.			

Larger capacity ↑ / Smaller capacity ↓. ORIGINAL FLOPPY → Standard floppy disk.

DD — Double-density (MFM, M²FM or GCR) FO — Flip-over: 2-side recording with 1 head 2 HD — Two-head: 2-side recording with 1 head on each side, full capacity on-line.

But some designs locate frequently used information, such as the software-operating system and key subroutines, on a few heavily used tracks of the disc. And heavy usage of a few tracks and light usage of others is determined by software, and seldom by the hardware design engineer.

Diskettes themselves can be dented, damaged, or devoured by media sensors and faulty clamping mechanisms, and made vulnerable to damage by doors that either aren't locked or aren't interlocked. Improved designs have been triumphantly announced—only to be recalled as quietly as possible when unexpected bugs developed. Don't count on the data sheet to show you that the mechanical arrangements are foolproof.

Many data sheets crow about "the unit's superior head design" which is said to give "the extremely low head/media wear." But few mention the head-loading force, let alone specify that it is a controlled quantity.

Shugart's design improvements in the 850/851 two-head band design allow the company to lower head loading from 15 to 8 grams. The result? A longer media and head life. The vendor should specify the force at which his heads are set, and guarantee it over all units. How much, for example, will that force vary on a single-sided unit as the head-load pad wears out?

Your pad or mine?

Even though data sheets say "no maintenance required," head load pads on a single-sided unit need to be replaced after 1000 to 2000 hours. And while dual-head designs eliminate the little pad holding the medium against the head, some new designs use big "squeegee" pads to help clean the disc and put the medium in tension. Check how often the pad must be replaced.

Check access times, too. Be sure to ask for maximums. Find out also if the "average" access includes settling time—it usually doesn't. The "average" is usually a third (not a half) of the maximum access time, although average latency is half the maximum rotational period. Vendors are inconsistent, but at least the numbers not shown on the data sheets are readily available.

Remember to question "hours" at every appearance on a data sheet. Head life and service life are stated in hours. What is meant? During power-on hours (POH), the drive is active only a small fraction of the time. What fraction is the manufacturer assuming?

Whether or not the drive manufacturer sells formatter/controllers specialized to his unit, ask him who else does. Ask how his electronics mates with the

← Typical Storage Specs →			
Capacity vs. Sectoring	No. of Tracks	Transfer Rate	Media Size
Kilobytes	Count	Kilobits/sec.	Package
1600 Hard 972 Soft (DD + FO or 2HD)	77 per side	500	8″ x 8″ envelope
800 Hard 486 Soft (FO or 2HD)	77 per side	250	
800 Hard 486 Soft (DD)	77	500	
400 Hard 243 Soft	77	250	↓
498.8 if DD & FO 218.8/249.4 if DD or FO 124.7 if 40 tk 109.4 basic	35 (40 opt.)	125 (250 if DD)	5¼″ x 5¼″ envelope

Until recently, most floppy applications have had no major dirt/dust problems, since the diskette stayed wrapped in an envelope lined with a dirt-removing material. Constant burnishing by the freshly cleaned medium cleans the heads, too.

But now a new component that is potentially dirt-sensitive has been introduced in some drives. Several vendors are offering metal-band actuator designs as the least expensive way to reduce track-to-track motion times. A metal band wrapped around a capstan replaces the traditional lead screw as the element transferring the motion from the stepping motor to the head assembly.

However, dirt buildup on the metal band may affect reliability by changing the effective radius of the capstan. So, more dirt means more head motion when the capstan rotates—and more track separation. Even a few-thousandths buildup across the 77 tracks of a

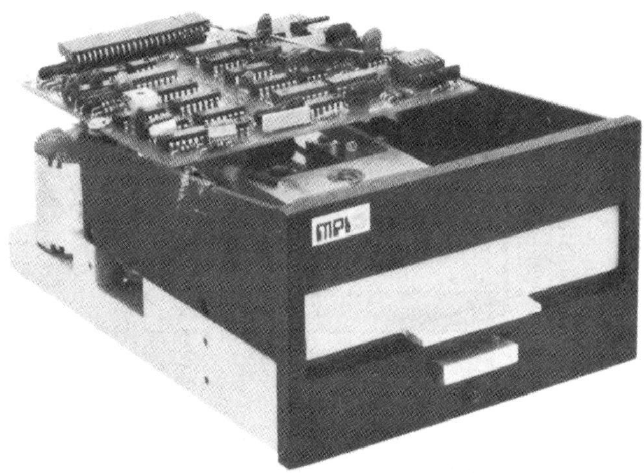

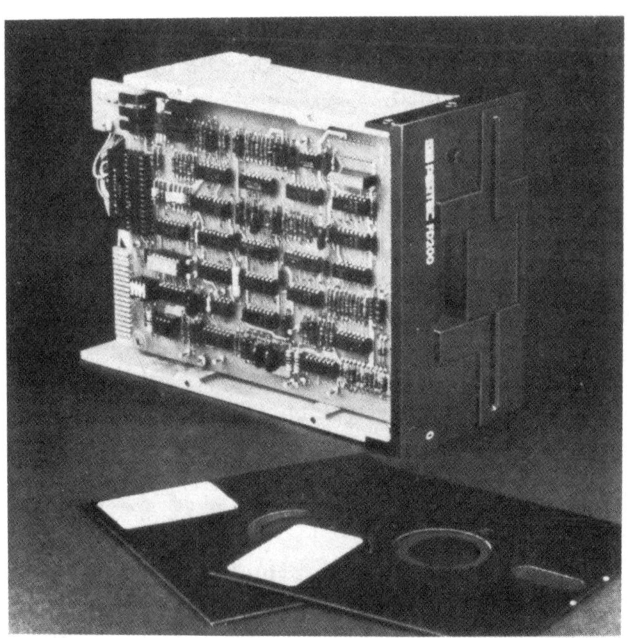

Western Digital 1771 controller chip, the NEC 372D, the SMSFDO 300, the Motorola MC 6843, the Intel 8271 or whichever ones pertain to your work. Request design examples and ask him to put you in touch with people who are using those controllers with his drives.

The controller determines how you'll handle double density—but the drive capabilities have to match. The encoding and decoding for modified frequency modulation (MFM) or modified modified frequency modulation (M²FM) or group-coded recording (GCR) are normally done in the controller. Discussion abounds as to which scheme is theoretically the best. Find out who's successful with each method for each drive you're considering. The bandwidth of the heads and electronics also affect your choice.

Don't forget dirt

A well-known and valuable feature of the floppy is that it doesn't have to operate in a "clean room." But how much dirt is acceptable? Data sheets list temperature and humidity limits but fail to consider the amount of dirt in the air. So beware.

Unless you can find it in print, the manufacturer isn't promising a floppy that will tolerate dirt. At least one vendor, Innovex, does have an enclosed filtered-air environment.

A micro-sized drive (top) from MPI is the only minifloppy to use a metal-band actuator. Its track-to-track time is 5 ms. Pertec's micro-sized floppy (bottom) boasts the same dimensions, mounting holes, interface signals, and voltage requirements as the Shugart SA400.

standard floppy can cause real problems, some experts warn.

Memorex and General Systems International have so far avoided a dirt hassle—no band. They have stayed with the lead screw, and made it play at 3 ms, the same as most metal-band actuators.

In the current Shugart product line, the single-head Models 800 and 801 use a lead screw. The dual-head Models 850 and 851 use a metal band and feature a decrease from 8 ms to 3 ms of track-to-track time. But too many changes are involved to upgrade an existing single-head model to dual-head.

Both Memorex and General Systems International claim to have a higher commonality of parts between their single-head and dual-head models than Shugart. Memorex will upgrade its single-head Model 550s to Model 552s for dual-head double-sided recording at the factory. GSI discourages such modifications because too many changes are needed, including head-loading hardware as well as the head carrier, but points to an 85% commonality of spare parts between its single-head FDD110s and double-head FDD220s.

Speaking of upgrades, how well can you foresee those your product may need later? And what do the manufacturers promise? Will you have to discard your floppies or merely modify them when double-track or some other change comes out? Data sheets seldom clear up such questions.

Get thee to a factory

For this reason and because many of the floppy-drive designs—and companies—are new, visits to the vendors' plants are valuable. Go with the idea of extensively questioning and examining the field performance of the unit you're considering, and the modes of failure. Down-to-earth discussions with satisfied—and dissatisfied—users of the products are also a must.

Put tough questions to every manufacturer you are considering, such as: "Is your mean-time-between-failures spec measured or calculated? If it is not based on field data, just how is it calculated?" Several data sheets candidly state that MTBF figures are calculated; that is, they are theoretical figures derived on paper from formulas—not factual data based on the real longevity of drives used in the field. Other manufacturers are not so candid; they omit the word "calculated." One even heralds "our MTBF rating," as if some outside authority had bestowed the 9000-hour figure after it was earned.

Keep your questions coming: "May I see the data that are the basis of your 0.5-hour mean-time-to-repair (MTTR) specification? What are the main failure modes of the model I am considering? If I sat down at your bench right now, how long would it take you to train me to repair all the kinds of failures that come up?

"How many repair people have you trained this way? How many are within service distance of my

Complete floppy-disc systems offer both hardware and software systems. Digital Systems' FDS-1 (top) includes one or two Shugart drives, an IBM-compatible controller, an Altair-IMSAI S-100 interface, and cables for connecting with Z80/8080 systems. Various Xebec models (middle) interface PerSci, Shugart, and Memorex drives to PDP8, PDP11, LSI 11, Nova, and Eclipse computers. Advanced Electronics Design (bottom) ties Memorex, Shugart (shown) and Pertec units to those five computers.

customers' locations? What tools and equipment will such a serviceman need, and how big a stock of parts? How do I test to ensure that I am reading 10^9 bits per soft error and 10^{12} bits per hard error? Can I test every unit to this spec? If not, how and when do I apply the spec?"

In a standard-density floppy, the data transfer rate is 250 kilobits per second. Figuring 10 bits per byte,

Table 2. Representative floppy drives

Notes: accept 8-inch square diskettes, access to 1.6 megabytes.

Company	Model No.	Model Designation	Capacity level and options (see Table 1)	Integration level (see Table 1)	Motor type	Head actuator	MTBF (hrs.)	MTTR (min.)	No. of Heads	Head life (wks.)	Track Life (days)	Read errors, recoverable	Read errors, unrecoverable	Seek error rate	Motion times (ms.) latency (av.)	headload	access, tk–tk	access, (av.)	settling	Units in rack width	Weight (lb.)	Special features
Calcomp	142M	Floppy Disk Drive	1, 2	1	AC	V leadscrew	note 1 / 7000	<30	1	note 2 / DES 5 yr. or 30,000h	note 7 / ?	10^{-9}	10^{-12}	10^{-6}	83	30	6	—	10	3E	16	Daisy chain, good read margins.
	143M	" " "	4MFM	1(3)	AC	"	"	"	2	"	?	"	"	"	83	30	6	—	10	3E (note 3)	16	Unique flat heads, opt'l. 1143M controller.
Control Data	9400	" " "	1	1(3)	AC	Leadscrew	4000	30	1	SVC 5 yrs. or 30,000h	—	10^{-9}	10^{-12}	10^{-6}	83	60	10	270	10	3	12	9474 subsystem
	9404	" " "	1, 2	1(3)	AC	"	4000	30	1	or 30,000h	—	"	"	"	"	60	10	270	10	3	12	interfaces 9404
	9406	" " "	4	1(3)	AC	Band (note 9)	8000	30	2	"	—	"	"	"	"	40	3	91	10	3	12	& 6's with 8080.
General Systems Int'l.	GSI-110	Flexible Disk drive	2	1(3)	AC	Leadscrew	6000	20	1	SVC 5 yrs. or 30Kh	7	10^{-9}	10^{-12}	10^{-6}	83	35	6	156	14	4	13	>55% read resolution on track 76.
	FDD-200	Flexible Disk drive	4MFM, M²FM	1(3)	AC	Leadscrew	6000	<20	2	SVC 5 yrs. or 30Kh	7	10^{-9}	10^{-12}	10^{-6}	83	35	3	128	14	4	11	3-bearing stepper, shielded pc
Innovex Corp.	200, 400 Series	Floppy disk drive	1, 2		AC	Leadscrew	>8500	<30	1	>15Kh typ	7	10^{-9}	10^{-12} est.	10^{-6}	83	30	8	—	8	4E	14	Filtered air, 35% better read margins.
	600 Series	Double-sided disk drive	4		(In development)				2	—	—	—	—	—	—	—	—	—	—	—	—	—
MFE	500 Series	Mayflower single-sided drive	1, 2		(In development)				1													
	700 Series	Mayflower Double sided drive	4MFM, M²FM	1	AC or DC models	Band	>10,000 if DC motor	—	2	4x10⁷ passes (note 5)	>10	$<10^{-9}$	$<10^{-12}$	$<10^{-6}$	83	35	3	—	15	4	10	Smallest, lowest power in DC version.
Memorex Corp.	550	OEM floppy	1, 2	1	AC	Leadscrew	9000	30	1	—	10	10^{-9}	10^{-12}	—	83	35	6	—	10	4	10.7	FRP frame, power saver on stepper.
	552	OEM dual-head floppy	4MFM, M²FM	1	AC	Leadscrew	9000	30	2	—	10	10^{-9}	10^{-12}	—	83	35	3	—	10	4	10.7	Factory can upgrade 550 to 552.
Micro Peripherals Inc.	B82	Flexible disk drive	1, 2, 4	1	AC or DC	Band	8000	30	2	DES 5 yr. (note 2)	7	10^{-9}	10^{-12}	10^{-6}	83	35	3	91	15	3	10	Compatible with Shugart, 30% less parts.
Per Sci, Inc.	70	Single floppy	1, 2	1(3)	DC	Voice-coil	6000	20	1	DES 5 yrs. or 15Kh	7	10^{-9}	10^{-12}	10^{-6}	83	40	10	33	0	4	15	1070 controller available (all models)
	277	Dual floppy	1, 2	2(3) (note 8)	"	"	"	"	2 (note 8)	"	"	"	"	"	"	"	"	33	0	4	20	Holds 2 independent diskettes.
	297	Two-sided dual floppy	4	2(3) (note 8)	"	"			4						"	35	"	33	0	4	22	All models have motor to insert disk & push-button to eject
Pertec, Inc.	FD400	Flexible disk	1	1	DC	Leadscrew	>10,000	—	1	20Kh	10	10^{-9}	10^{-12}	—	83	40	10	—	20	4	14	3 steps/tk., ferrite heads.
	FD5X0	"	1(2)	1	AC	"	"	—	1	"	10	"	"	—	83	40	10	—	20	4	14	Steel chassis, DD optional.
	FD511	"	1, 2	1	AC	"	"	—	1	"	10	"	"	—	83	40	10	—	20	4	14	Daisy chain, and extra control lines.

Company	Model No.	Model Designation	Capacity level and options (see Table 1)	Integration level (see Table 1)	Motor type	Head actuator	MTBF (hrs.)	MTTR (min.)	No. of Heads	Head life (wks.)	Track Life (days)	Read errors, recoverable	Read errors, unrecoverable	Seek error rate	Motion times (ms.) latency (av.)	headload	access, tk–tk	access. (av.)	settling	Units in rack width	Weight (lb.)	Special features
Remex	RFD1000	"	1, 2MFM	1(3-5)	AC	Stylus ball	—	—	1	>30Kh	>10	<10^{-9}	<10^{-12}	—	83	50	6	176	24	3E	15	PDP 8/11 interfaces available.
Shugart Associates	SA800	Diskette storage drive	1, 2	1(3)	AC	Leadscrew	5000HD 8000TYP	30	1	15Kh	7	10^{-9}	10^{-12}	10^{-6}	83	35	8	260	8	3E	13.0	Industry std. Controllers available.
	SA850	" " "	4M²FM	1(3)	AC	Band	"	30	2	"	7	10^{-9}	10^{-12}	10^{-6}	83	35	3	91	15	3E	13.0	8 gm head load force, down from 15.
Wangco, Inc.	76	Diskette drive	1, 2	1(3)	AC	Uni-ball	5000	30	1	DES 5 yrs.	N.A.	10^{-10}	10^{-12}	10^{-6}	83	16	6	168	14	3E	13	
	276	Dual head diskette drive	4	1	AC	Uni-ball	8000	30	2	DES 5 yrs.	N.A.	10^{-9}	10^{-12}	10^{-6}	83	35	3	90	15	3E	13	

Table 3. Representative micro/mini/floppies

Note: accept 5.25-inch-square diskettes,
hold 109.4 kilobytes on 35 tracks, one side } double for DD (double-density) (MFM,M²FM)
up to 498.8 kilobytes if options incl. 40, DD, FO } and/or double (again) if FO (flip-over recording)

Company	Model No.	Model Designation	Capacity level and options (see Table 1)	Integration level (see Table 1)	Motor type	Head actuator	MTBF (hrs.)	MTTR (min.)	No. of Heads	Head life (wks.)	Track Life (days)	Read errors, recoverable	Read errors, unrecoverable	Seek error rate	Motion times (ms.) latency (av.)	headload	access, tk–tk	access. (av.)	settling	Units in rack width	Weight (lb.)	Special features
Pertec, Inc.	FD200	Micro-sized	0, 40, DD, FO	1(5)	DC servo	Cam	—	—	1	20Kh	6	—	—	—	100	35	25	?	10	—	3.2	
Shugart Associates	SA400	Minifloppy	0	1(3)	DC	Cam	8000 (note 6)	30	1	?	6	10^{-9}	10^{-11}	10^{-6}	100	75	40	463	10	—	3 note4	
Micro Peripherals Inc.	B51	Micro-sized	0, 40, DD	1	DC servo	Band	10,000	30	1	DES 5 yrs	6	10^{-8}	10^{-10}	10^{-6}	100	35	5	75	15	—	3.0	Patented disk clamp, eject, band.
Wangco, Inc.	Model 82	MicroFloppy™	0, 40, DD, FO	1(3)	DC servo	Leadscrew	8500	30	1	Des. 5 yrs	N.A.	10^{-9}	10^{-12}	10^{-6}	100	60	30	370	20	—	3.5	8201 micro-controller available.

Notes:

1. MTBF figures are sometimes labeled "calculated" or "normal operations".

2. If head life is not stated, "DES" (design life) or "SVC" (service life) spec is quoted in this column.

3. "E" means estimated, where not stated by manufacturer. If H< 4.38, 4-wide is assumed.

4. Weight is "nominal", according to Shugart.

5. MFE quotes head life as >40×10^6 wear revolutions (>80 days of 24 hrs with heads loaded — absolute worst case, this is >11 weeks). Normal usage makes heads last much longer, since heads contact media a small fraction of POH (power-on hours). But all manufacturers leave "normal usage" undefined.

6. MTBF is 8000 power-on hours, but spindle motor is assumed to be on only 25% of those hours.

7. ED has quoted media life per track in terms of worst-case 24-hour days. Thus 3.5×10^6 wear passes becomes 7 days. Normal usage makes media last much longer, if duty cycles are low.

8. PerSci 277 and 297 are about the same size as most single-diskette drives, but each holds two independent diskettes, usable simultaneously.

9. CDC9406 was shown at NCC with leadscrew, but band is used in production units.

Original Source Microprocessor Manufacturers

The products cited in this report don't represent the manufacturers' full lines. For additional details, circle the appropriate number on the Reader Service Card. For data sheets and more vendors, consult ELECTRONIC DESIGN's GOLD BOOK.

Floppy drives

Calcomp, 2411 W. LaPalma, Anaheim, CA 92801. (714) 821-2011. (Joel Levine)

Control Data, P.O. Box 12313, Oklahoma City, OK 73112. (405) 946-5421. (Terry Hardie)

General Systems International, 1440 Allec St., Anaheim, CA 92085. (714) 956-7183. (Mike Krunic)

Innovex Corp., 75 Wiggins Ave., Bedford, MA 01730. (617) 275-2110. (Gary Bloch)

MFE, Keewaydin Dr., Salem, NH 03079. (603) 893-1921. (Jim Bartley)

Memorex Corp., San Tomas & Central, Santa Clara, CA 95052. (408) 987-1396. (Bob Erdman)

Micro Peripherals, 8724 Woodley Ave., Sepulveda, CA 91343. (213) 894-4076. (Keith Ullal)

PerSci, Inc., 4087 Glencoe Ave., Marina Del Rey, CA 90291. (213) 820-3764.

Pertec, 9600 Irondale Ave., Chatsworth, CA 91311. (213) 999-2020. (Bob Conti)

Remex (Ex-Cell-O), 1733 E. Alton St., Irvine, CA 92714. (714) 557-6860. (David Kolstrom)

Shugart, 415 Oakmead Pkwy., Sunnyvale, CA 94086. (408) 733-0100. (George Sollman)

Wangco, 5404 Jandy Place, Los Angeles, CA 90066. (213) 390-8081. (George Toor)

Systems

Advanced Electronics Design, Inc., 440 Potrero Ave., Sunnyvale, CA 94086. (408) 735-3555. (Jerry Kennedy)

Charles River Data Systems, Inc., 235 Bear Hill Rd., Waltham, MA 02154. (617) 890-1700. (Wm. Nimee)

DTC (Data Terminals & Communications), 1190 Dell Ave., Campbell, CA 95008. (408) 378-1112. (Herb Martin)

Data Systems Design, Inc., 3130 Coronado Dr., Santa Clara, CA 95051. (408) 249-9353. (George Fink)

Digital Systems, 6017 Margarido Dr., Oakland, CA 94618. (415) 428-0950. (John Torode)

Echo Science Corp., 485 E. Middlefield Rd., Mountain View, CA 94043. (415) 961-7145 (Bill Nichols)

Gnat Computers, Inc., 7895 Convoy Court, Unit 6, San Diego, CA 92111. (714) 560-0433.

Mupro, Inc., 424 Oakmead Pkwy., Sunnyvale, CA 94086. (408) 737-0500. (Donald Pantle)

North Star Computers, Inc., 2465 Fourth St., Berkeley, CA 94710. (415) 549-0858.

Peripheral Vision, P. O. Box 6267, Denver, CO 80206. (303) 777-4292. (John Taylor)

Scientific Micro Systems, 777 E. Middlefield Rd., Mountain View, CA 94043. (408) 964-5700.

Sykes Datatronics, Inc., 375 Orchard St., Rochester, NY 14606. (716) 458-8000.

Tri-Data, 800 Maude Ave., Mountain View, CA 94043. (415) 969-3700. (Herm Levin)

Western Telematic, Inc., 2435 Anne St., Santa Ana, CA 92704. (714) 979-0363.

Xebec Systems Inc., 2985 Kifer Rd., Santa Clara, CA 95051. (408) 988-2550. (Bob Sigal)

Media

BASF Systems, Crosby Dr., Bedford, MA 07130. (617) 271-4000. (John Healion)

Control Data Corp., 11615 "I" St., Omaha, NE 68137. (402) 333-0850. (J. D. Grimshaw)

Dysan Corp., 2388 Walsh Ave., Santa Clara, CA 95050. (408) 247-4109. (Wm. Harry)

EM&M Media Products, 1020 Timothy Dr., Santa Clara, CA 95133. (408) 298-7090. (Jack Smyth)

IBM Information Records Div., Rt. 522, Ridge Rd., Princeton, NJ 08540. (201) 329-1000.

ITC (Information Terminals Corp.), 322 Soquel Way, Sunnyvale, CA 94086. (408) 245-4400. (Bob Katzive)

K-Tronic Inc., 3260 Scott Blvd., Santa Clara, CA 95051. (408) 246-6830. (Ron Rader)

Memorex Corp., San Tomas and Central Expwy., Santa Clara, CA 95052. (408) 987-1000.

3M Co. Headquarters, 3M Center, St. Paul, MN 55101. (612) 733-1100.

Reading or writing 10^9 bits takes 4000 seconds or 67 minutes and 10^{12} bits takes 1111 hours.

But suppose soft errors start cropping up more often than every 67 minutes—and hard errors more often than every 1111 hours. Certainly, the burden of proof will be on you to show that you are maintaining and operating the unit correctly.

But what kinds of records will the manufacturer expect to see before he will even consider that it is *his* problem? How will you demonstrate to him that the "bug" is in the heads or electronics that he supplied, not in some infrequent glitch in your digital controller? Must you prove that you have never operated his floppy drive outside the temperature and humidity ranges he specified?

Does his spec apply only when you are using diskette media carrying his brand name? Or only when the diskette is recorded on his make of drive? Or only when it is recorded on the same drive that's reading it?

Find out if the manufacturer will work with you to correct any failures of *his* floppy drive in *your* system. He may plan to defend his unit by excluding your system as an unknown situation, and proving his drive meets specs in the environment at his factory. Perhaps previous customers have charged that the units were not meeting the MTBF, MTTR, or reliability specifications. How were these challenges resolved?

Apply hard questioning to burn-in and production testing as well. Does the manufacturer do margin testing? If so, how? In one method, specially prepared diskettes at Shugart contain track segments that are radially displaced by 1 to 10 mils, in 1-mil increments. Units that cannot read tracks displaced by ±0.008 in. don't get shipped. This provides an effective margin test on the read electronics. ■■

Simplify Low-cost Microprocessor Selection

HOWARD RAPHAEL
Intel Corp., Santa Clara, Ca.

The tremendous increase in available microprocessors has escalated the need for a reasonably straightforward way to select the right one for your application. Microprocessors can be split into two major groups—high-performance types with minicomputerlike capabilities and moderate to low-end performance units intended as replacements for complex logic. Most of the available processors fall into the latter classification. Picking the right μP from this group requires a painstaking and time-consuming two step process: first, point-by-point comparison; second, evaluation. However, tabulating most of the different μP specifications into three major areas—general-processor characteristics, minimum usable system characteristics and maximum usable system characteristics—makes selection of the one or two most likely candidates from a dozen or more very easy.

You'll need more than just tables

Once the best prospects have been selected, you can evaluate them by using applications-oriented comparisons of software and timing called benchmarks. Benchmarking depends heavily on your application, and many experts agree that a general test of execution time really doesn't provide a true comparison.

Don't just pick the μP with the lowest cost. You must also know how much you need in support circuitry, memory, power supplies, input/output requirements, among other things—everything that's necessary to make a completely operating system.

Of course, evaluate the general characteristics of each μP. Some of the important parameters such as word length, cycle times, memory capacity availability of working registers, manipulation capabilities and the available instructions make a good starting point for μP selection. Table 1 summarizes the characteristics of four and eight-bit processors, without regard to what an operating system may require.

Microprocessor *word length* defines the basic architectural data word size of the number of bits that can be entered every cycle. The *instruction length* describes the number of bits required for a command. Instructions can contain multiple words (often two or three words), although eight-bit words have now become a de facto standard for low-end μPs.

The *number of instructions* should be 50 or more to provide an adequate number of commands. Of course, the more instructions, the more convenience afforded the designer.

The speed at which a μP can complete an instruction, or its cycle time, must often be factored into the selection process. To give you a rough idea of various μP speeds, *best, average* and *worst-case cycle times* are provided in Table 1. Actual μP performance must be evaluated on an instruction-by-instruction basis since each μP's instruction-cycle duration will be different even for equivalent commands. In some cases, similar instructions on different μPs can require twice as much time on unit A as on unit B.

Separate the program and data

In many cases, the μP offers *separate program and data memories* so that the instructions and data are contained in two different memories. By separating memories in small systems, programs can be efficiently packed in read-only memory (ROM) storage while data held in random access memory (RAM) can be separately organized and addressed.

The addressing range of the μP is determined by the *range of the program counter* (PC). Maximum program sizes range from 50 to 80% of the maximum PC range, and efficient μPs have a majority of single-cycle instructions to keep program sizes small. However, since most μPs also have multicycle instructions, the range of the PC doesn't always indicate the maximum number of instruction words.

If when a μP uses a separately addressed RAM *data memory* to hold changing data values typical requirements are for less than 256 words of

Table 1. Basic microprocessor characteristics

	TI	Rockwell	National	National	National	AMI	Rockwell	Intel	GI	GI	Fairchild	National	Intel
Characteristic	TMS 1000, 1100, 1200 1300	PPS4/1	MM 5781/82	MM 5799	MM 5734	9209	PPS4/2	MCS-40	1640	1650	F8	SC/MP	8048
Word length	4	4	4	4	4	4	4	4	8	8	8	8	8
Instruction length	8	8	8	8	8	8	8	8	12	12	8	8	8
Number of instructions	46	50	45	45	45	28	50	60	27	27	70	46	96
Typical cycle time (μs)	12	24	10	10	14	15	5	10	1	1	6	20	2.5
Minimum cycle time (μs)	12	23	10	10	14	15	5	10	1	1	2	10	2.5
Maximum cycle time (μs)	12	60	20	20	28	30	10	20	2	2	13	46	5
Separate program/data memory	Yes	Yes	Yes	Yes	Yes	Yes	Yes	Yes	Yes	Yes	Yes	No	Yes
Program counter range (words)	2 k	1.3 k	2 k	1.5 k	630	756	4 k	8 k	256	512	65 k	65 k	4 k
Data memory range (words)	64/128	96	1 k	1 k	55	64	256	1 k +	32	32	65 k	65 k	320
Number of interrupts	0	0	0	0	0	0	0	1	0	0	Mul	1	2+
Number of levels of interrupt	0	0	0	0	0	0	0	1	0	0	1	1	1
Number of working registers	2	5	4	1	0	1	1	24	32	32	16	1	8/16
Number of register banks	–	–	–	–	–	0	–	2	–	–	–	–	2
Bit manipulation instruction	Yes	Yes	No	No	No	Yes	Limited	Limited	Yes	Yes	No	No	Yes
Nibble manipulation	Yes	Yes	Yes	Yes	Yes	Yes	Yes	Yes	Yes	Yes	No	No	Yes
Byte manipulation	No	No	No	No	No	No	No	No	Yes	Yes	Yes	Yes	Yes
Decimal arithmetic	No	Yes	Yes	Yes	Yes	No	Yes	Yes	No	No	Yes	Yes	Yes
Binary arithmetic	Yes	Yes	Yes	Yes	Yes	Yes	Yes	Yes	Yes	Yes	Yes	Yes	Yes
Indirect addressing	No	Yes	No	No	No	No	Yes	Yes	No	No	Yes	No	Yes
Indexing	No	No	No	No	No	No	No	No	No	No	No	Yes	No
Address stack depth	1	2	2	2	1	2	2	7	2	2	1	3	8
Full range jump	No	Yes	Yes	Yes	Yes	Yes	Yes	Yes	Yes	Yes	Yes	Yes	Yes
Relative jump	No	Yes	No	No	No	No	No	No	No	No	Yes	Yes	No
Number of conditional jumps	1	30	10	10	8	5	5	16	3	3	9	3	14
I/O expandability	Limited	No	Limited	Limited	No	No	Yes	Yes	Limited	No	Yes	Yes	Yes
Memory expandability	No	No	Yes	No	No	No	Yes	Yes	No	No	Yes	Yes	Yes

RAM (see Table 1). Most low-end μPs use separately addressed data and memory to facilitate organization of data values.

Often during processing, an external device may have to communicate with the μP. One way to do so is to interrupt the processor. The *number of interrupts* the μP can handle tells you how many devices can signal at the same time and be ranked and handled in turn. Every interrupt handled by the processor can be assigned a priority and the *number of interrupt levels* used to determine which input gets serviced first, second, and so on by the processor.

Interrupts come from many sources

However, a μP may have many sources of interrupts—but only one level. An example of a single level is the ability of a device to stop the main processing program and jump to a special service routine that is followed when an interrupt occurs. But if during execution of this new program a more urgent interrupt comes in (a higher priority), the complete interrupt routine being executed must be completed, and operation returned to the main program before the next interrupt can be handled.

On the other hand, more powerful machines are designed to accept another interrupt command even as they execute an interrupt. The process of storing the current routine and jumping to the next is called nesting and the number of possible levels is determined solely by the number of registers used to store the nested information. As you can see from Table 1, most low-cost μPs have only a single level of interrupt capability.

Data entering the processor are usually fed into one of the *working registers*. These registers are as long as a CPU word and can be manipulated by the instructions (the accumulator is considered a working register). Working registers often serve as a source or destination for data manipulated by an accumulator as well as data coming from or going to either an I/O-port, memory or the arithmetic-and-logic section. Ideally, all working registers should be accessible by all register instructions; when they are, they are called symmetrical.

Often, processor operations require that only a single bit in a word be altered. The ability of a μP to perform *bit manipulation*—setting, resetting, testing and so on—is a must for many I/O applications. Although you can circumvent this manipulation by using logic operations for setting, resetting and shifting data into the carry bit for testing, you will need more time for processing.

To process data in four-bit chunks (often referred to as nibbles), some μPs permit *nibble manipulation*—especially μPs intended to handle binary-coded decimal data. A good eight-bit μP should be able to handle both sizes of data words. Eight-bit processors, of course, have flexible *byte-manipulation* capabilities, but the mark of a good eight-bit unit is its ability to manipulate four-bit chunks of data.

Since a great deal of data appear in BCD form, the ability of a μP to do *decimal arithmetic* can be very important. Man-to-machine interfaces can be simplified if μPs can handle BCD data without having to convert to binary for each operation. Nevertheless, every processor chip is designed to handle *binary arithmetic*.

Accessing the available memory of each μP system is often done with direct addressing. But in cases where the address is not within the direct range, *indirect addressing* is available on some μPs to permit the unit to fetch an operand or data word from any memory location. Sometimes, an additional addressing scheme, called *indexing*, is available.

Indexing lets the μP add the contents of a predesignated register to the current address value and use the resulting sum as the new address. This technique is most advantageous when program memories are greater than 8-k words since addresses can be quickly modified. Indexing permits a block of memory to be rapidly pointed to from the current address, and is useful when you must access multiple data fields and tables without changing the basic address.

Stack depth limits subroutine nesting

During execution, a program will often jump to one or more subroutines. Depending upon the *address-stack depth*, the number of jumps can be restricted. This number can be especially important if subroutines must be nested. Three jumps should be the absolute minimum. Seven jumps are desirable if an interrupt operation must also be considered. Not only is the program-counter value stored in the stack, but during an interrupt all processor-status information can be stored there automatically.

Whenever the processor departs from sequential program flow, it jumps to a new address. If a *full-range jump* is possible (a jump to anywhere in the program up to full addressing range), simple programs can be written. Without an available full-range jump, multiple-page jumps are often required to reach the desired program point.

Program operation may be transferred to a location plus or minus some number of instructions from the location of the jump. When this type of *relative jump* is available, addressing can be made very simple. But when a program is developed with a symbolic assembler, relative jump

Table 2. Minimal system characteristics

Characteristic	TI	Rockwell	National	National	National	AMI	Rockwell	Intel	GI	GI	Fairchild	National	Intel
	TMS 1000, 1100, 1200 1300	PPS4/1	MM 5781/82	MM 5799	MM 5734	9209	PPS4/2	MCS-40	1640	1650	F8	SC/MP	8048
Number of required ICs	1	1	3	1	1	1	2	4	1	1	2	6+	1
Program memory size	1k/2k	1.3k	2k	1.5k	630	756	2k	1k	256	512	1k	2k	1k
Data memory (word)	64/128	94	160	96	55	64	128	80	32	32	64	256	64
PROM development available	Yes	Yes	No	No	No	No	Yes	Yes	Yes	Yes	Yes	Yes	Yes
PROM/ROM systems-identical (*Phys) (**Elec)	No Yes	No No	No No	No No	No No	No No	No Yes	No Yes	No Yes	No Yes	No Yes	Yes Yes	Yes Yes
I/O lines	23/25/28	31	18	18	24	33	36	21	24	24	32	23	27
I/O lines that can be inputs	4	31	5	5	4	9	30	17	24	24	32	11	24
Strobes, controlling flags and test lines	0	0	5	4	2	12	0	1	5	0	0	9	5
I/O lines that can be outputs	19/21/24	18	13	13	1	8	30	20	24	24	32	12	24
Bidirectional buses (I/O)	No	No	No	No	No	No	Yes	No	Yes	No	No	Yes	Yes
Timers	No	No	No	No	No	No	No	No	No	No	Yes	No	Yes
Timer resolution	–	–	–	–	–	–	–	–	–	–	8	–	8
Timer accuracy μs/bit	–	–	–	–	–	–	–	–	–	–	15.5	–	80
Event counter	No	No	No	No	No	No	No	No	Yes	Yes	No	No	Yes
Serial I/O	No	Yes	Yes	Yes	No	No	No	No	No	No	No	Yes	No
Clock on chip	Yes	Yes	No	Yes	Yes	Yes	Yes	No	Yes	Yes	Yes	Yes	Yes
Clock R/C controlled	Yes	Yes	No	Yes	Yes	Yes	No	No	Yes	Yes	Yes	Yes	Yes
Reset on chip	Yes	Yes	Yes	Yes	Yes	Yes	No	No	Yes	Yes	Yes	No	Yes
Reset separate pin	No	Yes	No	No	No	Yes	Yes	Yes	Yes	No	Yes	Yes	Yes
Power consumption (mW)	75	70	200	150	125	160	800	1000+	N/A	N/A	600	1000+	400
Low-power standby	No	No	No	No	No	No	No	Yes	No	No	No	No	Yes
Operating supply voltage	15 V	15 V	9 V	9 V	9 V	15 V	5 V,-12 V	15 V	15 V	5 V	5 V, -12-V	5 V, -12-V	5 V
Technology	PMOS	PMOS	PMOS	PMOS	PMC3	PMOS	PMOS	PMOS	NMOS	NMOS	NMOS	PMOS	NMOS
Package pin count	28/40	42	24/24	28	40	40/28	42/42	28	40	28	40/40	40	40

*Physical refers to pin compatibility between ROM and PROM parts.
**Electrical refers only to code compatibility.

instructions aren't as necessary. And, care must be taken in programming when relative jumps are used with multicycle instructions since a jump may inadvertently specify a noninstruction location.

External-system hardware can often determine when a jump occurs, and the *number of conditional jumps* can become important in many control applications. Conditional jumps are often performed after testing the carry flip-flop, special flags, test lines, accumulator bits, register values, and so on. The more conditional jumps available, the better.

The ease of *memory expansion*—if it can be expanded—can be an important factor, especially if high-level development languages are used. Memory expandability can often be likened with *I/O expandability*, since there are many combination circuits that contain RAM or ROM (or both) and I/O ports. However, a high degree of expandability permits dedicated peripheral I/O devices to feed into a single μP, which can cut system cost in the long run.

Look closely at a minimal system

Moving from basic processor characteristics to minimum usable system characteristics should give you a better idea of what's necessary to get a system going. Often, the *minimum number of required ICs* needed to support a system, including the μP, can be an eye opener.

As shown in Table 2, the number can range from one (just the μP) to more than six. The basic system includes the circuitry to generate the clock, handle 16 lines of I/O plus program and data-memory (ROM and RAM) storage.

While one-chip systems are often desirable, the basic system should be flexible and expandable. In many of the small systems, the *program memory* is on the processor chip. In general, at least 1 kword is desirable since it can cover about 70% of all current low-end applications. The *data-memory size* should also be as large as possible—64 bytes is comfortable, and no less than 32 bytes should be considered.

Being able to use programmable ROMs to develop programs is an absolute must. (Of course, the ultimate production line will use masked ROMs.) Without *PROM development*, the only other alternative is software simulation, which can cause several ROM mask iterations before all bugs are eliminated. If possible, *PROM/ROM systems* with identical pinouts for ROMs and PROMs should be used—they minimize the number of circuit alterations and allow rapid field changes with little work.

To control the transfer of data between the μP and peripherals, use the special *I/O lines* available from the μP. However, lines for interfacing only to specialized chips in multichip CPU organizations don't count.

I/O lines help determine flexibility

The number of *I/O lines that serve as inputs or outputs* can make the system more or less flexible than is readily apparent. For example, if a unit has 25 I/O lines but only four can be used as inputs, additional I/O devices may be required for certain applications to get more input lines—even though some output lines aren't used.

Special lines such as *strobes, test lines, flags and control lines* are convenient extensions of the I/O capabilities and should be considered a "bonus" for the extra control functions they provide. In many cases the I/O lines help control the data flow on a *bidirectional bus* that mates with all memory and peripheral circuits. However, some μPs use separate input and output buses to simplify their hook-up to systems.

Processors specifically designed for control applications often have a *timer* that can accumulate elapsed time. It can be an independent register fed by the system clock. To be a useful subsystem, the timer should: (a) operate independently of and simultaneously with the μP and (b) indicate an overflow by means of an interrupt when the terminal value is reached. These features, along with the control instructions included in the command set, allow total asynchronous operation between the timer and μP.

The *timer resolution and accuracy* must also be examined. For instance, an eight-bit timer register can accumulate 256 timing intervals, each as long as the period of the clock. When intervals of time longer than 256 periods must be timed, a software counter must be created to count the number of times the register timer overflows. By knowing the software counter status and how long the service routine takes, you can measure very exact long-time intervals.

Often you don't want to count clock pulses, but rather the occurrences of an external event. To this end some μPs include an *event counter* on the chip—it increments a register every time a transition occurs on the input line specifically enabled to record external event—and not clock—pulses. Instead of, or in addition to, offering parallel I/O capability, some devices provide a *serial I/O* capability. And when available, the serial I/O port should be capable of independent and asynchronous operation; otherwise it is little better than a software-controlled shift register.

Choose between internal or external clocks

To do all the timing, all processors need some form of *clock*. Many have the circuitry already built into the μP chip, with just the crystal or a

Table 3. Maximum operating system options

System support	TI	Rockwell	National	National	National	AMI	Rockwell	Intel	GI	GI	Fairchild	National	Intel
	TMS 1000, 1100, 1200, 1300	PPS4/1	MM 5781/82	MM 5799	MM 5734	9209	PPS4/2	MCS-40	1640	1650	F8	SC/MP	8048
Standard memory interfacing	No	No	Limited	Limited	No	No	No	Yes	No	No	Yes	Yes	Yes
Custom memory components with I/O	No	No	No	No	No	No	Yes	Yes	No	No	Yes	No	Yes
General purpose I/O peripheral	No	No	No	No	No	No	Yes	Yes	No	No	Yes	No	Yes-2
UART/USART	Yes	No	No	No	No	No	Yes	Yes	No	No	No	Yes	Yes
Keyboard display peripheral	Yes	No	On chip	On chip	On chip	On chip	Yes	Yes	No	No	No	No	Yes
DMA peripheral	No	No	No	No	No	No	No	No	No	No	Yes	No	Yes
Interrupt peripheral	No	No	No	No	No	No	No	Yes	No	No	Yes	No	Yes-2
Printer peripheral	No	No	Yes	Yes	No	No	Yes	No	No	No	No	No	No
Timer peripheral	No	No	No	No	No	No	No	Yes	No	No	Yes	No	Yes
Slave processor	Yes	No	No	No	No	No	No	No	No	No	No	No	Yes

resistor and capacitor needed to set the clock frequency.

For nonprecision applications, the R-C combination is truly a low-cost alternative. Once started, the minimal system should be easy to *reset*. This capability is often overlooked when a system is being selected. If the signal isn't generated on the chip or with a simple R-C network (during power-up), you must use a comparatively elaborate one-shot circuit that increases system cost.

Operating cost, or *power consumption*, can often limit the choice of usable μPs. Depending upon the technology used to build the μP and the clock frequency, power consumption can vary a factor of 10 or more. In case of power failure, some μPs can be transferred into a sort of *standby*, or "idle" mode to minimize power consumption.

Even the operating *supply voltages* play an important part in device selection—TTL-compatible ($+5$ V), single-supply operation is the most common requirement, but many processors or memory circuits require one or two additional supplies. The cost of additional power supplies must be added to the basic system cost.

To guarantee system operation, stay with well established technologies and avoid nonstandard packages whenever possible. Exotic technologies may be just beyond the current production capabilities while nonstandard packages may cause production handling problems.

If the μP family of components is expandable, the manufacturers should, ideally, have a large assortment of memory and I/O circuits available. Some of the more commonly sought-after peripheral and I/O support features are listed in Table 3. As indicated, many of the inexpensive μPs do not offer much in the way of peripheral support.

There are two major approaches to memory support for low-cost systems—off-the-shelf and custom memories. The custom memories are usually a form of ROM, PROM or RAM with a built-in I/O capability while the off-the-shelf units can be ROMs, RAMs or combinations thereof. Custom circuits can usually replace two or three standard memories with just a single circuit and thus decrease system cost.

I/O peripheral circuits can shave cost to the bone. Some peripheral control circuits are even more complex than the μP. These peripheral controllers usually operate independently of the μP and, since they permit the processor to perform another function simultaneously, often speed up system performance. ■■

Bibliography

1. Raphael, H., "Evaluating a Microcomputer Input/ Output Performance," *Electronics*, Aug. 19, 1976.

2. Raphael, H., "Interfacing μC Displays: Trade Offs and Techniques for Two Basic Strategies," *Digital Design*, September, 1976.

3. Raphael, H., and Hou, S., "Test Equipment For Microcomputers," *Machine Design*, Aug. 26, 1976.

Analysis of Microprocessor Instruction Sets

C. DENNIS WEISS, PH.D.
Bell Telephone Laboratories, Holmdel

The use of microprocessors, or MOS/LSI "computers-on-a-chip," requires programming skills. And that may seem to be a disadvantage. Hardware designers once concerned with such matters as latch selection, clock phases and propagation delay must now consider less familiar software-oriented factors like subroutine nesting, indirect addressing and computational algorithms.

However, a review of the basic vocabulary of microcomputer programming can help start you on the way to a microprocessor design. Moreover a review of the differing microprocessor instruction sets can establish a particular microprocessor's capabilities.

From a programmer's point of view, microprocessor instructions break down conveniently into the following:
- Data movement.
- Data manipulation.
- Decision and control.
- Input/output.

Data can be moved about between a variety of internal sources and destinations. The primary places are shown in Fig. 1. The most complex locations are those in memory—usually a RAM or RAM bank—since a variety of addressing modes can be used to specify location.

The *effective address* of a memory location to be read or written can be given *immediately* by bits in the instruction being executed (Fig. 2). In current microprocessors the immediate data may be 4, 8, 12 or even 16 bits long. Immediate data may be interpreted as a location (or displacement) in a previously selected page (or location) of memory.

The technique of *indexed addressing* permits a 16-bit address to be generated without providing all 16 bits in a current instruction. Were all 16 bits required, the instruction would necessarily be multiworded. The effective address is obtained when the instruction adds immediate data—say, 8 bits—to a designated register usually called the index register.

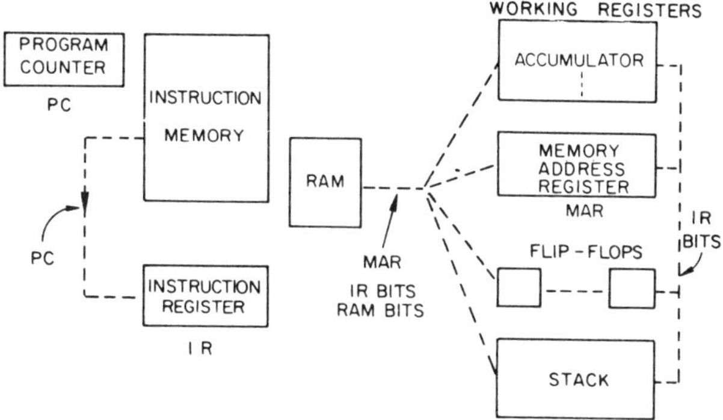

1. **Data flow among the major storage areas** is shown by broken lines. Bits in the storage locations control the flow.

In computers the index register may contain fewer bits than the immediate address. Hence the register appears to be a displacement with respect to the immediate address. Though the reverse is usually true with microprocessors, the same view can be taken, since we usually increment the index register to access successive words in memory. The index register can be thought of as a base register plus variable displacement.

An effective address may also be formed by *indirection*. In this case, a memory address is first computed by use of immediate data or by indexed addressing. Call this a direct address. Then, its contents are taken as the address of the actual memory location to be read or written. This is indirect addressing, a powerful technique that allows any memory location to serve as a memory address register; its content can be used to point to another possibly arbitrary word in memory.

Use addressing modes to advantage

An example follows on the use of various addressing modes (Fig. 3). Assume we write a routine to manipulate data stored in memory locations A_1, $A_2 \ldots A_n$. All references to these locations are by immediate addressing.

How to compute effective address

1. Use immediate data, given in the current instruction word.

2. Use the contents of the memory-address register, which can be manipulated separately.

3. Add together immediate data and a base, or index, register. This technique is called indexed addressing.

4. Use the contents of a memory location which itself is computed using all of the above. This technique is indirect addressing. An example follows:

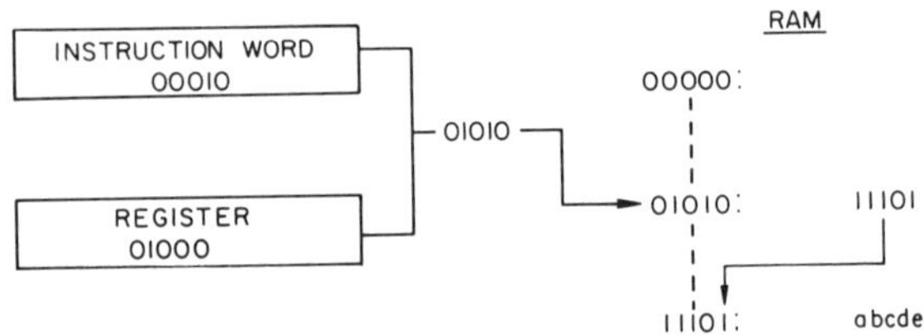

The final address is 11101 and the data finally accessed are abcde.

2. **An effective RAM address** can be formed from immediate data, address register, index register or a combination of techniques.

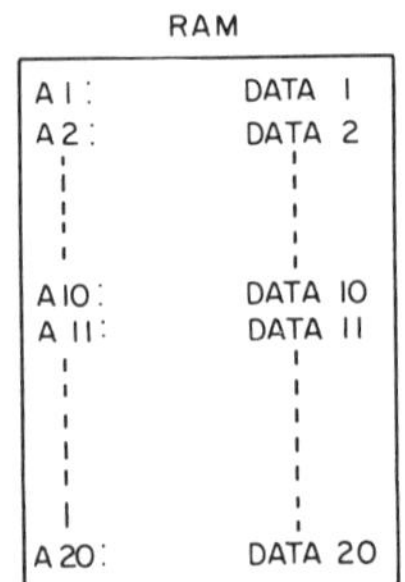

Computation required:
$G_1 = F(\text{Data } 1,...,\text{Data } 10)$
$G_2 = F(\text{Data } 11,...,\text{Data } 20)$

■ In the program to compute G_1 and G_2, data must be referred to by addresses.

■ If $A_1,...,A_{10}$ appear as immediate addresses in the program to compute G_1, this program will not compute G_2.

■ If the program uses a memory-address register to point to Data, the register can be initialized either to A_1 or A_{11}. The program then increments the register to compute G_1 or G_2.

■ If indexed addressing is available, then a program which computes G_1 will do G_2 if we first add 10 to the appropriate index register.

■ Indirect addressing would provide the most flexibility in this kind of problem.

3. **An example of data movement** illustrates the effect of different addressing modes.

We can apply the routine to different blocks of data, either by successively loading each block in locations $A_1...A_n$, or by modifying the instructions in the routine to refer to new memory locations. Either alternative can lead to inefficient programming, while the latter alternative is, in fact, impossible if the program is stored in a ROM.

Now consider the case where the original routine used indirect addressing, so that $A_1...A_n$ contain addresses of data. A simple change of the contents of $A_1...A_n$ allows the routine to operate on a new block of data located in a different block of memory. Of course, indexed addressing can be used to achieve the same flexibility.

If the new data locations have the same relative displacements as the original block of data, a reinitialization of the index register allows the routine to access new data. Indirect addressing is not even required in this case. But when the relative displacements are not the same, indirect addressing becomes more useful.

Accumulator—the essential register

Microprocessors generally have several working registers. However only a single register, usually called an accumulator, is essential, so long as it has access to read/write memory and there are instructions permitting immediate addressing and data manipulation between the accumulator and a memory word. With indirect addressing, even the function of index registers can be accomplished with memory.

The major significance of working registers lies in access time and the bit efficiency of instruction words. It takes far fewer bits to specify one of several previously defined working registers than a memory location. Whether these registers are in an external memory or in the CPU is irrelevant, so long as they can be referenced efficiently. But a faster execution time can be obtained with registers that are separate from memory. They can be accessed for read and write operations without users incurring excessive memory-cycle delays.

The quantity of registers may not be as significant as their quality. For example, can each register be incremented and tested for zero, or is only the accumulator so equipped? If each can, then each register can be used for counting and program loop control.

Which registers can you use for indexed addressing, if any? Can all registers be loaded directly from memory, or can they be loaded only from the accumulator? Which registers can be used as a source or destination for arithmetic/logic operations?

It's difficult to say how many registers are

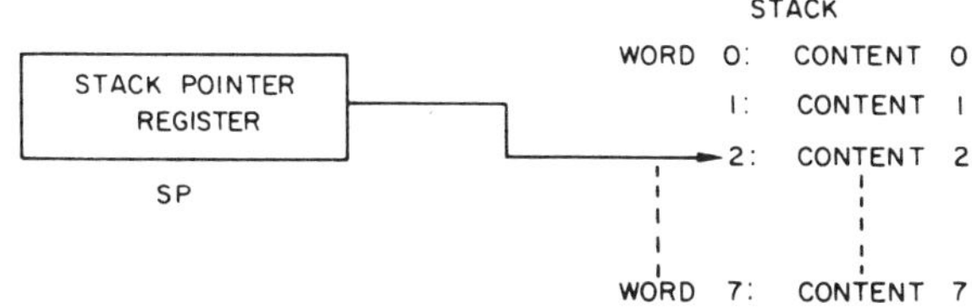

Current SP value	Operation	Next SP value
2	PUSH	3
7	PUSH	0
2	POP	1
0	POP	7

- TO WRITE data, or PUSH onto Stack, store in location addressed by SP. Then increment SP.

- TO READ data, or POP from Stack, decrement SP. Then read data from location addressed by SP.

4. **Last-in, first-out stacks** are a common feature of microprocessors. The order of instructions contains address information within the stack.

DATA FORMATS
width: 4, 8, 16 bits, 25 digits
encoding: binary, BCD

ARITHMETIC FUNCTIONS

add
- with or without carry bit
- between accumulator and register, memory or immediate data
- multiple precision possible
- possibly with skip if carry out used

subtract - not always.

multiply / divide { by subroutine or special purpose hardware

increment/decrement

LOGIC FUNCTIONS
complement

rotate / shift } with or without extra carry/link bit

AND
OR
EXCLUSIVE-OR
compare accumulator (with register, memory or immediate data) and skip

5. **Data manipulation instructions.** Missing instructions may be performed by a subroutine.

needed in general, or even in any particular application, and the number varies widely in current microprocessors. Some have stack-oriented registers that can only be accessed in a last-in, first-out basis (Fig. 4). This orientation is not a serious limitation, since algorithms can often be planned so the required data always are on top of the stack. Stacked registers have the advantage of being more numerous than individually addressed registers. Also, instruction bits

are not required to address them. A stack instruction can refer to only one register, the top register of the stack.

Memory-address registers may be the ordinary working registers, or specially designated ones, such as the program counter. A key register in any computer, this counter points to the next location in memory for an instruction-fetch operation. In addition it's common to have an independently controlled register that points to a read/write memory location. Instructions to load and store the program counter are extremely important, since they permit modification of the instruction sequence. A special advantage results when the counter can be loaded or modified by a value in the accumulator or other working register. This simplifies the control of a program's sequence through computed or external data. Otherwise we would have to rely solely on test-and-branch, subroutine call or fixed jump instructions in program store— where the instructions may not be modifiable.

For example, suppose a microcomputer system must perform certain functions that are selected by an input data word, interpreted as a command for some service. How do we translate this input-bit configuration into the desired computer response? We want to go to a certain program location associated with that command. If we can load the program counter with data, the input command word can be encoded directly as an instruction address. The loading of a portion of the counter causes sequencing to begin immediately at the desired program location.

Alternatively, we can use the input data as an index to enter a table containing program location addresses and load the appropriate address into the counter to cause the desired jump. If program instructions are stored in writable memory, we can modify the address information in a jump instruction before executing it, according to the requirements of the input data.

But if the program is in read-only memory, and the program counter cannot be loaded with data, we must resort to something as complex as the execution of a possibly lengthy decision routine. This routine consists of a sequence of stored instructions that contain all possible desired jumps. Repeated testing of the input data sequences through the decision routine in such a way as to arrive at the desired jump instruction.

One of the most sophisticated addressing modes is found in the National IMP-16. It uses immediate and indexed addressing, either with respect to the program counter or one of two index registers. In addition the IMP-16 permits indirect addressing, either with or without the use of indexing, to compute the effective address. The 256 lower order addresses in the RAM can also be specified with use of an 8-bit field in the current instruction word.

The simplest data-movement instructions are found in 4-bit microprocessors, such as the Rockwell Microelectronics PPS and Intel 4004. These, as well as the 8-bit Intel 8008 machine, also require separate instructions to load or manipulate a memory-address register, through which all memory references are made. The 8008 contains a single 16-bit memory address register, with 14 bits actually used. The Intel 8080 permits six 8-bit working registers to be used in pairs to provide three 16-bit memory address registers. In addition a 16-bit address for memory reference can be specified by two immediate bytes in certain load and store instructions.

The Fairchild PPS-25 has a unique instruction field for memory references. A mask-programmed repertory of six fields permits assignment of one of six predefined fields in each 25-digit (100-bit serial) register. Only the selected data field is affected by the data movement or arithmetic instruction. A separate program-controlled pointer permits access to any single-digit (4-bit) field.

Data manipulation capabilities

Generally the arithmetic capabilities of microprocessors are limited to addition and subtraction, and usually in a binary format (Fig. 5). The Fairchild PPS-25, however, features decimal arithmetic performed on 4-bit BCD-encoded digit fields. And several other machines include special instructions for handling BCD fields. Apart from the PPS-25, data words vary from 4 to 16 bits, so that multiple-word arithmetic is often required. Care must be taken that carry bits are added into the successively more significant fields—a capability that is always available.

Multiply and divide functions must be performed by subroutines in most systems. Or they can be performed in microcode for microcomputers like the National Semiconductor GPC/P, which are microprogrammable.

Microprocessors, especially those designed primarily for calculator applications, may not allow logic operations. For example, the Intel MCS-4 and Fairchild PPS-25 don't have operations like AND, OR, EXCLUSIVE-OR. However, they do permit complement, shift and rotate operations. The usual rotate or shift is by 1, but the National IMP-16 features rotation by an arbitrary amount in a single 16-bit instruction containing immediate data. The execution time is, of course, a function of the number of shifts called out. However, the instruction bit efficiency is high.

When shift and logic operations are omitted, they can usually be accomplished by a sequence

JUMP
CALL } can be conditional or unconditional
RETURN

BRANCH } always conditional
SKIP

JUMP

Location	Instruction
k:	i
k+1:	i+1
*k+2:	i+2 = JUMP to location m
¦	¦
¦	¦
¦	¦
m:	j

*At this point, the PC was loaded with m rather than being incremented to k+3.

CALL

Same as JUMP except that PC content is saved so we can return to instruction at k+3. A RETURN instruction performs the restoration.

A user can select either an on-page (short) or arbitrary (long) JUMP address in the Rockwell PPS, Intel 4004 and Fairchild PPS-25.

6. Some instructions change the order in which other instructions are executed.

of other instructions that are available. For example, "shift left by 1" is equivalent to the addition of a binary number to itself. As long as an individual register bit can be tested—say, by rotation into a carry flip-flop—all logic operations can also be performed whether or not individual instructions for them exist. However, considerable additional time will be spent.

Increment and/or decrement—critical arithmetic functions—can be accomplished along with test-and-skip functions. Such multiple-function instructions are particularly useful in controlling passes through program loops. For example, the Rockwell PPS has a 1-byte instruction that adds a 4-bit immediate field—say, the number 1—to the accumulator. If a carryout is generated (when the register reaches its maximum value), the next instruction word is skipped, but the carry flip-flop itself is not disturbed. The National IMP-16 has an analogous 1-word (16-bit) instruction.

A similarly powerful instruction in the Intel 4004 permits incrementing any one of 16 4-bit registers. If the result is zero, the next instruction in sequence is taken; if nonzero, a jump occurs to an immediate location on the same ROM page designated by the second byte of the current instruction. Again, the accumulator and carry flip-flops are not affected. Here, a 2-byte instruction is used that provides a more flexible jump instead of a skip.

An interesting extension of the increment/

decrement capability occurs in the National IMP-16. A memory location can be incremented or decremented with skip if the contents become zero. This feature permits efficient use of memory locations as counters for control functions. Also, the processor's addressing modes specify the effective address of the memory word to be incremented or decremented.

The Intel 8080 also permits a single memory location to be incremented or decremented. Internal flip-flops are affected, so a conditional jump instruction can be used later to test the memory content for zero.

An unusual and powerful feature of the decimal arithmetic in the Fairchild PPS-25 is the ability—through mask-programmed options—to

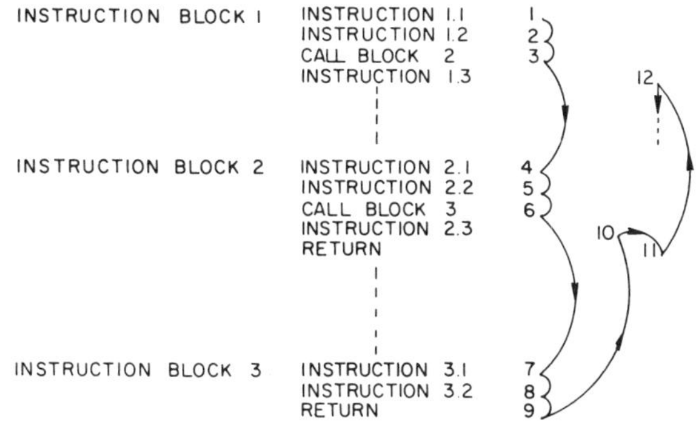

7. **CALLS are nested to a depth of two** in this example. Illustration shows the order of execution.

specify one of six fields over which any arithmetic function is to operate. The words are organized with a maximum of 25 decimal BCD 4-bit fields. Hence part of a register can be treated as a mantissa and part as an exponent. Appropriate arithmetic can be performed on these fields under program selection. Otherwise we would have to mask out or store different data separately. An individual decimal field can also be singled out by reference to a pointer register, which is itself under program control.

Decision and control capabilities

Microprocessors use the common convention of sequencing through instructions in order, unless directed otherwise by a decision-and-control type of instruction. The instruction changes the value of the program counter (Fig. 6).

Microprocessors execute JUMPS, CALLS or BRANCHES. The program counter may be changed unconditionally by a JUMP or CALL instruction, or conditionally, depending on the outcome of a specified test. These instructions are called conditional JUMPS, conditional CALLS or BRANCHES.

The difference between a JUMP or BRANCH on the one hand and a CALL on the other (conditional or otherwise) has to do with whether or not the program counter is saved. In a CALL, the program counter (or counter plus 1) is saved. Thus the counter can conveniently be restored to point to the instruction that would have followed the CALL had the instruction stream not been changed by the CALL. The RETURN instruction restores the counter to the instruction following the last executed CALL. RETURNS can be conditional, as well. If the condition is not satisfied, the counter is not restored but is simply incremented once again. It then points to the instruction stored after the conditional RETURN.

A further distinction can be made as to the ability to nest CALLS. Such nesting is illustrated in Fig. 7, where a series of CALLS transfers the program counter to a sequence of instruction blocks. By an execution of a series of RETURNS, the counter eventually returns to a location in the original block.

CALLS and JUMPS can be crucial

The use of conditional CALLS and JUMPS is absolutely crucial to programming (Fig. 8). Essentially they allow programs to respond to inputs rather than simply to deliver the same answers to the same programmed questions. A program must do different things, depending on the condition of the machine: Has a carry been generated? What is the current computer result? Is the number zero? (If it is, don't divide by it.) Has an interrupt or new command been issued? And so on.

All microprocessors allow such conditions as "carry bit set?" and "accumulator = 0?" to determine whether or not a JUMP, CALL or BRANCH is to be executed. Some permit branching as a result of logic levels presented on direct input lines, or individual bits in registers, or program-set flip-flops, or register parity, or a stack-full condition, or still other requirements. Again, the absence of one condition can almost always be overcome by the use of extra program steps. In a common situation, JUMP or CALL occurs if a condition is TRUE. But a symmetrical instruction in which the FALSE condition triggers the JUMP or CALL does not exist. By use of an extra unconditional JUMP or CALL, of course, the deficiency can be overcome.

The address loaded into the program counter when an unconditional JUMP or CALL is executed—or when a conditional JUMP or CALL or BRANCH is executed—may be specified in the same variety of ways in which memory is addressed: immediate or indexed direct; or indirect, through a memory location which itself is

TYPES OF CONDITIONS (JUMP, CALL, RETURN)
True or False on
- carry FF
- zero register (usually Accumulator)
- sign (most significant bit) of register
- parity of register
- programmer controlled flip-flop
- test input

If condition fails, do next instruction in sequence.

3-WAY BRANCH CONDITIONS (FAIRCHILD PPS-25)
example: if $(A) < (R)$, $PC \leftarrow PC + 4$ bit immediate data
$(A) > (R)$, $PC \leftarrow PC +$ another 4-bit field
$(A) = (R)$, $PC \leftarrow PC + 1$

SKIP CONDITIONS
- if $(R) \cap M = 0$, skip
- if $(R) > M$, skip   } National IMP-16
- if $(R) \neq M$, skip
- if Flip-Flop = 1, skip
- if R (lower) = 4-bit immediate   } Rockwell PPS
data, skip

COUNT AND JUMP/SKIP
- increment R and if $\neq 0$, do short JUMP (Intel 4004)
- increment (decrement) M and skip if zero (National IMP-16)
- $(A) \leftarrow (A) + M$ and skip if carry out
- $(A) \leftarrow (A) + 4$ bit immediate field and skip if carry out   } Rockwell PPS

NOTE: (A) = contents of accumulator
      (R) = contents of register R
       M = contents of memory location currently addressed.

8. **A summary of conditional instructions** shows the variations possible for JUMP, CALL, RETURN, BRANCH and SKIP.

specified by an immediate or indexed mode. The obvious reason for using JUMPS is to get to a new section of the program. For example, all work routines in some systems may report back to a main executive routine by an unconditional JUMP.

Unconditional CALLS allow us to use one copy of a sequence of instructions, a subroutine, and to enter it from many different routines. For example, a multiply subroutine can be called whenever required in any instruction sequence. With a CALL, a single RETURN as the last subroutine instruction causes the program counter to return to the sequence immediately following the CALL. A nesting facility enables the programmer to write subroutines that themselves call on other subroutines to perform operations. Thus several arithmetic subroutines might call a still simpler subroutine that shifts a register a certain number of places.

The Rockwell PPS microprocessor allows unconditional JUMPS to one of 64 locations on the current 64-word page. The locations are specified by 6 bits of data in the 12-bit JUMP instruction. Unconditional *long* JUMPS provide an immediate 12-bit address in the two successive words of the instruction. The CALL and

RETURN instructions are also unconditional.

The short CALL in Rockwell's PPS is an example of indexed immediate and indexed indirect program-counter addressing. The instruction itself specifies an immediate partial address consisting of the six low-order bits of an address. These bits are indexed by a fixed page address, called page 60. When the directly addressed word on memory page 60 is read, its 8-bit content is used as the low-order bits of the program counter. The high-order 4 bits of the counter are automatically set to 1110. Thus the first JUMP is made to an address given indirectly by any one of 64 locations on page 60.

The final JUMP seeks any one of the 256 locations on pages 56 through 59—pages with 6-bit addresses whose high-order 4 bits are 1110. When the CALL is executed, the current program counter is pushed, or placed in the upper register of a two-level stack. The current contents of the top stack register displaces to the second stack register, whose contents, in turn, are lost. Execution of the next RETURN instruction pops the stack.

All conditional instructions in the Rockwell PPS microcomputer are of the form "SKIP next instruction if condition holds." The skipped instruction could be chosen to be an unconditional CALL or JUMP, thereby giving the equivalent of a conditional CALL or JUMP for the complementary condition.

The Intel 8008 has conditional and unconditional JUMP, CALL and RETURN instructions. The CALL and JUMP use 14-bit, immediate addresses only (and thus a 3-byte instruction), and CALL uses a seven-level stack for pushing and popping the program counter. There is, however, a single byte unconditional CALL instruction that pushes the counter and replaces it with an address consisting of all zeros except for bit positions 3 through 5. These are given as immediate data in the instruction. Hence eight short, but frequently used, subroutines can be located in the lower order 64 locations of memory, accessible by exceptionally fast and short CALLS. The 8008 accepts and executes such an instruction on its input bus upon receipt of an interrupt signal. This feature enables direct control by external devices of JUMPS to routines that handle interrupts.

Microprocessor has stack pointer

The Intel 8080 contains a 16-bit register called a stack pointer, which is incremented and decremented automatically by CALL and RETURN instructions. The current program counter is stored in (for a CALL) or loaded from (for a RETURN) a RAM location whose address is given by the contents of the stack-pointer register. This permits arbitrary depth nesting of CALLS. But since the memory locations must be reserved for this use, a limit must be set on the depth.

In the National IMP-16, all registers and condition flip-flops can be pushed or popped from the internal 16-level stack, thus providing a convenient way to save the entire state of the processor. Registers and condition flip-flops can also be saved in or restored from the RAM stack area in the Intel 8080, but not in the Intel 8008. This capability is particularly important in interrupt-handling applications.

An unusual feature of conditional instructions in the Intel 8008 and 8080 is the way in which three of the condition flags—ZERO, PARITY EVEN, and SIGN BIT 1—are interpreted. They refer to the register last referenced by an instruction that might change a condition.

The Fairchild PPS-25 has a very flexible control structure. It uses unconditional JUMPS to an address within the same ROM, as specified by 8 bits of immediate data from the JUMP instruction. These 8 bits are interpreted as a signed-2's-complement number that is added to the address of the current ROM location. The feature permits jumping forward or backward a specified amount from the current location. A separate ROM-select instruction changes the high-order bits of the program counter, permitting a JUMP to a new ROM page.

Conditional JUMPS can lead to either two-way or three-way branches. A two-way BRANCH is an ordinary JUMP instruction. Three-way BRANCHES involve either two different modifications of the program counter (both using immediate data) or execution of the next sequential instruction. A pair of instructions selects the desired conditional mode.

CALLS in the PPS-25 are accomplished in two steps. First, the current program-counter value plus 1 must be stored in one of two fields in a special status register. Then an unconditional JUMP or conditional JUMP or BRANCH is executed. The execution does not itself save the content of the counter. A RETURN is accomplished by reloading the counter with the current content of the appropriate status-register field, again after the counter automatically increments once. This second incrementing ensures a skip over the JUMP or BRANCH instruction that followed the original counter storage instruction.

The National IMP-16 exploits its 16-bit instruction word to permit flexibility in generating the addresses for unconditional JUMP and CALL instructions. The counter is loaded with an effective address that is computed from an 8-bit immediate-data field (a signed-2's-complement displacement) that is added to the 16-bit

content of an index register. If the indirect mode is selected, this address is used to access a memory location whose content becomes the value for the counter. In the CALL instructions the current counter value is saved in a 16-level stack. The RETURN instruction retrieves the counter value from the top of the stack and adds to it 7 bits of immediate data from the instruction itself.

The Intel 8080 has an instruction that transfers the 16-bit content of two working registers into the program counter, thus causing an unconditional JUMP. The JUMP address originally in the working register could have been obtained by a computation or table look-up operation. The National IMP-16 provides this same flexibility, since the effective JUMP address can be based on an index register content. Or it can be based on the content of one of the 256 lower order RAM locations, in which case an indirect memory-reference mode would be selected.

The conditional instruction in the IMP-16 is a JUMP and provides an 8-bit displacement (7-bit magnitude plus sign) that is added to the current counter value. One of 16 condition flags can be tested, including several externally and internally controlled flip-flops.

Input/output capabilities

The nature of the microcomputer interface and the I/O instructions vary considerably from one system to another (Fig. 9).

A basic scheme employed in the Intel 8008, 8080 and the National IMP-16 provides bits on the address bus for both input and output instructions. With an INPUT or OUTPUT enable pulse, these instructions can be used to select an I/O device. Then the microprocessor either puts out the accumulator contents as OUTPUT data or gates the input bus content to the accumulator. The address-bus bits in the Intel machines come from the current instruction word; in the IMP-16, they are more general, being formed by an addition of immediate data from the instruction and the content of an internal working register.

The Rockwell PPS system uses immediate data for device selection, but then it provides a bi-directional data exchange in the same cycle. The 4 bits in the accumulator go out on 4 bits of the instruction-data bus. This is followed by a loading of the accumulator from the remaining 4 bits of the same 8-bit bus. The INPUT instruction for the Intel 8008 also outputs the accumulator before loading it from the main instruction-data bus. Hence every executed INPUT instruction can also be used to output data to the same peripheral address.

The Intel-4004 uses I/O ports that are asso-

Example: Intel 4004
(I/O ports are associated with special ROM and RAM devices bus-connected to the 4004 microprocessor)

Ports
- a RAM output port (4 bit, latched)
- a ROM I/O port (4 bits, mask programmable to specify direction)

Selection
- one (or two) set-up instructions select a ROM and RAM device

Data transfer
- (A)←input port bits on ROM
- ROM output PORT bits←(A)
- RAM output latch←(A)

Example: National IMP-16
Selection
- (R) + 7 bit immediate field is transmitted as a 16-bit device address/enable, accompanied by an I/O enable signal. It is sent to the Address Resister.

Data transfer
- A←(external device)
- (external device)←A

9. **Input/output instructions combine** a selection and data-transfer operation. These can be triggered by successive instructions or by a single combined instruction.

ciated with the ROM and RAM devices of a complete MCS-4 system. A ROM and RAM are selected by separate instructions. The I/O port of the ROM—each of 4 bits is mask-programmed as either an input or output terminal—and the latched RAM OUTPUT port can be read or written with an appropriate 8-bit instruction.

The Fairchild PPS-25 uses a set of I/O commands to control special I/O devices designed for use in this system. In addition it contains an unusual direct 8-bit (serial) input to the ROM address register. Data on this input are added to the ROM address register. Also, a special instruction loads serial data into the active status register, where each bit can be interrogated as an individual flag.

Bibliography:

"IMP-16C Application Manual," Publication No. 4200021B, June, 1973, National Semiconductor, Santa Clara, Calif. 95051.

"MCS-4 Microcomputer Set Users Manual," Revision 4, February, 1973, Intel Corp., Santa Clara, Calif. 95051.

"PPS-25, Programmed Processor System Preliminary Users Manual," October 25, 1972, Fairchild Semiconductor, Mountain View, Calif. 94040.

Wickes, W. E., "Parallel Processing System (PPS), Application Notes," Publication 2518-D-17, January, 1973, Rockwell Microelectronics Div., Anaheim, Calif. 92803.

"8008 8-bit Parallel Central Processor Unit, Users Manual," Revision 4, November, 1973, Intel Corp.

"8080 Preliminary Specifications," Revision 1, Intel Corp.

MOS/LSI Microcomputer Coding

C. DENNIS WEISS, PH.D.
Bell Telephone Laboratories, Holmdel

Engineers who incorporate MOS/LSI micro-computers in their designs face a critical need: conversion of system algorithms into instructions that can be loaded directly into the system's memory.

IC manufacturers are giving more and more attention to this phase of design, generally called coding, with improved tools and techniques to simplify the designer's task.

The basic tools available are these:

- Assemblers.
- Editors.
- Loaders.
- Compilers.
- Microprogramming.

Fig. 1 shows the primary function of the first four tools. In addition hardware or software simulators are available for program testing and error locating.

Assembly language: the most appropriate

An assembly language, the most common for microcomputer programming, has these features: symbolic operation codes; labels that refer to memory locations—instruction or data; and symbolic names for operands, such as registers, condition flip-flops and test conditions of conditional instructions (Fig. 2).

For example, in the Fairchild PPS-25 the instruction[1]

$$(R_{ij}) \leftarrow (A_j) + (R_{kj})$$

replaces the contents of register R_i with the sum of the contents of the accumulator and register R_k. However, only a designated field, j, in each register is involved in the addition. The Fairchild assembly-language equivalent reads

ADD Y, X, T.

Here Y represents the name of a destination register, X the name of a source register and T a previously selected code that represents the field over which addition is to take place. The possible codes of T, with their meanings, include the following:

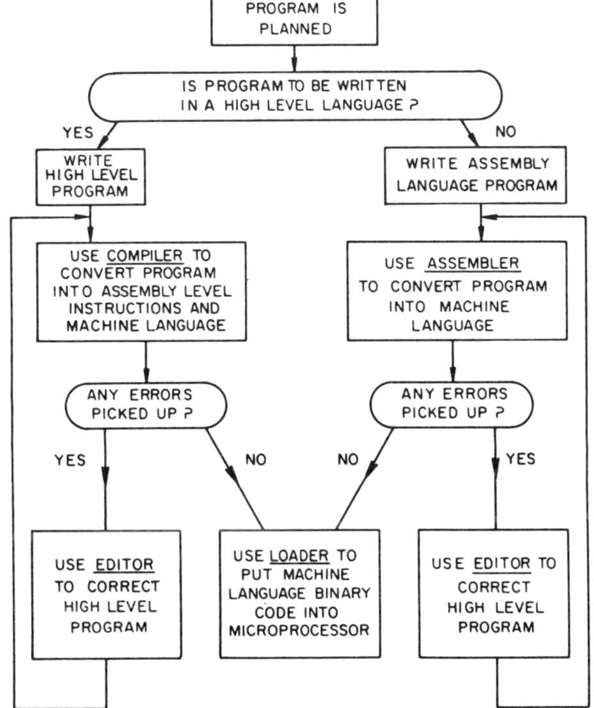

1. **Preparation of the binary code** to be placed in read-only memory can be simplified by use of a compiler or assembler and an editor and loader.

TOTAL:	Total field,
FRAC:	19 (left-most) digit fractional or mantissa field,
LSD:	Least significant digit,
PFIELD:	Digit selected by pointer register.

In the Intel 8008, consider this conditional CALL instruction: PC↓S and (PC) ← 14 bit immediate field, if condition holds; otherwise do next instruction. PC refers to the program counter and S represents a last-in, first-out stack.

Such an instruction in the Intel assembly language is written

CTX PLACE.

X refers to C, Z, P or S, which mean, respective-

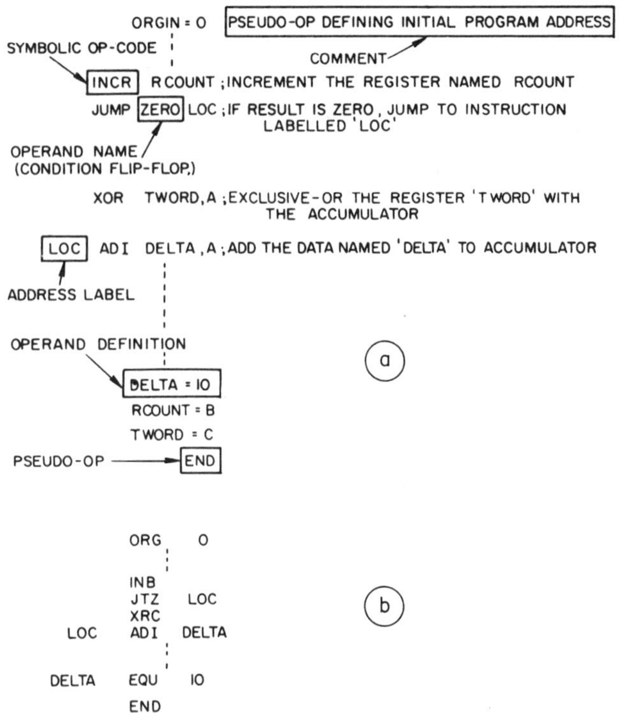

2. **Part of an assembly-language program** (a) illustrates the basic language features. The same program segment appears in the Intel 8008 assembly language (b).

A line of source tape

This says LOAD register ACφ indirectly, through the address given by adding 10 (octal) to the current value of the program counter (denoted by·)

A line of the list tape

10 = line number in assembly language program (on source tape)
000 = location of the instruction
9109 = hexadecimal representation of the 16-bit machine language word
LD ACφ, @ .+10 = assembly language statement written by programmer on source tape

A line of the object tape

This is a 16-bit machine language equivalent of the instruction above.

3. **The assembler,—a program,—converts a source tape** to a list tape and absolute object tape in this example from the National IMP-16.

ly, Carry = 1, Result Zero, Parity Even and Sign Bit 1. PLACE is the label associated with any other instruction in the sequence being assembled.

Hence the statement

       CTP   STEP1

causes the microcomputer to call STEP1 conditionally. The processor saves the program counter and replaces it by the address labeled STEP1, if the parity of the register last operated upon was even. Otherwise the instruction that follows would be executed.

The sequence

       INB
       CFP   STEP1
       JMP   STEP2

increments register B, calls to STEP1 if the parity of register B is odd or performs an unconditional JUMP to STEP2 if the parity is even.

The assembler can read a source tape or file with statements written in the symbolic assembly language (Fig. 3). Also, the assembler can construct various tables from the source file and produce an output object tape, or file, with binary numbers for the microcomputer.

For example, in the Fairchild PPS-25,

       ADD B,C, FRAC

appears in the object code as

       000100101010.

From left to right, 000 is the operation code for ADD; 100 is the Fairchild code for the B register; 101 is the code for the C register, and 010 represents the mask-programmed code to select the left-most 19-digit field of a register.

For the Intel 8008,

       CTP   STEP1

appears as the 3-byte instruction,

       01111010
       00110000
       xx001110.

STEP1 is assumed to be an instruction stored at binary location 00111000110000. The last two bytes give, respectively, the low 8 and high 6 bits of the address. The bits marked x are "don't cares" for the 8008. The assembler could substitute any bit pattern, since the machine ignores these locations.

The assembler—a program

The assembler is a program that must be run on some computer. One assembler program—from Intel—can be loaded into several pROM or ROM chips and executed by a microcomputer of the type for which it is assembling. These are called "hardware assemblers," because they run on the hardware itself.

A more common situation is one in which the

```
                NUMBERS OCTAL
                ORIGIN 0
ENTRY 1 LOAD R1, MEM 1
        LOAD R2, MEM 2
* * *   'LOAD' IS UNDEFINED OP-CODE * * *
ENTRY 1 COMPARE R1, R2
* * *   DUPLICATE ADDRESS LABEL * * *
        JCOND PLACE
* * *   'PLACE' is UNDEFINED ADDRESS
        LABEL * * *
* * *   OPERAND MISSING * * *
        JUMP FINISH
        STORE R1, MEM; if R1 > R2, EX-
        CHANGE
* * *   'MEM' UNDEFINED * * *
        STORE R2, MEM 1
FINISH  HLT
* * *   'HLT' IS UNDEFINED OPERATION * * *
MEM 1   = 1732
MEM 2   = 1840
* * *   NUMBER IS INVALID OCTAL * * *
          END


                NUMBERS OCTAL
                ORIGIN 0
ENTRY 1 LOAD R1, MEM 1
        LOAD R2, MEM 2
ENTRY 2 COMPARE R1, R2
        JCOND GREATER, PLACE
        JUMP FINISH
PLACE   STORE R1, MEM 2; if R1 > R2, EX-
        CHANGE
        STORE R2, MEM 1
FINISH  HALT
MEM 1   = 1732
MEM 2   = 2040
        END
```

4. An assembler provides error messages that start with
"***" in a program with errors (top). The corrected
program appears at the bottom.

assembler itself is written in Fortran. With
minor modifications, the program can be run on
any computer that compiles Fortran programs.
Thus the designer prepares source programs, assembling them on some other computer, to obtain the object tape for the microcomputer. The
Fortran-written assemblers are often made available to users through various national time-sharing, computer-service companies.

Assemblers contain pseudo-operations

Assemblers provide more sophisticated features. These are usually pseudo-operations, or assembler instructions, that do not assemble into
microcomputer instructions directly but control
the assembly of instructions that do. The more
significant and common psuedo-ops are as
follows:

■ NUMBER SYSTEM (B,O,D). If B is writ-
ten, all literals that appear in operand fields are
interpreted as binary numbers. Similarly O and
D establish octal and decimal modes.

■ ORIGIN. The statement ORIGIN 256D
causes the next instruction to be stored at location 256 (decimal). Consecutive locations are
used until another ORIGIN statement appears.

■ COMMENTS. It's common to intersperse
English text in a source file that contains assembly language. With the selection of a symbol,
such as "/" or ";" or ":", the assembler ignores
all symbols to the right of the selected one on
each line of source text. But the assembler re-
produces the symbols in the final list file.

■ EQUAL. A statement such as R1 = PLACE
establishes that PLACE, and R1 can be used in-
terchangeably as names of register R1. The statement DATA1 = 53D causes the contents of
DATA1 to be taken as 53 (decimal).

■ DATA GENERATING STATEMENT. A
statement such as TABLE D 7, 53, 29 creates
three data words stored in successive locations in
memory. The first location is labeled TABLE.

Assemblers give error messages

The ability of assemblers to detect and point
to a variety of errors in source statements is
one of their most valuable features (Fig. 4).
These errors are syntactic—they deal with misuse of the actual language. Assemblers normally
cannot catch logic errors in the program, errors
of intent or other subtle problems. A statement
that contains an error is printed in the list file
with a code letter—a flag—beside it. Or the entire error message may be printed.

Some common errors that can be detected include duplicate address label, undefined label and
unrecognized instruction mnemonic (due perhaps
to the misspelling of an operation code). Other
detectable errors include undefined operand field
names, wrong number of operands and an in-
valid number in the number system chosen. In
addition an assembler could be made to detect
the error of an address referred to the same
ROM page, as in a short JUMP when a long
JUMP is required.

Not all errors of syntax are flagged in current microprocessor assemblers. For example,
when the labeled address for a JUMP or CALL
instruction is not the start of an executable instruction, the error is not generally detected.

A macro facility—a deluxe feature in assemblers—is very useful when similar sections of

code are used repeatedly but variations preclude the use of conventional subroutine techniques. A macro consists of a sequence of code or a routine that is defined with such parameters as data values, addresses, labels or even instructions. An expansion of a macro involves a specific copy of this sequence in which all parameters have assigned values.

For the assembler to produce an expansion of the macro, only a single statement need be written—if you assume that the macro definition has already been given to the assembler. This statement appears at the location at which the expansion is to begin, and it contains a list of the values to be assigned. The assembler creates the complete expansion where requested.

Editors make changes

Editors are interactive systems that allow designers to prepare a program, or text, and to make changes with simple commands. Time-sharing services, which provide remote access to microcomputer assemblers, have such editor systems. Hence designers can prepare assembly-language programs and correct them. They can add documentation and store, combine and retrieve programs. And they can output programs onto paper tape and printers with relative ease.

Once a program has been written, assembler-flagged errors corrected and a binary object tape, or file, created, the program must be loaded into the memory of the microcomputer system.

Assembled programs can be loaded into mask or field-programmable ROMs. They can also be loaded into RAMs, in which case a small bootstrap loader is required. The latter may be a minimal program loaded into several ROMs or pROMs. This bootstrap program has just enough capability to read an object tape of a complete loader program, which is placed on a tape reader under microprocessor control. More often, the bootstrap loader contains the entire loader program, and all RAM space is available to load the application program.

Application programs can be conveniently tested in RAM before they are committed to ROMs or pROMs. However, if they are to be used in RAMs in the final system, a startup or restart procedure is needed. The procedure permits bootstrapping of the microcomputer into operation. A permanent loader is required in read-only memory.

Advanced loader features

The most elementary binary loader simply reads successive words on the object tape and writes them into successive locations of RAM

A PL/M statement

DECLARE (X,Y,Z) BYTE; IF X > Y THEN Z = X − Y + 2; ELSE Z = Y − X + 2

An equivalent set of assembly language statements for the Intel 8008

```
          ORG 4000
BEGIN     LLI LOW X
          LHI HIGH X
          LAM;          accumulator contains X
          LLI LOW Y
          LHI HIGH Y
          LBM;          B-register contains Y
          SUB;          Subtract B-register from
                        accumulator
          JTS LOC2;     if result negative, jump
                        to LOC2.
LOC 1     ADI 2;        add 2 to accumulator
          LLI LOW Z
          LHI HIGH Z
          LMA;          store answer in the loca-
                        tion for Z
          JMP FINISH
LOC 2     LCI 377
          XRC;          accumulator bits
          ADI 1:        complemented
                        2's complement of X-Y in
                        accumulator
          JMP LOC1
FINISH    HLT
LOW X     EQU 70;       word address of X
HIGH X    EQU 10;       page address of X
LOW Y     EQU 71
HIGH X    EQU 10
LOW Z     EQU 72
HIGH Z    EQU 10
          ORG 4070
LOC X     DEF 0;        X = 0 initially. Value as-
                        signed  elsewhere
LOC Y     DEF 0;        Y = 0 initially
LOC Z     DEF 0;        Z = 0 initially
```

5. **A short, readable compiler statement** corresponds to many assembly-language statements.

memory. The loader generally starts at a fixed origin. A relocating loader is more complex and not generally available. The reloading loader uses a special object tape and the desired origin data to automatically adjust the program addresses and load the resulting binary instructions.

With a basic binary loader, the same flexibility can be achieved by reassembly of the original source tape or file, but with a change of the origin using a suitable ORIGIN pseudo-operation.

Another feature of more advanced loaders is linking capability. Here program segments or routines with undefined labels or names can be loaded. The loader supplies missing cross references between the separate routines. Again, this feature can be achieved by reassembly of the entire collection of programs.

Compilers translate languages

A compiler is a program that accepts as input data another program, written in a so-called

- Errors in basic system design
    difference between intended or desired opera-
        tion and that achieved
- Errors in basic algorithms
    incorrect algorithm
    wrong strategy
    algorithm takes too long to execute
    arithmetic accuracy or precision unsatisfactory
- Errors in implementation
    logic error
        off by one count
        conditions reversed
        data stored in wrong order
        microcomputer hangs up in a loop
        data destroyed by overstore
        wrong register used
    coding errors
    wrong instruction
- Errors in hardware
    marginal operation
        races
        propagation delays too great
    wiring error
    interface signals incorrect
    peripheral device operated improperly

6. Many potential sources of error exist in a microcomputer design.

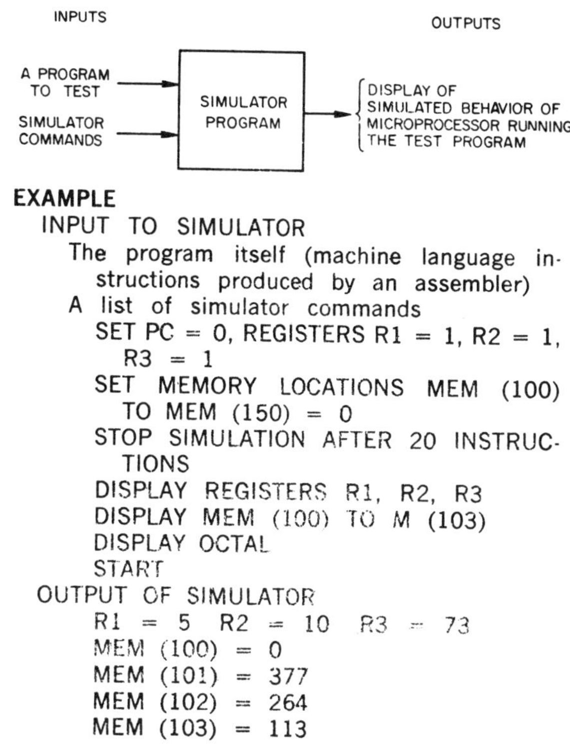

EXAMPLE
    INPUT TO SIMULATOR
        The program itself (machine language in-
            structions produced by an assembler)
        A list of simulator commands
            SET PC = 0, REGISTERS R1 = 1, R2 = 1,
                R3 = 1
            SET MEMORY LOCATIONS MEM (100)
                TO MEM (150) = 0
            STOP SIMULATION AFTER 20 INSTRUC-
                TIONS
            DISPLAY REGISTERS R1, R2, R3
            DISPLAY MEM (100) TO M (103)
            DISPLAY OCTAL
            START
    OUTPUT OF SIMULATOR
        R1 = 5   R2 = 10   R3 = 73
        MEM (100) = 0
        MEM (101) = 377
        MEM (102) = 264
        MEM (103) = 113

7. Commands to a simulator allow designers to verify
that a program is correct.

source language. The compiler then outputs another program, written in what is called the
target language. The latter can be either the
assembly language or a machine language.

The source language is usually a high-level
language, in which the instructions or commands
are much more powerful than those of the target
language. Examples of source languages are
FORTRAN, COBOL, APL, ALGOL or PL/1.

Compilers make the programmer's job easier
because they provide a language that requires
fewer statements for an algorithm. Compilers
eliminate the need to write detailed codes to
control loops, to access complex data structures,
or to program formulas and functions.

For example, a compiler from Intel has a subset of PL/1 instructions as its source language.
The subset language is called PL/M.[2] An example
from PL/M illustrates the powerful nature of
the source-language instructions:

    DECLARE (X,Y,Z) BYTE;
    IF X > Y THEN Z = X − Y + 2;
    ELSE Z = Y − X + 2.

The PL/M statements are converted by the
compiler into a sequence of assembly-language
instructions. The instructions compute Z after
they test to see if X > Y. If X is bigger, then
Z = X − Y + 2 is computed. If X ≦ Y, then
Z = Y − X + 2 is computed. X, Y and Z refer
to the contents of three, single-byte locations established by the DECLARE statement.

Fig. 5 shows an equivalent sequence of instructions written directly in the assembly language
of the Intel 8008. Notice how much more difficult the instructions are to understand, despite
the comments. And notice the increased amount
of writing required, even without comments.

The use of higher-level languages has its limitations. Although errors may be reduced because of the lessened detail, new problems can
be caused by failure to understand all the con-
ventions built into the compiler. There is also
invariably some loss in efficiency in compiler-
generated code.

If you rely too heavily on a compiler, your
mode of thinking may be too far removed from
the actual microcomputer capabilities. While
programs are compact, easy to read and much
easier to write, the net result may be excessive
storage space and slower execution.

One solution is to write routines that are typical for an application in both the compiler's
source and assembly languages. The comparison
helps to determine any loss of efficiency and
how significant the loss may be.

A compiler that produces assembly-language
code—and not simply machine-language words—
permits the use of an assembly listing for tests
and verification. Also, such a compiler lets the
designer eliminate redundant data movement.

Microprogramming tailors designs

Some microcomputers—the National GPC/P,[3] for example—can be tailored to design requirements through use of a mask-programmed control ROM. In effect, the designer can choose, within limits, the basic machine-language instruction set if he writes the microprogram.

This flexibility simplifies use of a microcomputer as an emulator of another computer. The instruction set of the other computer is micro-programmed into the microcomputer control ROM. Execution of a program instruction corresponds to selection of the equivalent micro-routine.

Microprogramming can also be used for critical, short routines in applications where speed is of the essence. The routines can be executed faster when written in the basic control language of the microcomputer. A single machine-language instruction triggers the routine.

The microprogram instructions are more elemental than the usual machine-language instructions. Each instruction controls limited, simple operations in the microcomputer. A sequence of instructions is required for most machine-language instructions. Hence many instructions are required for an entire computational routine.

Simulator tests programs

Many potential sources of error exist in a microcomputer program of even modest complexity (Fig. 6). A software simulator provides one of the most useful tools for testing programs.

Input data to the simulator consist of an assembled program, or object file, written for the microcomputer. In addition various commands are available to control the simulated execution of the program (Fig. 7).

The simulator output contains representations of the contents of various registers, flags and memory locations. These are shown as they would appear inside the microcomputer. The simulator commands allow designers to obtain selected outputs at simulated instants. A listing of simulator commands similar to those for the Intel 4004 and 8008[4,5] appears in Fig. 8.

- Start simulation.
- Stop simulation after a given number of cycles of simulated instructions.
- Stop simulation when the processor reaches a specified instruction or memory location.
- Stop simulation when the contents of a specified memory location are altered.
- Display any registers, flags, program counter, stack contents, I/O ports, or memory locations specified in a command and range-list.
- Trace the simulated microprocessor by displaying elements such as registers whenever an an instruction is fetched from the memory region specified in a range-list.
- Display the number of instruction states used by the microprocessor since the last simulator initialization.
- Set specified memory locations, registers and I/O ports to specific values to initialize a run.
- Interrupt the simulated microprocessor and force a CALL instruction.

8. **A variety of simulator commands** is available to test microcomputer programs.

- Hardware exercisers
- Test programs for RAMs
- Logic subroutines for microcomputers which do not have basic logic type instructions
- Decimal arithmetic routines
- Transcendental function routines
- Data format conversion routines
- Teletype or tape drive interface programs

9. **Program libraries** contain frequently used programs.

As with all computer systems, microcomputer program libraries are beginning to form, with contributions from vendors and users. A brief listing of frequently used programs appears in Fig. 9.

References:

1. "PPS-25, Programmed Processor System Preliminary Users Manual," October 25, 1972, Fairchild Semiconductor, Mountain View, Calif. 94040.
2. "A Guide to PL/M Programming," July, 1973, Intel Corp., Santa Clara, Calif. 95051.
3. "General Purpose Controller/Processor (GPC/P)," Publication No. 4200005A, National Semiconductor, Santa Clara, Calif. 95051.
4. "MCS-4 Microcomputer Set, Users Manual," Revision 4, February, 1973, Intel Corp.
5. "MCS-8, 8008 Simulator Software Package," November, 1972, Intel Corp.

Low-cost Design Aids Simplify Microprocessor Development

SAMUEL DERMAN

The explosive proliferation of the microprocessor industry is more than matched now by a rapid increase in the number of μP design aids.

Anyone interested in designing μP-based equipment is immediately confronted with a bewildering variety of teaching aids, learning aids, design aids, development aids, evaluation kits, software and hardware-development aids and kits and on and on.

And because the microprocessor field is both new and growing, exact definitions of these aids simply don't exist.

Aids currently range from tiny devices, whose simple circuitry (less than \$200) is controlled by a few switches and mounted on a single printed circuit (PC) board, to highly sophisticated, computer-based behemoths, bearing a price tag that often runs to tens of thousands of dollars.

Particularly important are the hardware design aids—mainly one or two PC boards—on which the designer can put together a breadboard version of his μP-based system. The price range, approximately \$100 to \$900, is low enough to permit just about anyone to join the μP generation.

Although at first glance it might seem that the cost of a particular design aid should bear a direct relation to its complexity and to the amount of memory it provides, such is not always the case. The amount of memory is certainly a factor, but there are other contributors:

■ Speed. Cheaper units run at a 1-MHz rate rather than at 2 MHz or faster.

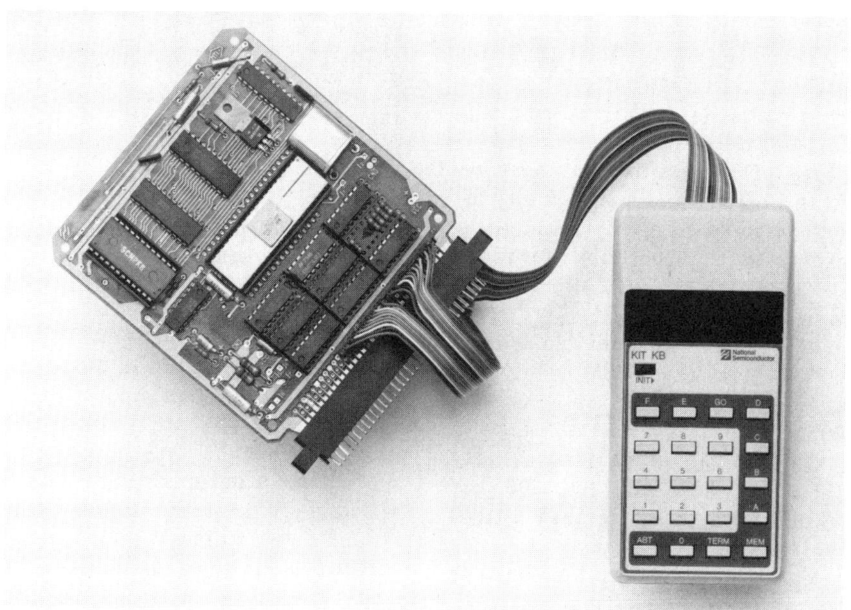

Input/output capability at low cost for National Semiconductor's SC/MP kit is provided by a hand-held hexadecimal keyboard and display. A 21-wire flat cable supplies the connection to the μP board.

The EVK 300 from AMI is one of a series of four PC boards for designing 6800-based systems.

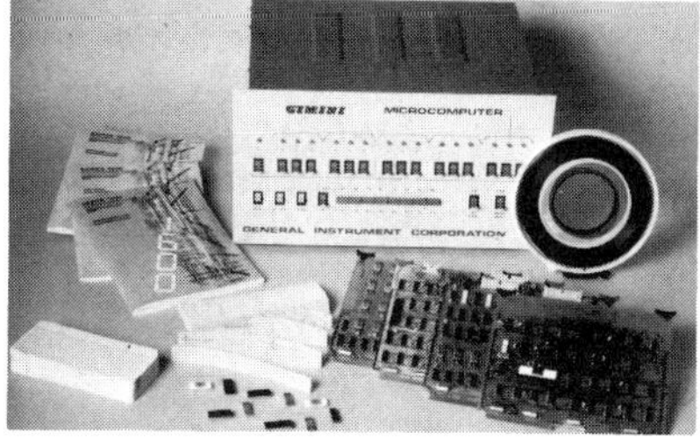

Designing with the 16-bit CP1600 μP is made easier by General Instrument's Gimini microcomputer.

■ Documentation. The greater the amount of material provided, the higher the price, in general.

■ The desired market. Equipment aimed mainly for the hobbyist or experimenter usually is made with low-quality components. The result is a low price. Some large semiconductor manufacturers, however, unwilling to compromise their reputation, produce only quality kits—for anybody—that sell for a relatively higher price.

Other semiconductor firms shooting primarily for large-volume sales of their particular μPs may offer design aids at zero profit, or even below cost, to encourage engineers to design with their product.

Consequently, classifying hardware-design aids simply by selling price can be misleading. Categorizing them by the μP they support avoids such a pitfall.

Getting started with the 6800

A simple and inexpensive tool for designing systems based on the 8-bit M6800 μP is the MEK68002 evaluation kit from Motorola, Austin, TX. Except for the power supply, all parts needed to complete the μP-based system and get "on line" are provided.

Consisting of two PC boards, the $225 kit is configured to allow programs to be entered manually through a 24-key hexadecimal keyboard or via an asynchronous interface adapter for an audio-cassette tape recorder. By avoiding an expensive teletypewriter terminal, the designer can get started at a minimal cost. A 6-digit LED display monitors both the data and address buses. Four other 6800 prototyping kits, all from American Microsystems in Santa Clara, CA, range in price from a low $152 to a hefty $950. The EVK 99, 100, 200 and 300 all have the same basic 10-1/2 in. × 12-in. PC board.

For anyone willing to buy or borrow his own TTL buffers, clock generators and power supply, the EVK 99 can get them off and designing with the 6800. In addition to the 6800 MPU, the EVK 99 comes equipped with four 128 × 8 RAMs, a peripheral interface adapter (PIA), a 1 k × 8 ROM and an asynchronous communications-interface adapter (ACIA). The ACIA allows the system to communicate bidirectionally with such serial-data I/O peripherals as a standard teletypewriter.

The EVK 100 ($295) provides 2 kbytes of ROM, 512 bytes of RAM, and totally buffered MPU lines. Built on a PC card with two edge connectors, one for the MPU bus and one for I/O, the EVK 100 can even be expanded to the EVK 300.

Programming the S6834's 512 × 8 erasable and electrically programmable memory (EPROM) is available in the higher-priced EVK 200 ($512). A 1 kbyte random-access memory gives the EVK 200 greater design capability.

Signetics' Adaptable Board Computer provides a system of jumper wires for changing the board configuration. Additional components may be added.

The EVK Model 300 ($950) features 2 kbytes of ROM (with an S 6831), 512 bytes of EPROM, 1 kbyte of RAM, and three PIAs (58 input/output lines). A ROM-subroutine program library and a selectable DMA mode augment the system's versatility.

However, none of the EVK units comes configured with a keyboard. Since external terminals are required to read the program in, their cost must be added to the "get started" expenses.

Although low-cost keyboard entry permits aspiring designers to get started with a small initial investment, a penalty must be paid. The size of the programs that can be entered via a manual keyboard is limited, and the maximum number of program steps is about 150.

Still more μP support

An evaluation kit from RCA in Somerville, NJ, for its 8-bit CDP-1802 COSMAC μP comes with a PC board, byte-input and output ports, a terminal interface, a ROM containing a utility program of commonly required functions, and a RAM for storing the user's program.

With a user-supplied terminal and a single 5-V power supply, the CDP18S020 Evaluation Kit becomes a compact computer system for the evaluation of COSMAC programs and prototyping systems. The kit costs $249. A pocket-sized miniterminal, soon to be available as an add-on for the board, contains both keyboard and digital display and should sell for under $300.

The difference between higher-priced development systems with higher capability and the low-cost hardware designs is clearly illustrated by RCA's more expensive ($3000) CDP18S004 COSMAC Development System. It has 11 plug-in PC cards; fits onto a 19-in. rack; and features editor, assembler and debug programs—and permits complete software development.

An SC/MP kit ($99) from National Semiconductor, Santa Clara, CA, comes supplied with PC board, parts and documentation. However, an external teletypewriter is required for inputting and outputting information.

A recently introduced portable keyboard from National interfaces with the SC/MP kit. The handheld keyboard ($95) avoids the teletypewriter, so the user's initial financial outlay stays low.

Besides a hexadecimal, six-digit display, the keyboard provides keys for inputting commands and hexadecimal data. A 21-wire flat cable connects the keyboard with the PC board.

ABC for the beginner

Two different design aids from Signetics, Sunnyvale, CA, fit into the low-cost category.

For $190, the novice designer can assemble the Adaptable Board Computer (ABC), a flexible prototyping system based on the 8-bit 2650 μP.

ABC includes 512 bytes of read/write memory, two latched I/O ports and three-state buffers on data, address, and control lines. The basic board configuration can be altered by a system of jumper wires and by adding more components to the board.

For those beginners designing with the Signetics 8 $\times$ 300 bipolar μP, an evaluation kit, designated the 8 $\times$ 300KT 100 SK, is available for $299. The kit's single board includes a 250-ns, 8-bit-μP central processing unit (CPU), four input/output (I/O) ports for interfacing external devices, and 256 bytes of working data storage. The 8 $\times$ 300 can be used with any bipolar or TTL-compatible integrated circuits.

A complete single-board system, including CPU, memory, and I/O, is available from Intel, Santa Clara, for designing with the 8-bit 8080 μP. Intel's SDK-80 kit interfaces directly with most terminals (75 to 4800 baud), and boasts 2-μs instruction-cycle time. The board comes with 2 kbytes of ROM (expandable to 4 k) and 256 bytes of RAM (expandable to 1 k).

Although it's a full microcomputer on a single board, the Apple Computer developed by Apple Electronics in Palo Alto includes a large breadboard area for the engineer to develop his own interface circuitry.

The Apple uses the 8-bit MOS Technology 6502 μP, and comes not only with up to 8 kbytes of RAM, but also with all the electronics needed to interface directly with a video terminal.

A peculiar price of $666.66 may put Apple close to the upper edge of the low-cost spectrum, but it also gives the purchaser a video link that operates six times faster than a standard teletypewriter. The Apple system is formatted to display 960 characters in 24 rows of 40 characters each. Since Apple's video-display section contains its own 1 kbyte of memory, all 8 kbytes of RAM are available to the user for programming.

Two design aids, the SE1 and 2 from Texas Instruments in Houston, allow the 4-bit TMS 1000 μP family's on-chip mask programmable ROM to be replaced with external PROM. Consequently, the designer can develop and modify programs before committing them to final hardware.

Both devices are 64-pin dual in-line packages (DIPs). For $43.66 ($26.95 in quantities over 100), the SE1 provides a 64 $\times$ 4 RAM on chip and offers access to 1024 $\times$ 8 bits of external ROM. For $61.12 ($37.33 for 100 or more), the SE2 provides twice the ROM and RAM density of the SE1.

To supply data and control functions, the designer connects a CRT or teletypewriter.

Complete systems

Other systems are complete microcomputers that don't need the breadboarding space. The PC board (or boards) is complete as it stands. To simulate his system, the designer connects his particular I/O devices, including any necessary supplies, or clocks, then programs the μP to accommodate this hardware.

A complete, factory-assembled system for evaluating the IM6100

A design aid for the MC 6800 μP is Motorola's MEK6800D2. Programs can be entered through the system's keyboard or via audio cassette interface.

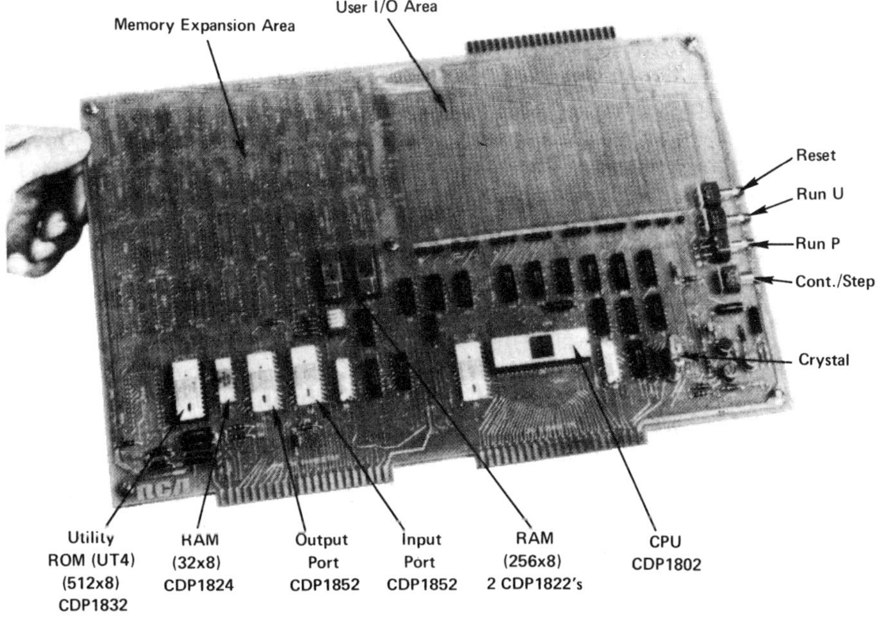

Low-cost design support for RCA's COSMAC is provided by the CDP 18SO20. This unit comes with a 512-byte ROM and a 256-byte program RAM.

Intel's SDK-80 is a complete 8080 microcomputer on a single PC board. Instruction-cycle time is 2 μs.

CMOS μP comes from Intersil, Cupertino, CA. Intercept Jr., which is called a tutorial system by its manufacturer, features one PC board (10 in. $\times$ 11 in.) that mounts all components, including batteries.

A single, 12-key keyboard on the unit is used for both operation entries and numerical entries. In fact, each key can enter either a single numerical value or one of three different program operations.

There is no ambiguity. The operator simply keys in his instructions and the numerical data, and a program built into a ROM decides that the entry is to be interpreted either as a numeric or an instruction or a command.

The Intercept Jr. is also the first low-cost ($281) design aid to provide op-coded control functions right on the keyboard, according to Gopal Ramachandran, Intersil's application engineer. The microcomputer comes configured with a 1024 $\times$ 12 CMOS ROM (the IM6312) and a 256 $\times$ 12 CMOS RAM. Memory addresses as well as data are displayed simultaneously in octal language on two, 4-digit LED displays.

Four standard "D" cells supply the required voltage. To compensate for aging batteries the microcomputer is designed to function at supply voltages as low as 4-1/2 V. A receptacle can be added to permit operation from a standard 110-V-ac-to-6-V-dc adapter.

SC/MP, F8 and Z80 support

For SC/MP design capability more advanced than the SC/MP kit permits, National Semiconductor supplies a Low Cost Development System (LCDS) with a single chassis. The chassis contains six-digit hex display, PC board, control switches and circuitry—all controlled by a 16-key dual-function keyboard.

For $499, the LCDS includes the following capabilities:

- Displaying the contents of the SC/MP program counter, registers and accumulator.
- Altering the components of the SC/MP program counter, registers and accumulator.
- Displaying the contents of any memory location.
- Interrupting the execution of the user-generated program at any point.

Anyone designing with the 8-bit F8 μP can be helped by the F8 Micro Pro from Fairchild in San Jose, or by the F8 Survival Kit from Mostek, Carrollton, TX. Both aids include a user-operating system for loading, debugging and modifying software, 1 k of RAM, four 8-bit I/O ports, teletypewriter interface, timer and Fortran IV cross assembler. The designer operates the two systems by attaching either a 100 or 300-baud ASCII terminal and a +5 and a +12-V supply. Both Micro Pro and Survival Kit come assembled for $185. (An unassembled version from Mostek is available for $147).

There is a major difference, however. The Survival Kit begins its 1000-byte debug program in memory location zero, which may interfere with the designer's program. On the other hand, the Micro Pro's debug program starts at some high location in memory to avoid such a problem.

A compact, one-board development system with 8 kbytes of memory for the Z80 8-bit μP is available from Zilog in Cupertino, CA. The Z80-MCB comes with the following features:

- A timer chip with four programmable timer-counter circuits for varying the baud rate so that the Z80-MCB-system speed can be matched to that of peripheral, electromechanical devices.
- A programmable, serial I/O port with RS-232 or current loop interface for hooking up to a teletypewriter or cathode ray tube (CRT).
- 4 kbytes of RAM.
- A PC board, smaller than that of most design aids of this type (only 7 7 in. $\times$ 7.5 in.).

The Z80-MCB sells for $475 in quantities of 1 to 9, $435 in quantities of 10 to 24, and $400 for quantities of 25 and over.

Two plug-in accessory boards for mating with the Z80-MCB are also available from Zilog. A floppy-disc controller card, the MCD ($745 in 1 to 9 qty), controls up to four floppy discs, contains 12 kbytes of RAM, two ports for parallel I/O. and a ZDOS operating system.

A RAM memory card containing 16 kbytes of memory, the Z80-MCB ($750), can support up to four such cards for a total of 64 kbytes of RAM.

The 8080 and 6502 revisited

Both the 8080 and the 6502 μPs are also supported by design aids that come complete on a board. Two single-board 8080 μP-based computers from Intel, the SBC 80/10 and the SBC 80/20, provide programmable synchronous/asynchronous interfacing with the RS 232 or a teletypewriter. The 80/10 requires an optional adapter for the teletypewriter. A 1-kbyte memory is provided with the 80/10 and 2k with the 80/20.

The keyboard-controlled, single-card KIM-1 from MOS Technology, Norristown, PA, is a complete microcomputer for designing with the 6502 μP. Besides its 23-key keyboard, the MOS design aid ($245) contains the electronics needed to interface with either an audio-cassette tape recorder or a teletypewriter terminal. With control from the keyboard, KIM-1 can generate hard-copy printout and read or punch paper tapes. A six-digit LED display provides on-board readout.

The memory, which consists of 2048 bytes of ROM and 128 of RAM, can be expanded to 65 k.

Every extra bit helps

Sixteen-bit μPs provide advantages not offered by the 8-bit devices. For example, more precise calculations can be made at higher speeds but such a capability requires complex support equipment and, ultimately, more money. Although the high cost of such equipment places them out of the low-cost category they must be included as a necessary adjunct to 16-bit μP design.

Measuring only 7.7 in. × 5 in. Zilog's Z80-MCB provides 4 kbytes of RAM with capacity up to 4 kbytes of ROM. A single 5-V source powers it.

For example, the sophisticated, 16-bit "Gimini" from General Instrument Corp., Hicksville, NY, costs $3500. Built around GI's CP-1600 N-channel MOS μP, the Gimini provides a host of capabilities, including:

- Separate data, address and control buses.
- Direct addressing up to 65 k words of memory.
- Nested interrupt system.

Although Gimini comes housed in a cabinet, its ICs and other circuitry are mounted on PC plug-in boards. A card cage behind the front panel holds four PC boards, with space and connectors for nine more.

All control and timing signals as well as data and address buses are fully buffered and available to expand the memory. A cable assembly allows interfacing to a teletypewriter or to a paper tape reader/punch.

Another 16-bit μP, National Semiconductor's PACE, is supported by the PACER, manufactured by Project Support Engineering, Sunnyvale, CA.

For $1195, PACER provides such sophisticated features as the ability to examine and modify the contents of any computer register or memory location, hexadecimal to decimal conversion, and full alphanumeric display. ■■

Program Microprocessors
with Software Design Aids

DAVE BURSKY
Electronic Design

While grateful for the circuit simplification microprocessors permit, the designer is not so pleased with the difficulty and high cost of programming them. Designers have almost learned to live with the programmer's rule of thumb: Three to five lines of valid code represent a good day's work.

The meager output is understandable, however: With over 40 available μP types—and each with a different instruction set—the designer/programmer can't be an expert in them all. Changing from one to another requires preparation and time.

To remedy the costly bottleneck many companies that make or use μPs offer myriad forms of programming aids—from simple programs that help you develop your own to full libraries of working programs for use on your system.

Software support is available in four basic levels and in almost as many forms:

- If you're familiar with machine language, you can work directly with the microprocessor in hexadecimal notation. For large programs, however, working in hex can be extremely cumbersome.

- If numbers bother you, go one step away from machine language and do the programs in assembly language—mnemonic equivalents of the hex codes. Once the program is written, however, you'll have to convert it back to hex.

- If you don't like mnemonics, go down one more level to a more English-like language (such as Basic) with special operators or even a more simplified form called Tiny Basic. However, complex languages like Basic require more

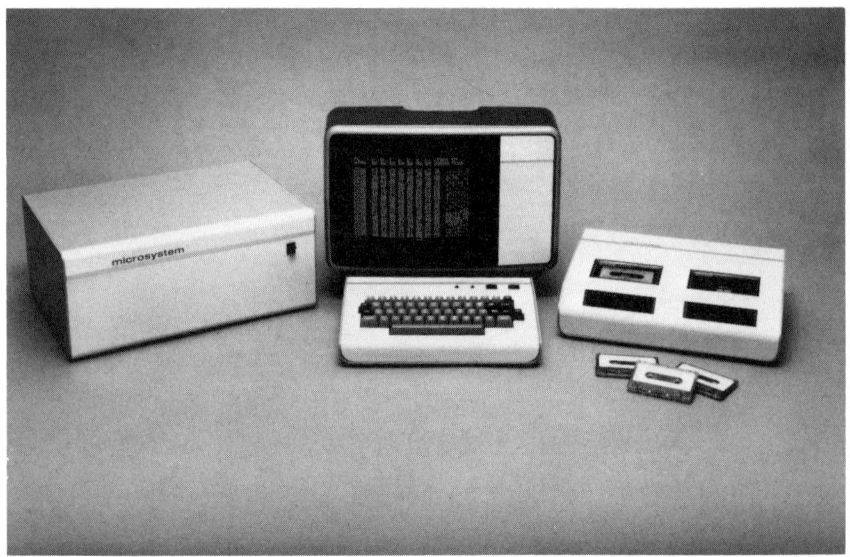

Low-cost cassette tapes and CRT monitors can be used by such development systems as this one from Microkit, Santa Monica, CA. Important to any software-development system, however, is the support literature for the programs.

memory support and are not often as efficient (with more lines of machine code to do a specific task) in the long run.

- If you're most familiar with programming large computers in such languages as Fortran, PL/1, or Cobol, you can also use these languages as the fastest route to a program. However, these languages are the most inefficient.

Software in many forms

You can purchase the software, for use on in-house computer systems, in the form of firmware ROMs, paper-tapes, mag-tapes, floppy discs, card decks or source listings. And, if no in-house computer is available, a terminal and any one of the many time-sharing serv-

ices offer viable alternatives with high-level languages, simulators and emulators.

For short microprocessor programs, say 200 lines or less, you can readily put the program together by hand. A pencil and paper are the only tools absolutely necessary to hand-assemble and compile a program. Almost every μP vendor offers pads of specially lined paper to permit you to keep track of all points by setting up columns for instructions, address data and comments. Even non-μP vendors have picked up on this method, and some companies, like Walton Electronics in Bethany, OK, offer pads of coding forms.

But aside from some demonstration routines, few programs are less than 200 lines long. Typical

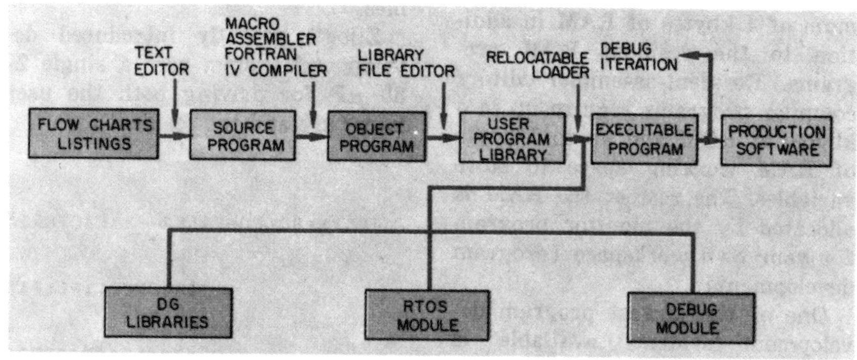

A general program-development cycle, as suggested by Data General, can be a long and tedious process. However, for microNova users, real-time operating systems, large software libraries and debug aids can speed programming.

lengths range from 200 to 4000 lines (often equatable with 500 to 8 kbytes of memory). For programs longer than 200 lines you'll end up whittling a lot of pencils unless you're sharp in hex notation. Vendors who have foreseen this problem offer a wide variety of assemblers, debuggers, compilers and disassemblers to help you.

Software for microprocessor-program development can be split into two major groups—resident and nonresident. Resident software consists of programs written in the instructions of a specific microprocessor and designed to run on a system that uses that microprocessor. Nonresident software consists of programs that run on one processor (typically, a minicomputer or larger) for the benefit of developing the software of another processor (typically, a μP).

Most of the microprocessor-development systems, from the $100 kit to the $10,000 work station, come with some form of resident software. In the lower-cost systems, the software, usually minimal, appears in the form of ROMs —often referred to as firmware. The more expensive development systems usually contain either mag-tape or floppy-disc drives, which permit large support programs.

Three basic programs permit software development: resident assemblers, editors and debuggers. Another program usually included in most utility packages is some form of communications routine that permits the microcomputer to communicate with a teletypewriter or other I/O device.

Each of the various μP manufacturers offers his own version of an assembler, editor, debugger or other program—and the available

features and capabilities vary widely. For example, the Kitbug ROM included in the SC/MP kit from National Semiconductor, Santa Clara, CA, requires 512 bytes of memory and enables you to:

■ Initiate execution of your program at any point desired.

■ Establish breakpoints within your program to allow execution of selected program segments.

■ Examine memory contents and SC/MP registers to determine if your program is producing the desired results.

■ Change the contents of any memory location.

■ Alter the contents of SC/MP registers to set up conditions.

■ Communicate with the SC/MP via a teletypewriter control routine.

Motorola, Phoenix, AZ; Fairchild, Mountain View, CA; RCA, Somerville, NJ; Intel, Santa Clara, CA; Signetics, Sunnyvale, CA; and MOS Technology, Norristown, PA, all offer similar ROMs in their evaluation boards. But in most cases, you can't buy just the ROM —it comes with the entire package.

The ROMs from Motorola appear to offer the widest range of capabilities. Seven ROM-based programs are available. The smallest is the monitor included with the Educator 2. It has six commands that are intended to handle binary-entered instructions and data. Jbug, which comes with the two-board Evaluation Kit 2, offers eight commands and is designed to handle data from a hex keyboard. Available with the Micromodule μP board is Microbug, a monitor and assembler with 13 commands and an RS-232 interface routine.

Two versions of Minibug, one that uses the peripheral interface

adapter as an RS-232 port and one that uses the asynchronous interface adapter to do the RS-232 interface, are available with the Evaluation Module 1 and the Evaluation Kit 1, respectively. A five-command program known as Mikbug comes with the Evaluation Module 1.

The most complex program is EXbug, which provides 34 commands and requires 3 kbytes of ROM. Of the 34 commands, 26 are used for interactive debugging.

Only the EXbug and Mikbug ROMs are available by themselves, for $200 and $18.15 respectively.

Included on the MOS Technology Kim microcomputer board is the Kim monitor, which resides in two 6530 ROM/RAM and I/O circuits. The monitor program, called TIM (terminal interface monitor), communicates with you over a full-duplex port and adjusts the data speed to that of your terminal. I/O routines similar to SC/MP also come with TIM. Coming soon are ROM-based line editors, assemblers and even a mathematics package.

Even nonmicroprocessor manufacturers are developing firmware that helps you cut μP-program development time. Wintek, Lafayette, IN, for instance, has ROM programs called Fantom I and Fantom II designed to support the 6800 μP. Fantom I is similar to Motorola's Mikbug, and has five basic commands that let you load, examine, print and display data and instructions as well as initiate programs. Fantom II is a 1-kbyte loader and diagnostic program that, in addition to the commands used in Fantom I, permits you to operate the μP in the single-instruction step mode, examine instructions in memory, dump memory to console, and examine/modify the A, B, condition-code and, index registers and program counter.

ROMs limit programming ease

Most of the ROMs in the small systems permit you to work only in hexadecimal—a severe limitation when you have to develop a lengthy program. The next step up is to get a system that offers a program that can assemble and then compile assembly language listings.

The program necessary to do the assembly usually requires several kbytes of memory. Resident programs in Motorola's EXORciser, Intel's Intellec-MDS, Zilog's development system, Fairchild's Formulator and RCA's development system are often sold with a minimum of 4 kbytes of RAM in addition to the resident ROM programs. Resident-assembler/editor/compiler programs require up to 4 kbytes of ROM and up to 1 kbyte of RAM working space to store variables. The rest of the RAM is allocated by the monitor program for your own workspace (program development).

One of the largest program development systems available is Intel's 8080-based MDS-800. The minimum system consists of 16 kbytes of RAM, 2'k of ROM, an 8080-based microcomputer, hardware interfaces and software drivers for TTY, CRT, floppy discs, line printer, high-speed paper-tape reader/punch, and PROM programmer. A system monitor is included in the resident ROM for program loading, debugging and execution.

A resident assembler, written in Intel's PL/M, a high-level system programming language, occupies 12 kbytes of RAM and translates symbolic 8080 assembly-language instructions into machine-operation codes. Also available is a text editor that permits manipulation of entire lines of text or individual characters within a line. The text editor requires 8 kbytes of RAM and is also written in PL/M.

A resident PL/M compiler program that is designed to operate on the dual floppy disc-based MDS system has been introduced recently by Intel. However, a full 65-kbyte memory is necessary to support the $10,000 system. Specially developed routines in the disc control system permit up to 200 files to be packed onto the disc. To provide maximum code storage, the disc-monitor program keeps track of the empty space and the location of files.

Zilog's recently introduced development system uses a single Z-80 μP for driving both the user hardware and the resident monitor. The system monitor permits programs to be entered into memory, then edited; assembled and loaded for execution.

A debug ROM module allows user-designated operations to be stored in an independent memory

Development programs for M6800 microprocessors are available in just about every format from Motorola.

and the user to specify an operation that can stop processing and cause the system to go into the monitor mode. In addition, all operations preceding the suspension are stored in an independent memory and can be examined to find errors.

With two 2650 μPs to speed program development, the Twin system from Signetics can offer many advantages. Software includes an operating system, a file-management system, debugging software, a text editor and a resident macro-assembler.

The dual-μP structure provides a common (user) memory space and a master processor/operator system that is independent of the user system.

Mini-like micros have software

For the μPs that approximate full minicomputers, such as the 6100 from Intersil, Cupertino, CA,

```
PL/M-80 COMPILER     FACTORIAL GENERATOR - PROCEDURE


                 $OBJECT(:F1:FACT.OBJ)
                 $DEBUG
                 $XREF
                 $TITLE('FACTORIAL GENERATOR - PROCEDURE')
                 $PAGEWIDTH(80)


   1             FACT:
                 DO;

   2    1        DECLARE NUMCH BYTE PUBLIC;

   3    1        FACTORIAL: PROCEDURE (NUM,PTR) PUBLIC;
   4    2           DECLARE NUM BYTE, PTR ADDRESS;
   5    2           DECLARE DIGITS BASED PTR (161) BYTE;
   6    2           DECLARE (I,C,M) BYTE;

   7    2           NUMCH=1; DIGITS(1)=1;
   9    2           DO M = 1 TO NUM;
  10    3              C=0;
  11    3              DO I = 1 TO NUMCH;
  12    4                 DIGITS(I) = DIGITS(I) * M + C;
  13    4                 C = DIGITS(I)/10;
  14    4                 DIGITS(I) = DIGITS(I) - 10 * C;
  15    4              END;

  16    3              IF C <> 0 THEN
  17    3              DO;
  18    4                 NUMCH = NUMCH+1;  DIGITS(NUMCH) = C;
  20    4                 C = DIGITS(NUMCH)/10;
  21    4                 DIGITS(NUMCH) = DIGITS(NUMCH) - 10 * C;
  22    4              END;
  23    3           END;

  24    2        END FACTORIAL;

  25    1        END;
```

Programming in PL/M, Intel's high-level language, can slash the time needed to develop 8080 software. English-like commands replace many lines of hard-to-write assembly-language statements. A PL/M compiler in the Intellec development system can cut the cost of time-shared program development costs.

the LSI-11 from Digital Equipment Corp., Maynard, MA, the TMS-9900 from Texas Instruments, Dallas, TX, and the microNova from Data General, Southboro, MA, a wealth of available software and programming aids already exists.

Data General, for example, has a diskette-based disc-operating system for the microNova with such utilities as an editor, assembler, relocatable loader and symbolic debugger. A real-time Fortran IC program also can run on the microNova.

Digital Equipment Corp.'s user library, DECUS, provides many programs that can be used on the 6100 since the 6100 emulates, to a great extent, the PDP-8 minicomputer originally developed by DEC. And for LSI-11 program development, DEC offers a wide range of compatible PDP-16 software.

A new language, developed by RCA and Forth, Manhattan Beach, CA, is designed to run on the Cosmac development system. Dubbed microForth, this language is an interactive program that can compile assembly-language statements directly into RAM. An 8 kbyte system is recommended to hold microForth. About 2 k of RAM workspace is available.

Other new languages are being developed by outside (non-IC manufacturers) companies and individuals to make programming easier. One such program is a string-oriented language called SLP that permits large arrays of instructions to be assembled with fast and compact listing.

Scelbal, developed by Scelbi Computer Consulting, Milford, CT,

Software Definitions

Machine code: commands for the μP system, often written in binary or hexadecimal format. Machine code is often referred to as machine language or object code.

Assembly language: commands for the μP system written in mnemonic form. Typically, three letter abbreviations, called mnemonics, are used to represent each instruction, and each mnemonic can usually be equated to one machine-code instruction.

High-level: commands for computer systems where each instruction is actually equated to many machine-code instructions strung together.

Monitors: programs that control the operation of the entire computer system. They often contain routines that tell the computer how to communicate with the outside world and how to allocate resources.

Editors: programs that permit data or instructions to be manipulated and displayed. Their most common use is in the preparation of new programs.

Assemblers: programs that permit you to represent instructions, addresses and data in symbolic form (character strings that represent machine instructions, addresses, data, among others). An assembler automatically translates symbols into their corresponding numerical values. It permits symbolic addressing by assigning values to labels used to indicate program-jump locations.

Compilers: programs that usually translate an assembled program into a complete machine-code listing. No matter how many times a section of code is used in the assembled program, it will be translated only once and put in its proper place.

Interpreters: programs that, much like the compiler, translate an assembled program into a complete machine-code listing on a line-by-line basis. If a statement is used in a program 10 times, it will be translated 10 times.

Disassemblers: programs that do the opposite of compiler programs. Given a machine-code program listing, the disassembler turns it back into an assembly listing, with mnemonic representations, for troubleshooting purposes.

Debuggers: programs that help track down and eliminate errors that occur in the normal course of program development.

Cross-assemblers and cross-compilers: programs that are usually designed to run on a large computer for the purpose of translating instructions for use on another processor, usually a μP.

Simulators: programs that help to evaluate a μP by duplicating all logic operations within the software of a large computer.

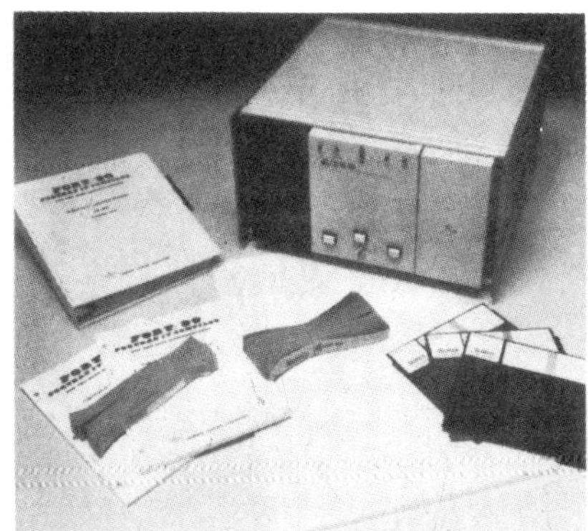

A resident Fortran compiler for 8080 software development is available on a floppy-disc system offered by Realistic Controls, Cleveland, OH.

and originally intended to run on the older 8008 μP, is similar to Basic in capabilities. The language operates in an interpretive mode— both the user and the resident programs must be held in RAM. When a run command is given, the resident program converts each line of high-level language program into executable code.

Slam, a symbolic language adapter for microcomputers, works on 8080-based equipment. Developed by Penn Micro, Lancaster, PA, Slam is an interpreter-type language with editing capability and English-like instructions.

Pull apart programs to debug

Not only is there a wide variety of languages that assemble assembly-language listings, but there is also a specialized group of programs called disassemblers that rip apart an assembled listing to help in the debugging. MOS Technology's MDT development system has such a program. Tranti Systems, North Billerica, MA, has a similar program in its Model 8000 universal programming system.

The MDT system's assembler assembles from a source tape or

```
                  LEVEL I ASSEMBLY LANGUAGE
                  ────────────────────────────────

FL LOC  COSMAC CODE     LNNO SOURCE LINE
    0000                   1 .. THIS SAMPLE CALCULATES THE ARITHMETIC
    0000                   2 .. AVERAGE OF TWO NUMBERS.  THE NUMBERS ARE
    0000                   3 .. STORED IN TWO ADJACENT LOCATIONS
    0000                   4 .. POINTED TO BY REGISTER R2.  THE
    0000                   5 .. RESULT IS STORED IN THE HIGH ORDER BYTE
    0000                   6 .. OF REGISTER 3.
    0000                   7 .. -------------------------------------------
    0000 42                8 LDA R2
    0001 E2                9 SEX R2
    0002 F4               10 ADD
    0003 F6               11 SHR
    0004 B3               12 PHI R3
    0005                  13 .. -------------------------------------------



                  LEVEL II ASSEMBLY LANGUAGE
                  ────────────────────────────────

FL LOC  COSMAC CODE     LNNO SOURCE LINE
    0000                   1 .. THIS SAMPLE CALCULATES THE ARITHMETIC
    0000                   2 .. AVERAGE OF TWO NUMBERS.  THE NUMBERS ARE
    0000                   3 .. STORED IN TWO ADJACENT LOCATIONS
    0000                   4 .. POINTED TO BY REGISTER R2.  THE
    0000                   5 .. RESULT IS STORED IN THE HIGH ORDER BYTE
    0000                   6 .. OF REGISTER 3.
    0000                   7 .. -------------------------------------------
    0000 42E2F4F6B3        8 @R2!+@'R2/2->R3.1
    0005                   9 .. -------------------------------------------



                       FORTH LANGUAGE
                       ──────────────────

       THE EXAMPLE BELOW CALCULATES THE AVERAGE OF ANY TWO NUMBERS.
       THE NUMBERS ARE ENTERED FROM THE TERMINAL AT EXECUTION TIME.
       THE FIRST LINE STATES THE FORTH DEFINITION.
       THE SECOND LINE IS AN EXAMPLE OF ITS EXECUTION AND PRINT OUT.
       .. -------------------------------------------------------------

        : AVR + 2 /
        12 46 AVR . 29
```

Programming the Cosmac μP from RCA can require knowledge of assembly language, a higher symbolic assembly language, or an interactive language called microForth—depending on the money spent for software development.

RAM, has six character labels and symbols, permits free-form entry of the source statement, delivers a symbol table, puts error flags on listings and delivers an assembled program in executable code. Once the assembler has done an assembly, the disassembler can pull the listing apart and give back the mnemonics from the hex code. Of course, the disassembler does even more, such as setting program traps, goes forward or backward one instruction, shows next or last cycle of operation and more.

A text-editor program comes with the MDT. Available text-manipulating routines include load text buffer, insert or delete a line or character, step forward or backward one character or one blank, go to top or bottom of text index up or down one line, find a specified string of characters and provide output to printer/punch.

Time-sharing cuts capital costs

Because of the accessibility of large computers or time-sharing services, many of the μP vendors have developed programs written in PL/1, Fortran, Cobol and other languages that will deliver microprocessor-compatible machine code. National CSS, Norwalk, CT; General Electric Information Services, Bethesda, MD; First Data, Waltham, MA; United Computer Systems, Kansas City, MO; and Tymeshare, Cupertino, CA, are just some of the firms that offer a wide variety of μP-development software.

All the programs offered on time-sharing systems are designed to run on large computers—the IBM 360/370, the GE Mark 111a, and even the DECsystem 10s. Cross-assemblers, cross-compilers, debuggers, simulators and other programs are available for μPs and bit-slice processors. Each company's programs offer slightly different features, so make sure you know the capability of the various time-sharing programs before you hook up.

The familiarity of engineers with Fortran and PL/1 makes these two languages the most popular choices, although Cobol is favored by most programmers. Cross software typically operates faster than resident software and often has more commands or a library of available routines to select from.

A high-level system often permits you to develop the program for a μP before the actual hardware can be prototyped—sometimes even before a dollar is spent for hardware, since complete simulators are available for some μPs. Cross-assemblers are commonly available in Fortran, versions of PL/1, and assembly language. Some assemblers can even produce more than one machine-code format to allow for absolute and relocatable code listings.

Compilers and integrator programs in PL/M, PL/W, PL/Z, MPL, Forth, Cobol and Fortran are available, and there are probably others still to be found. Programs in PL/M, PL/W, PL/Z and MPL are all optimized by the IC vendors to work only for their μPs.

The last type of program just starting to appear is a resident form of Fortran. Motorola has available a condensed form of Fortran that runs on the EXORciser system and is available on floppy disc. However, it will burn up quite a bit of RAM—about 16 k is needed to hold the program. ∎∎

Peripheral Chips: Functions and Problems for Microprocessor Systems

ANDY SANTINI
Electronic Design

Peripheral chips are becoming more and more important to microprocessor systems because they provide the interface circuitry and hardware to perform functions the μP can't handle, extending the capabilities of the CPUs themselves. In fact, over the next few years, the peripheral chips' share of the market for microprocessor-system components will grow as the CPU and memory shares decline (see graph). But as the influence and complexity of peripheral chips grow, so do the problems of testing and deciding when—and when not—to use the devices.

Running benchmarks

For one thing, it is becoming increasingly difficult to employ standardized benchmark tests to select a microprocessor. Rather than consider a CPU's features alone, many engineers are concerned with specific tasks and how easy or difficult it is to apply the microprocessor and its peripheral chips. So the peripheral chips available with one CPU may make that CPU seem more desirable than a superior CPU without the peripherals. "You can't just run a microprocessor through its paces and say it's the best," says Dan Abenaim, engineering manager of GenRad Inc.'s Electronic Instrument Division in Concord, MA.

Peripheral chips are also making it much more difficult to test microprocessor-based printed-circuit boards, says GenRad engineer Mark S. Mayes. "Peripheral chips can be more complex than processors, and there are often more of them on a board." While an 8080A CPU chip has fewer than 5000 transistor equivalents, a floppy-disc controller or a synchronous-data-link controller has the equivalent of over 22,000 transistors on a chip, says David House, marketing manager at Intel's Microcomputer Division in Santa

Clara, CA. In addition, a CRT controller contains about 15,000 transistors per chip, and even a relatively simple keyboard/display controller has about 6000, says House.

Searching for sources

Moreover, a CRT controller may represent 25 to 30 SSI and MSI chips, according to Art Gruszynski, product manager at National Semiconductor in Santa Clara, CA, which leads to another problem—alternate sources.

"We're talking about large-scale systems on a chip," says Gruszynski. "The more you do that, the more the buyer becomes dependent on the supplier." As a result, buyers are unwilling to commit to designs that use peripheral chips available from only one source.

"There's still a considerable re-

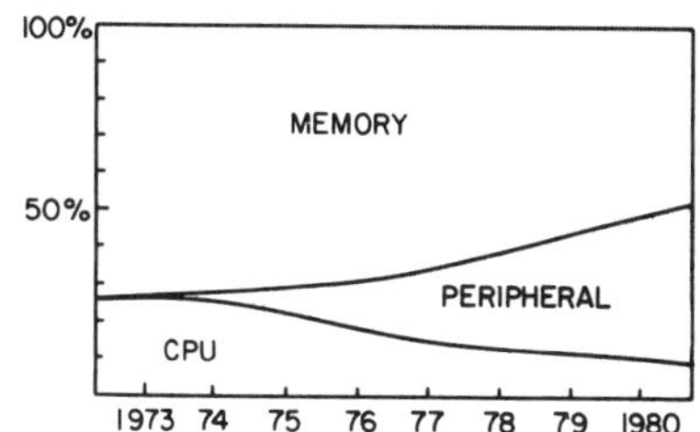

Microprocessor peripheral chips are getting so important, they will account for more than 40% of the dollar volume in μP-system sales by 1980.

sistance in peoples' minds to buying a sole-source product," says David F. Millet, microprocessor product manager at NEC Microcomputers Inc., Lexington, MA. While NEC is the only source for some of its peripheral chips, the firm is negotiating for alternates.

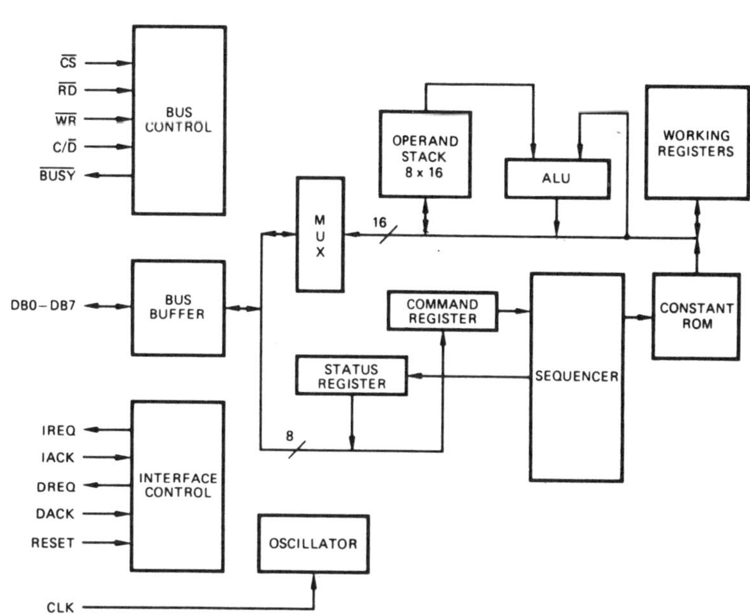

Plugging in a peripheral chip can add calculatorlike functions to a microprocessor-based system. This AMD circuit calculates trigonometric and logarithmic functions without tying up a lot of CPU time.

And Texas Instruments is negotiating for alternate sources for its 9900-series devices.

Trading software for hardware

But sometimes peripheral chips aren't needed at all. "A microprocessor can do any job without sophisticated I/O chips, if it has enough time," says W.J. Dennehy, microprocessor-product marketing manager at RCA Solid State Division in Somerville, NJ. Peripheral chips are needed only when the CPU isn't fast enough to perform a specific task, or when there isn't enough time in the microprocessor's program to perform the function in software, says Dennehy. On the other hand, when high speed is demanded, or when the CPU has too many other tasks to perform, a universal asynchronous receiver/transmitter (UART) should be used, not software, according to Dennehy. In other cases, code conversion and formatting can be written into software. Storing a UART program in ROM costs about 32 cents —a good deal less than the cost of an additional chip, according to NEC's Millet.

If a minicomputer's CPU devotes just half its time to assigned tasks, that's too much, Dennehy says. Because the computer is employed in general-purpose systems, other, often unforeseen demands must be satisfied in the time remaining. But since, by and large, microprocessor CPUs aren't used in general-purpose applications, over 90% of the CPU's time can be dedicated to specific tasks, says Dennehy. Since operations can be handled in software, additional chips are unnecessary.

"If you're going to build a lot of something, you want to get your chip count down to nothing," Dennehy adds. That requires putting as much into software as possible.

Signetics' Weissberger agrees that some functions could be done in software, but complex tasks like synchronous data link control demand too much of a microprocessor's time and are best left to external hardware. "It takes a lot of overhead, and even the fastest bit-slice microprocessors can't do it," he says.

"The tendency is to use more and more the intelligence you're building into the system," says National's Gruszynski, so anything that can be off-loaded from the CPU should be performed elsewhere. For example, the

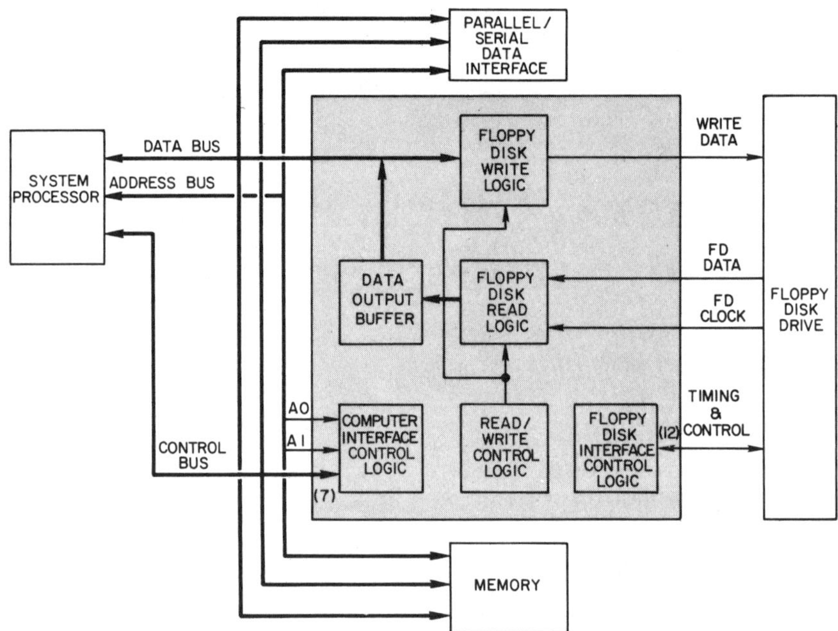

Peripheral chips tie peripherals to microprocessor systems, too. This National/Western Digital circuit interfaces a floppy-disc drive to a multiplexed three-state data bus.

microprocessor can scan a keyboard, but such a burden is better left to special-purpose peripheral chips.

Adding functions

Indeed, peripheral chips are often called upon to extend the capabilities of the CPU itself. For example, the Am9511 arithmetic processor unit from Advanced Micro Devices Inc. of Sunnyvale, CA, adds a number of calculatorlike mathematical functions to processor-oriented systems, which reduces the software necessary to perform these functions.

Besides the four basic arithmetic functions—add, subtract, multiply, and divide—the 9511 can perform trigonometric and inverse trigonometric calculations, square roots, logarithms and exponentiation and can store such constants as pi and e. Its operating mode can be either fixed point, with single or double precision (16 or 32 bits), or floating point, with single, 32-bit precision.

Like other peripheral chips, CPU extensions take some of the burden that system software would otherwise have to handle. And by quickly performing functions in hardware, they increase time in the CPU for other functions.

Without external arithmetic processors, even relatively simple operations like multiplication would be time-consuming for most microprocessors, which perform multiplications by adding and shifting data. Some microprocessors, like Texas Instruments' TMS 9900, have built-in facilities for single-instruction multiplication, but must handle more complex calculations in software.

On the other hand, the 9511 takes data from the microprocessor, performs a function, and returns the result over an 8-bit bidirectional data bus. The device can be connected to the system through a conventional programmed I/O port, or through a faster direct-memory-access (DMA) controller.

Gaining access

The DMA controller is itself a useful peripheral device. By transferring data between memory and outside devices without passing the information through the CPU, a DMA controller, like Mostek's MK3854 for the F8, can take over some of the CPU's tasks, again leaving the microprocessor available for other operations.

In the IM6102 from Intersil Inc., Cupertino, CA, a DMA controller is incorporated with memory extension and interval-timer circuitry. A silicon-gate CMOS device that interfaces with the IM6100 microprocessor through the data bus and handshake lines, the IM6102 operates from dc to 8 MHz and requires a single, 4 to 11-V supply.

The IM6102's real-time clock circuitry can be used to accurately measure and count intervals or events, as required by data acquisition and data processing systems. Similar functions can be added to 6800-based systems with the MC6840 programmable timer from Motorola Semiconductors, Austin, TX.

The 6840 has three 16-bit binary counters, three corresponding control registers and a status register. The counters are under software control and may be used to generate system interrupts as well as output waveforms.

For 9900-based systems, Texas Instruments offers the TMS 9901 programmable systems interface, which includes a real-time clock, interrupt-control circuitry, and I/O ports. An n-channel, silicon-gate device, the 9901 operates from a single, 5-V supply and has TTL-compatible inputs and outputs.

The 9901's clock consists of a 14-bit counter that functions as an interval timer by decrementing to zero, issuing an interrupt, and restarting at the programmed start value. The clock can also function as an event timer since, whenever the device is switched to the clock mode, the current value of the clock is stored in a register.

Six dedicated and nine programmable interrupt inputs are sampled and gated with their respective mask bits. If an interrupt input is active and enabled by its mask bit, the signal is passed to a priority encoder, which converts the highest priority signal to a 4-bit binary code. The code and the interrupt request are fed to the CPU at the proper clock time.

Communicating with peripherals

Besides extending CPU functions, microprocessor peripheral chips can interface the processor with external circuits and devices. These interface chips are either communications-oriented devices or circuits to interface microprocessors to such peripherals as floppy-disc drives and cassette recorders.

An example of the latter type is the FD1771 floppy disc formatter/controller from Western Digital Corp., Newport Beach, CA. An alternate source for the device is National Semiconductor Corp., Santa Clara, CA. As a formatter, the 1771 divides a disc according to IBM 3740 standards, with sector lengths of 128, 256, 512, or 1024 bytes. Discs can also be divided into non-IBM sector lengths from 16 bytes to 4 kbytes in 16-byte increments.

As a controller, the 1771 seeks any

track, restores to track zero, steps ±1 track, reads and writes single or multiple sectors, and reads the identification field. The chip is programmed by the system's software, which—along with data, status, and control information—is transferred over a three-state bidirectional bus.

A similar floppy-disc controller, the μPD373, is available from NEC Microcomputers Inc., Lexington, MA, along with the μPD371 tape-cassette controller, which contains the circuitry needed to read data from, write data into, and control the motion of a digital cassette recorder. The μPD371 also converts data from 8-bit parallel to phase-encoded format, and vice-versa, as well as generates and detects cyclic-redundancy check (CRC) codes.

Chips by type, too

Some peripheral chips complement particular microprocessor types. Intel offers a line of devices for its microprocessors, Motorola for its 6800, Zilog for the Z-80, Fairchild for the F-8, and Mostek for its versions of the Z-80 and F-8. Other chips can be used with any microprocessor, or at least with any that has an 8-bit bidirectional data bus. And some more general-purpose products, like analog-to-digital and digital-to-analog converters, can be considered microprocessor peripheral chips when they are applied in μP-based systems.

Many of the latest converters are designed with microprocessor-based systems in mind, among other systems, says Ivar Wold, director of systems development at Analog Devices, Norwood, MA. The converters' digital-data terminals have three-state, byte-addressable configurations to minimize interface circuitry by permitting direct connection to the bidirectional data bus of the microprocessor.

Even where multiple converters are necessary, interfacing can be simplified with a peripheral-interface adapter (PIA) like the MC6820 from Motorola, says Dave Kress, product-marketing specialist at Analog Devices Semiconductor in Wilmington, MA. As shown in the figure, eight d/a converters can be interfaced to a 6800-type microprocessor through a single PIA.

Where digital data are to be transmitted to other devices, such as CRT terminals, a common approach is to process signals from the microprocessor through a UART. Asynchronous systems are simpler than synchronous systems, especially when a UART is employed. "A UART saves

Talking to the analog world is simplified by feeding μP digits through a peripheral interface adapter to as many as eight digital-to-analog converters.

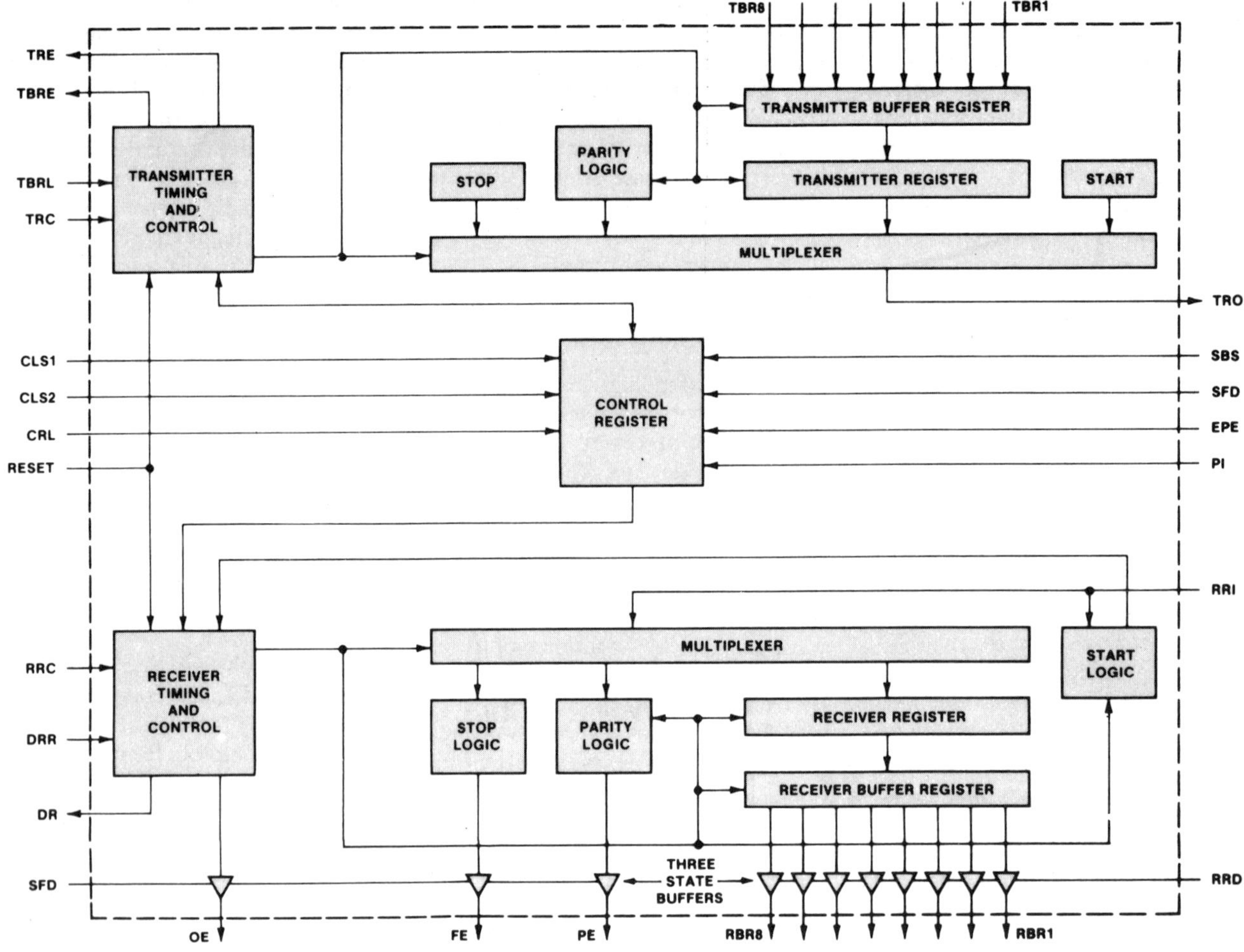

When digital data are transferred from one system to another, as from a CRT terminal to a microcomputer, the number of lines needed can be cut by employing an asynchronous receiver/transmitter such as the HD-6402/HD-6403 from Harris Semiconductor, shown here, to convert from parallel to serial and back.

logic cost," explains Ed Zander, product manager for the Micro Nova line at Data General Corp., Southboro, MA.

Pin-compatible synchronous and asynchronous control devices represent Texas Instruments' approach to receiver/transmitters. Instead of using a serial interface with the processor, the TMS 9902 asynchronous and TMS 9903 synchronous controllers interface directly to 8-bit buses and operate from single, 5-V supplies. Because the 9902 is housed in an 18-pin package and the 9903 in a 20-pin package, a board design that leaves space for 20 pins can accept either device. So by simply changing one IC and the program, a designer can change from synchronous to asynchronous links. This can be less expensive than incorporating a universal synchronous/asynchronous receiver transmitter, with its 40-pin package, into a system, says Tom Miller, TMS 9900 program manager at TI in Houston, TX.

Even the latest microprocessors, like Intel's single-chip 8085, have peripheral chips available. For CPU functional expansion, Intel offers timer, direct memory access, and interrupt controller chips. There are general-purpose I/O devices, universal synchronous/asynchronous receiver/transmitters (USART), and memory interfaces.

Aiming at common needs

In addition, Intel has just begun production of peripheral chips that perform "the four functions we found most prevalent," says Intel's House. The 827X peripheral series includes the 8271 floppy-disc controller, the 8273 synchronous data link controller, the 8275 CRT controller, and the 8279 keyboard and display controller.

The 8271 can control two single-sided for one double-sided drive in an IBM 3740 soft-sectored format. If the sectors are assumed to have no faults, the 8271 can drive four units. Programmable functions include record length, step rate, settle time, head-load time, and head-unload index count.

The 8275 CRT controller has screen and character formats that can be programmed by feeding data into the device's registers. The registers appear to the microprocessor as if they were memory locations. In addition, the controller can detect light-pen outputs for changing data on the CRT screen.

Among the peripheral chips available for the Z-80 microprocessor, from Zilog and Mostek, are the Z80-PIO parallel I/O controller and Z80-CTC counter-timer. The interrupt control logic for these devices is included on the chip, so a separate interrupt controller chip is not always necessary when they are employed.

The latest Z-80 peripheral chips include a serial I/O controller and a direct memory access circuit. The DMA chip controls data transfers between two ports, which may be either system memory or peripheral I/O devices. The circuit can also search a block of data for a particular byte, with or without a simultaneous transfer. ∎∎